Joyce Carol Oates
Conversations 1970–2006

Joyce Carol Oates
Conversations 1970–2006

Edited by Greg Johnson

Ontario Review Press ✦ Princeton, NJ

Ontario Review Press
9 Honey Brook Drive
Princeton, NJ 08540

Distributed by W. W. Norton & Co.
500 Fifth Avenue
New York, NY 10110

Library of Congress Cataloging-in-Publication Data

Oates, Joyce Carol, 1938–
    Joyce Carol Oates: conversations, 1970–2006 / edited by Greg
Johnson.— 1st ed.
        p. cm.
    ISBN 0-86538-118-6 (paper)
    1. Oates, Joyce Carol, 1938 —Interviews. 2. Novelists,
American—20th century—Interviews. 3. Fiction—Authorship. I.
Johnson, Greg, 1953– II. Title. III. Title: Conversations, 1970–2006.

    PS3565.3.A8Z465 2006
    813'.54—dc22
    [B]
                                                    2006049545

Contents

Preface

These twenty interviews with Joyce Carol Oates need little by way of introduction: they speak eloquently for themselves.

"Language," Oates remarked in her 1970 National Book Award acceptance speech for her novel *them*, "is all we have to pit against death and silence," and in the majority of these interviews Oates speaks insightfully and at length about such various topics as contemporary fiction, her literary and philosophical influences, her reading, her writing habits, feminism, boxing, and the conception and ensuing writing process that bring her individual works of art into being. Unlike some writers, who retreat into an ivory tower and refuse to discuss their work, Oates has said that "we human beings are on this earth to communicate with one another," and except for a brief period early in her career, when she shied away from discursive remarks about her writing, she has been available for more than thirty-five years to literary journalists who have wished to undertake serious discussions of her work and other related issues.

This collection has aimed to be carefully selective in showing the arc of her career between 1970 and 2006, including only those interviews that illustrate significant moments in her writing life and, most important, those that are substantial and significant in their exploration of her fiction, drama, and poetry. Most of the inclusions here were written-out rather than "live" interviews, reflecting Oates's wish to think out her answers and phrase them carefully. Thus a number of brief "publicity" interviews undertaken to promote a particular book have not been included; nor have other pieces that merely repeat information given in these longer and more probing conversations. Naturally this book is indebted to Lee Milazzo's 1989 compilation, *Conversations with Joyce Carol Oates* (University Press of Mississippi), but the majority of the interviews collected here were either not included by Milazzo or have appeared since his book was published. This gathering, therefore, hopes to make a new and substantive contribution to the burgeoning field of Oates scholarship.

Although Oates began publishing books in 1963 with her debut collection *By the North Gate*, interviews from the first decade of her career are somewhat rare. At that time, she avoided publicity and preferred to concentrate on her writing. Betty Lee's semi-comical essay "Tracking the Elusive Author," in which the intrepid journalist literally stalked the novelist until she consented to a brief conversation, illustrates Oates's reserve as a young writer. However, 1972 was something of a transitional, if not a watershed year, since it saw the appearance of a *Newsweek* cover story on Oates and another, fascinating interview with Joe David Bellamy, originally published in *The Atlantic*, in which readers got their first extended look at Oates's phenomenally productive writing life. Later in this decade, Oates gave another lengthy, insightful interview to her friend Robert Phillips for the famous *Paris Review* series of conversations with contemporary authors.

Certain of these interviews have been included because they shed light on facets of Oates's writing outside of her predominant genre of fiction. Her interview with *Ohio Review* in 1973, "Transformation of Self," focuses on her poetry, at which Oates has worked with her usual industry through most of her career, and Laurence Shyer's provocatively titled "The Sunny Side of Joyce Carol Oates" explores the author's playwriting, which engaged her especially in the 1980s and early 1990s. Another turning point came in 1980 with Lucinda Franks's "The Emergence of Joyce Carol Oates," originally published in *New York Times Magazine*, an interview that coincided with the publication of Oates's magical-realist family saga, *Bellefleur* (the first novel she wrote after moving in 1978 to Princeton, New Jersey, where she still resides), and that showed a new openness to the curious eyes of a literary world that saw Oates as a fascinating enigma in contemporary letters.

Throughout the 1980s, the 1990s, and into the new century, Oates has continued to make herself available to journalists on a selective basis, granting a lengthy interview to *Playboy* magazine in 1993 and, a decade later, even conducting with the Swedish journalist Stig Bjorkman a very long conversation, excerpted here, that became a book-length work published in Sweden. This piece, along with the one by Aida Edemariam for *The Guardian* (U.K.), suggest the extent of Oates's international reputation. Especially for this volume, she has granted this editor yet another lengthy interview, "Fictions of the New Millennium," which focuses on her work since the year 2000 and thus brings the book up to date.

Thanks are due to all the writers who contributed to this project; to Raymond J. Smith, editor of Ontario Review Press; and most importantly, of course, to Joyce Carol Oates herself, who offers in these many interviews a fascinating look at her life, her writing, and the creative process.

Greg Johnson
Atlanta, Georgia

Chronology

1938   Born in Lockport, New York.

1945-52   Attends one-room schoolhouse in a rural area near Millersport, New York.

1956   Graduates from Williamsville Central High School; begins undergraduate studies at Syracuse University on a New York State Regents Scholarship.

1959   Wins fiction contest administered by *Mademoiselle* magazine for "In the Old World," her first nationally published short story.

1960   Graduates from Syracuse University as class valedictorian. Begins study toward her M.A. in English at the University of Wisconsin.

1961   Marries Raymond J. Smith, a doctoral student at Wisconsin. Receives her M.A. degree. Moves to Beaumont, Texas and begins Ph.D. studies at Rice University, but soon leaves the program in order to concentrate on her writing.

1962   Begins teaching English at the University of Detroit.

1963   Her first book, the story collection *By the North Gate*, published by Vanguard Press.

1967   Begins teaching appointment at the University of Windsor. Wins a Guggenheim fellowship for the academic year 1967-1968.

1968   Publishes her fourth novel, *them*, which wins the National Book Award for 1970.

1974   With her husband, Raymond J. Smith, co-founds the literary magazine *Ontario Review*.

1978   Begins teaching in the Creative Writing Program at Princeton University.

1980   Publishes *Bellefleur*, her first New York *Times* best-seller.

1987   Named the Roger S. Berlind Distinguished Professor in the Humanities at Princeton, a position she continues to hold.

2000   Publishes the novel *Blonde*, a national best-seller.

2000   *them* is reprinted by the Modern Library in a revised edition.

2001   *We Were the Mulvaneys* is selected for the Oprah Book Club, becomes a #1 best-seller on the New York *Times* list and sells approximately two million copies.

2003   *A Garden of Earthly Delights* is reprinted by the Modern Library in a revised edition.

2003   Receives the Common Wealth Award for Distinguished Service in Literature.

2005   Receives the Prix Femina Étranger for *The Falls*.

Tracking the Elusive Author

Betty Lee

Originally appeared in the *Toronto Globe & Mail*, March 14, 1970. Reprinted by permission.

Ever since the news came through on March 3 that 31-year-old University of Windsor lecturer Joyce Carol Oates had won the U.S. National Book Award for fiction, the university switchboard has been jammed with calls from local well-wishers and from curious newspaper and television journalists everywhere.

I was one reporter who wanted to know more about the young writer who beat out such literary giants as Philip Roth, Vladimir Nabokov and John Cheever (all of them authors of widely discussed novels last year) for the 1969 fiction honors. After several telephone assaults on the university's nerve-frayed department of English, I finally connected.

"But I simply have no time for interviews," Miss Oates breathed hastily into the phone. "I've got a full-time teaching job, you know. I've been away from it too long as it is." The voice was uptight. Tired. "In any case," she continued before hanging up abruptly, "the whole thing is completely unimportant."

Well, the only way to track a story like that is to begin with available sources. The pickings are dismally slim: some dust-jacket notes issued by Miss Oates' publishers, Vanguard Press; a few brief biographical pieces printed in literary publications and book review sections. Even after the big awards announcement (she won the prize for her most recent novel, the hauntingly tragic *them*), there was little personal material about the author published in the North American press.

Research did turn up the information that Joyce Carol Oates was born in Lockport, New York State, that she is married to another U.S.-born University of Windsor English professor, Raymond Smith. And that she joined the university's faculty of English as author-in-residence two years ago after a teaching stint at the University of Detroit.

Her career as a writer has been impressive. She has had seven books—short stories, poetry, novels—published since 1963. Two works of fiction, *A Garden of Earthly Delights* and *Expensive People*, were nominated for the 1967 and 1968 National Book Awards. She was a winner of the 1968 Richard and Hinda Rosenthal Award of the National Institute of Arts and Letters and was awarded a Guggenheim for her work in 1967. Oates' short stories appear frequently in all of the major U.S. anthologies.

With this intelligence in my notebook, I began tracking Joyce Carol Oates in Windsor. A visit to the university turned up a zero. The author lectures just twice a week and the rest of the time her office door is shut tight. She is not listed in the telephone book either as Smith or Oates (two harried Windsor residents named Oates have recently threatened to have their phones disconnected) and the university's English department crankily refuses to divulge her home address.

Not only that, everyone connected with the university has obviously become heartily sick of reporters trying to pry the information out of them.

"Nothing personal," apologized John Sullivan, head of the English department, when I popped the same question. "It's just that we promised to do this for Mrs. Smith when she first came to us in 1967. She's a very private person, you know."

After more quizzing, he revealed a few more facts about the elusive author-lecturer. No, Mrs. Smith does not have the reputation for being a recluse though she and her husband are not exactly known as social gadabouts. At university gatherings, Mrs. Smith can be charming and witty, according to Dr. Sullivan. "But just when you think you've got close to her as a person, she turns it off again." The English department apparently considered throwing a party to celebrate the book award but decided against it "in case the Smiths would be embarrassed."

Dr. Sullivan agreed it was a pity the university was not reflecting in Joyce Carol's current glory because of her aversion to publicity. "However," he sighed, "I suppose it's strictly her own business." Channel 4 in Detroit did manage to confront her with a camera and microphone for a somewhat terse interview. The Windsor Star also infiltrated but the yes-and-no copy had to be beefed up with quotes from old book jackets. *The Detroit News* dreamed up its own interview and—according to Dr. Sullivan— has now been wiped off Mrs. Smith's list of eager markets for her acclaimed literary criticism.

The English department chief provided me with a prospectus of Joyce Carol Oates' current lectures (creative writing, Kafka, Yeats and contemporary poets) and the names of several students who were in her classes. Later, I met Fritz Logan, a young man who exuded stunned admiration of Mrs. Smith's literary talents. He agreed that the author was a Very Private Person who felt newspaper interviews were redundant because "just about everything people need to know about her is in her books."

"For Joyce," said Fritz, "writing is a work of art. She doesn't want to sell her books on the basis of a public image." He showed me a rare interview with the author which had been published last year in *The Lance*, the university's student newspaper. Some of the quotes helped add to my notebook of Oates information: "I think of most newspapers sort of as comic books. That one is entertained by them but doesn't get beyond the superficial treatment of news."

And: "I admire Thomas Mann very much. Mann is one of those extraordinary people. You can lose yourself forever in Mann. I also like Dostoyevsky. Fantastic energy. Then of writers who are writing today, I like John Updike. And I like people who are anonymous. People who write for small magazines."

Ah-ha! Anonymous people. Admired. "Even her friends find it difficult to ask Joyce for an autograph," said Fritz.

After the Logan interview I went to the Windsor Public library to check the city directory. The Smiths were not listed. The librarian smiled warmly when I asked if Joyce Carol Oates' books were popular with Windsor readers. They certainly were and the copies available were always on the reserve list. Had she ever considered inviting the well-known author to speak in the library to her fans? "Oh no," she smiled a little nervously. "I hear she is a very private person."

Back at a telephone I checked with an increasingly irritated department of English about Mrs. Smith's upcoming lecture schedule. One was listed for the following morning at 11 so I positioned myself outside Joyce Carol Oates' office door and waited for my subject to arrive. She turned up around 10:30, dressed in a dark blue dress and a fluffy wool coat. She is small, very thin and when her extraordinarily large, dark eyes turn themselves on you, you get the creepy feeling you are being photographed for posterity.

She looked surprised and a little annoyed when I introduced myself. But I was there in her office, wasn't I? After politely reminding me that she had a lecture in a few minutes, she agreed to answer some questions.

Yes, she had two more books in the works. A volume of short stories which would be published this fall and another novel which was a story about the generation gap. Yes, she hated interviews, publishers' parties and autograph sessions. The week in New York was awful. She tried to avoid curious reporters because she believes she does not come across as a very interesting person in interviews. "Besides," she added solemnly, "I simply don't like being made a fuss over."

So far, she and her husband have not made a decision about becoming Canadian citizens. They are happy in Canada but feel it is too soon to tell whether they want to live here permanently. With a sigh which revealed she must have answered the same question before, she said she felt Saul Bellow, John Updike, Jean Stafford and Doris Lessing were doing "extraordinary work" with the contemporary novel. Canadian poets, she feels, are making a special mark in the literary field.

The novel, she said, would always be her favorite literary form. "Short stories are like snapshots. The novel is a sustained vision of a complete world." At that moment, I got the feeling she might have been happy to talk some more about herself. But a bell rang somewhere, the big eyes blinked apologetically and Joyce Carol Oates pushed back her chair. "I'm very tired, you know," she said. Then the Very Private Person walked off down the corridor.

Oates

Alfred Kazin

Originally appeared in *Harper's*, 1972. Reprinted by permission.

Sunday noon on Riverside Drive in Windsor, Ontario, which is not as far away as you would think. Detroit looms up just across the Detroit River—a concentrated industrial silhouette of piers, storage tanks, factory fronts, dead just now in the frosty February stillness. It's certainly quiet, genteel-quiet in the exquisite little house, on the river, of Professor and Mrs. Raymond Smith, Americans who both teach at the University of Windsor. There's peacefully enveloping snow on the ground all around us, Detroit is in front of you but looks far away, and there's a Mozart symphony on the hi-fi just behind the sofa where Mrs. Smith— Joyce Carol Oates—is enduring the interview.

Obviously the Mozart is a help to a very private person who gamely responds to every question put to her, but who volunteers nothing—not even a smile. She sits beside me on the sofa, taking me in with those extraordinary dark eyes that have been described as "burning in a dove's face." In her photographs ("I take terrible pictures, don't I?" she says in her schoolgirl voice) those eyes seem almost too large to be natural. But when you finally see her, you realize that she just freezes up before a camera. Her eyes seem friendly enough, are as inquisitive as the rest of her, and just as timid.

She has not been easy to get hold of; no one I know has even met her! And now that I have jetted to Detroit this Sunday morning, taxied across the International Bridge at Windsor, and am finally sitting with her in her pretty, proper little house, but listening to her with some difficulty through the Mozart, I realize to my dismay that we are soon going to exhaust all biographical items relating to Joyce Carol Oates, and that I will have no excuse not to return to New York this very afternoon.

The problem is not only that she is shy, doesn't drink or smoke, has no small talk, no jokes, no anecdotes, no gossip, no malice, no verbal embroidery of the slightest kind, and is as solemn as a graduate student taking an oral examination, but also that we are free-associating questions and answers so fast that I am rapidly making my way through whatever she *will* talk about. We are getting through this a mile a minute, and while she confirms the sense I get from her fiction an extraordinary and even tumultuous amount of purely mental existence locked up behind the schoolgirl face, I didn't expect this much of a rush. I had rather looked forward to a leisurely look around at Windsor, at the university where she is associate professor of English, at "Canada" even if it does look straight at Detroit. But Joyce Carol Oates is shy, *very* reserved, and moves as fast as a writer has to; she also says things like, "I'm not very interesting," "I'm not much," "I'm really not very ambitious." *Herself* is not a big issue with her. She is the most fortunate of writers: she has the instinctive self-confidence of a writer who has been writing stories since she was a child, but no ego, no sense that Joyce Carol Oates is important. In fact, Joyce Carol Oates is not exactly here. When I asked her about her daily routine, what she would do this Sunday, she said with some wonder at my question: "Why, write a story. I have several in my head just now." "And when will you finish it?" "Why, tomorrow morning." She'd also cook dinner. "I do enjoy cooking. Doesn't every woman?"

At thirty-three she looks and sounds like an altogether demure, old-fashioned, altogether proper student intellectual from another generation (or another country) who is dying to get back to her books. Though she is obviously startled by all the attention she has been getting lately, and is absurdly respectful to the middle-aged critic who is trying to draw her out, the extraordinary *amount* of mental life in her fascinates me. All sorts of filaments are hanging in the air, suggestions for innumerable stories, people, relationships. She obviously can't wait to get back to her desk.

So talking to her everything goes fast-fast-fast—like Oates knocking out one story after another at her electric typewriter. Joyce Carol Oates is a square, a lovely schoolmarm, but her life is in her head; her life is all the stories she carries in her head. And when I say "carry," I do not mean that she is plotting a story there, thinking it out, "working it over," as writers say, against the day when they finally get down to the heart-crushing business of *writing* it, as writers do, with many cigarettes, many cups of coffee, many prayers, shrieks of despair, imprecations, and curses against fate. *Dollars damn me*, said poor old Herman Melville. *Though I wrote the gospels in this century I should die in the gutter.* Poor old Joseph Conrad had positively to be roped in his chair. *Every morning, when I can't put it off any longer*, said a poor old writer of my acquaintance, *I feel I am on trial for my life and will definitely not be acquitted.*

This is not the case with not-poor, not-old Joyce Carol Oates. She writes, she is said to write, the way Mozart wrote down the score already written out in his head. Mozart was just a secretary! And Joyce Carol Oates, who will begin a story on Sunday and finish it on Monday, has four—or is it ten?—stories in her mind just now. Her latest novel (at the time this is written), *them* (1969), was her fourth published novel in the past seven years, during which she also published three collections of short stories; had two plays produced off-Broadway; finished a fifth novel, a book of poems (*Anonymous Sins*), a book on tragedy, and many short essays and reviews. She even has two completed novels in manuscript that she will "probably" not publish, for they may get in the way of new novels she is planning to write. In the same soft, matter-of-fact, young-girl voice in which she expresses some wonder at the profusion of manuscripts in her house (she's had to move some of it to her university office), she says very quietly, without boasting, without any feeling of strangeness, that she's also written stories "taking off" from actual stories by Chekhov and Joyce, and one "taking off" from Thoreau. It is called "Where I Lived, and What I Lived For."

In New York, where writers talk about "Oates" without knowledge and without mercy, it is reported that her agent jokingly complained once that as soon as one story went out to a magazine, another came in, thus producing a happy and profitable glut on the literary marketplace. Obviously Joyce Carol Oates leads an altogether austere, hard-working existence straight out of the hard-pressed Thirties in which she was born— a period that haunts her as the great example of the unrelieved social crisis which is her image of America, and which recurs in her novels *A Garden of Earthly Delights* and *them*.

She comes from that colorless, often frozen and inhospitable lonely country in western New York, outside of Lockport, where her father is a tool-and-die designer. It was only with a New York State Regents' Scholarship and a scholarship from Syracuse University that she was able to go to college. Her frugality, simplicity, and even academic solemnity are what you would expect of a scholarship girl whose father is a blue-collar worker, belongs to the United Automobile Workers, and whose family contains recent immigrant strains in addition to the English "Oates" line. She has a Catholic background. She is going to Europe for the very first time this summer. Even her not smoking and drinking, her partiality to soda pop, her belief in the classroom, remind me of the simpler ideals and routines of working-class families during the Thirties. Her biography on book jackets reads like an application for a job: . . . *received her elementary education in a one-room schoolhouse and then attended city junior and senior high schools...majored in English and minored in philosophy. . . class valedictorian . . . Phi Beta Kappa . . . on a fellowship from the University of Wisconsin she earned her master's degree in English. . . at Wisconsin she met her future husband, Raymond Smith, who is a specialist in eighteenth-century literature . . . Miss Oates's love for writing is almost as old as she is . . .*

Since she writes so easily, she probably has more time for reading than many writers do ("I'm just beginning to read D.H. Lawrence!"), even though she has a full teaching schedule and is obviously a dedicated teacher. "I have three geniuses in my writing class this term." She likes every writer you ask her about. Sitting with her, talking to her rush-rush-rush, seeking out a young woman who will not be sought out, I nevertheless find myself happily looking at and listening to her unbelievable "old-fashionedness." Some of her expressions come straight out of the schoolroom of *my* youth: "And when I have written my story, I copy it out on *good paper*." Good paper! This is the way good little girls and boys in public school talked in 1929, before Joyce Carol Oates was born!

But perhaps she isn't a good little girl? Though she has so little vanity that you might think writing is her hobby, I am fascinated by the intense dislike she arouses—perhaps especially among women writers, who would like to put her down as a freak. One reviewer pointedly asked her to stop writing. Another, in a general attack called "Violence in the Head," complained of the story "What Death with Love Should Have To Do" (in the collection *Upon the Sweeping Flood*): "The plot crystallizes the motif of sex and death, a sort of lumpen *Liebestod*, that reappears in the novels. There is an authentic feeling in these stories," wrote Elizabeth Dalton, "for the physical ambience of poverty, for the grease stains, the stale smells, the small decorative objects of plastic. What seems less authentic, however, is the violence itself and the rather programmatic way it is used to resolve every situation. . . ." Miss Dalton said of the first novel, *With Shuddering Fall*: "Through the transparent implausibility of the plot there looms a sado-masochistic fantasy which endows the heroine with tremendous power." She complained of *them*: "One reason for the oddly blank effect of all the horror is the lack of structure and internal impetus in the narrative. Events do not build toward a climax, or accumulate tension and meaning, but seem simply to happen in the random and insignificant way of real life." Another woman writer complained that "Oates is entirely undramatic. Dullsville."

These complaints come more often than not from women, I believe, because Joyce Carol Oates is, more than most women writers, entirely open to *social* turmoil, to social havoc and turbulence, to the frighteningly undirected and misapplied force of an American powerhouse like Detroit. It is rare to find a woman writer so externally unconcerned with form. After teaching at the University of Detroit from 1962 to 1967, she remarked that Detroit is a city "so transparent, you can hear it ticking." When publishing *them* (which deals with the 1967 eruption of Detroit's blacks) she described Detroit as "all melodrama." She has an instinct for the social menace packed up in Detroit, waiting to explode, that at the end of the nineteenth century Dreiser felt about Chicago and Stephen Crane about New York. The sheer rich chaos of American life, to say nothing of its staggering armies of poor, desperate, outraged, and by no means peaceful people, presses upon her; her fiction, Robert M. Adams has noticed, takes the form of "retrospective nightmare." What Elizabeth Dalton disapprovingly called "violence in the head" expresses, I suspect, Joyce Carol Oates' inability to blink social violence as the language in which a great many "lower class" Americans naturally deal with each other.

So a writer born in 1938 regularly "returns" to the 1930s in her work. *A Garden of Earthly Delights* begins with the birth on the highway of a migrant worker's child after the truck transporting the workers has been in a collision. I would guess that Joyce Carol Oates' constant sense of Americans in collision, not to overlook characters who are obsessed without being able to *talk* freely, perhaps rubs the wrong way critics who like events to "build toward a climax, or accumulate tension and meaning." Oates is unlike many women writers in her feeling for the pressure, mass, density of violent American experience not known to the professional middle class. Praising a little-known social novel by Harriette Arnow, *The Dollmaker*, Oates said:

It seems to me that the greatest works of literature deal with the human soul caught in the stampede of time, unable to gauge the profundity of what passes over it, like the characters of Yeats who live through terrifying events but who cannot understand them; in this way history passes over most of us. Society is caught in a convulsion, whether of growth or death, and ordinary people are destroyed. They do not, however, understand that they are "destroyed."

I do not know how applicable this is to *The Dollmaker*, a book I have not read. But this view of "literature" as silent tragedy is a most illuminating description of what interests Oates in fiction and of what she is trying to do in her novels. Her own characters seem to move through a world wholly physical in its detail, yet they touch us and frighten us like disembodied souls calling to us from another world; "they live through terrifying events but cannot understand them." This is what makes Oates a new element in our fiction, involuntarily disturbing. She does not understand why she is disturbing. She is "radical" not programmatically but in her sweetly brutal sense of what American experience is really like. She knows that while "history" is all we save from death, people caught up in the convulsion of society cannot see the meaning to their lives that history will impose. Life as we live it, trying to save ourselves as we go, is really images of other people; hence the many collisions in Oates's work, the couplings that are like collisions, the crash of people against metal and of metal with metal. As Faulkner said, "It's because so much happens. Too much happens." People are literally overpowered by their experience.

Oates is peculiarly and even painfully open to all this, selfless in her imagination, so possessed by other people that in an author's note to *them* she says of the student who became the "Maureen Wendall" of the novel, "Her various problems and complexities overwhelmed me . . . My initial feeling about her life was, 'This must be fiction, this can't be real!' My more permanent feeling was, 'This is the only kind of fiction that is real.'" This capacity for becoming one's characters (Keats called it "negative capability") makes Oates a sometimes impenetrably voluminous historian of lives, lives, lives; you feel that you are turning thousands of pages, that her world is as harshly overpopulated as the subway, that you cannot distinguish the individual sounds within this clamor of existence.

On the other hand, much contemporary fiction by Americans, women and men, is not only peculiarly personal, moodily self-assertive, but dominated by a social anxiety that mistakenly traces itself to personal instability. There are "Danger" signs now posted around every personal landscape. Much of contemporary American fiction is based not only on the amazingly expansive sense of self that is the privilege of middle-class society—"I" means movement, money, the ability to take a chance—but personal vulnerability, the risk we take every day of being exposed, totally, to the destructiveness of our own power.

The middle-class American, traditionally expansive in his estimate of life, now feels peculiarly threatened by "history." This expresses itself more as open social conflict than as individual anxiety; but the anxiety is real enough, and shows itself as the typically American rhetoric of bitterness—to have moved up so far, yet no longer to feel safe in anything! This is why so many women writers now express perfectly the complaint that the individual, never before so aware of its wants and possibilities, has never felt so betrayed. Women writers are now the spokesmen for the frustration of the educated, professional middle class.

Oates is feminine all right, and a woman writer whose sensibility can sometimes detour you through empty country. Her titles— *With Shuddering Fall, By the North Gate, Upon the Sweeping Flood, A Garden of Earthly Delights, The Wheel of Love*—often taken from English Renaissance poems, are almost comically appropriate to what she writes about. She once told an interviewer from *Cosmopolitan* that she is always writing about love. "The emotion of love, probably that's the essence of what I'm writing about, and it takes many different forms, many different social levels . . . I think I write about love in an unconscious way. I look back upon the novels I've written, and I say, yes, this was my subject. But at the time I'm writing I'm not really conscious of that. I'm writing about a certain person who does this and that and comes to a certain end."

What she means by love, you notice, is an attraction of person to person so violent that it expresses itself as obsession and takes on the quality of fatality: the emotions of her characters are stark physical truths, like the strength or weakness of one's body. But she herself is the most intensely unyielding lover in her books, as witness the force with which she follows so many people through every trace of their feeling, thinking, moving. She is herself obsessive in her patience with the sheer factuality of human existence. This evident love for the "scene" we Americans make, for the incredible profusion of life in America, also troubles Joyce Carol Oates, I would guess. Every writer knows himself to be a little crazy, but her feeling of her own absurdity is probably intensified by the dreamlike ease with which her works are produced. It must indeed trouble her that this looks like glibness, when in point of fact her dogged feeling that she writes out of love is based on the fact that she is utterly hypnotized, positively drugged, by other people's experiences. The social violence so marked in her work is like the sheer density of her detail—this and this and this is what is happening to people. She is attached to life by well-founded apprehensions that nothing lasts, nothing is safe, nothing is all around us. In *them*, the best of her novels, Maureen Wendall thinks:

Maybe the book with her money in it, and the money so greedily saved, and the idea of the money, maybe these things weren't real either. What would happen if everything broke into pieces? It was queer how you felt, instinctively, that a certain space of time was real and not a dream, and you gave your life to it, all your energy and faith, believing it to be real. But how could you tell what would last and what wouldn't? Marriages ended. Love ended. Money could be stolen, found out and taken . . . or it might disappear by itself, like that secretary's notebook. Objects disappeared, slipped through the cracks, devoured, kicked aside, knocked under the bed or into the trash, lost . . . Her clearest memory of the men she'd been with was their moving away from her. They were all body then, completed.

The details in Oates's fiction follow each other with a humble truthfulness that makes you wonder where she is taking you, that is sometimes truly disorienting, for she is all attention to the unconscious reactions of her characters. She needs a lot of space, which is why her short stories tend to read like scenarios for novels. The amount of concentration this involves is certainly very singular, and one can well understand the vulnerability, the "reedlike thinness," the face and body tense with listening that her appearance gives off. My deepest feeling about her is that her mind is unbelievably crowded with psychic existences, with such a mass of stories that she lives by being wholly submissive to "them," the others. She is too burdened by some mysterious clamor to *want* to be an artist, to make the right and well-fitting structure. "The greatest realities," she has said, "are physical and economic; all the subtleties of life come afterward. Intellectuals have forgotten, or else they never understood, how difficult it is to make one's way up from a low economic level, to assert one's will in a great crude way. It's so difficult. You have to go through it. You have to be poor."

Yet admiring her sense of reality, so unpresuming, honest, and truly exceptional, I have to add that the problem of dealing with Oates is that many of the things she has written are not artistically ambitious enough. They seem written to relieve her mind of the people who haunt it, not to create something that will live. So much documentation of the suddenly frightening American situation is indeed a problem in our fiction just now; the age of high and proud art has yielded to a climate of crisis. Oates' many stories resemble a card index of situations; they are not the deeply plotted stories that we return to as perfect little dramas; her novels, though they involve the reader because of the author's intense connection with her material, tend, as incident, to fade out of our minds. Too much happens. Indeed, hers are altogether strange books, haunting rather than "successful," because the mind behind them is primarily concerned with a kind of Darwinian struggle for existence between minds, with the truth of the universal human struggle. We miss the perfectly suggestive shapes that modern art and fiction have taught us to venerate. Oates is perhaps a Cassandra bewitched by her private oracle. But it is not disaster that is most on her mind; it is, rather, the recognition of each person as the center of the coming disturbance. And this disturbance, as Pascal said of divinity, has its center everywhere and its circumference nowhere.

So her characters are opaque, ungiving, uncharming; they have the taciturn qualities that come with the kind of people they are—heavy, deracinated, outside the chatty middle class. She speaks in them, but *they* are not articulate. They do not yet feel themselves to be emancipated persons. They are caught up in the social convulsions and they move unheedingly, compulsively, blindly, through the paces assigned to them by the power god.

This is exactly what Oates's work expresses now: a sense that American life is taking us by the throat. "Too much" is happening: we will disappear. Above all, and most ominously, it is a world in which our own people get "wasted." There is a constant sense of drift, deterioration, the end of things, that contrasts violently with the once-fond belief in the immortality of art. Oates is someone plainly caught up in the "avalanche" of time.

The Dark Lady of American Letters

Joe David Bellamy

Originally appeared in *The Atlantic Monthly*, 1972. Reprinted by permission.

"I feel a certain impatience with generalizations, especially my own," Joyce Carol Oates wrote in her reply to my preliminary questions, mailed off to her just a few days before, "but I'll try to think out coherent answers to your questions.

"Art is mostly unconscious and instinctive; theories obviously come later in history, in personal history, and are therefore suspicious. Any kind of verbal analysis of any kind of impulsive art is dissatisfying. This isn't a way out of answering difficult questions—though I am always eager to find a way out of questions of any kind—but something I believe in very strongly."

Unlike her previous letter, written out in her careful, elegant hand—in which she gave her consent to this interview-by-mail—this letter was crowded onto the page, typewritten single-spaced in shotgun style with "X"ed-out corrections, almost without margins, as if the pages themselves had seemed scarcely large enough to the writer to contain the potential deluge of language—or so I imagined.

This was not the first time I was to be surprised by the promptness of her replies. I was undecided whether to be gratified by this swiftness or simply flabbergasted. Surely she had more pressing things to do than to write to me. Surely she was attending to those pressing matters, whatever they were, in addition to writing these letters. Such productivity struck me as mildly terrifying.

Though hardly out of character. Winner of the 1970 National Book Award for fiction, as well as numerous other prizes for her writing through the years, Joyce Carol Oates has been producing work (especially fiction, but also poetry, plays, criticism, and reviews) at an astounding rate since the publication of her first collection of stories, *By the North Gate*, eight years ago: five novels published, three more collections of stories, two books of poetry, two plays produced off-Broadway, a book on tragedy, on and on.

The interview which follows is an edited version of our correspondence, including all material that seemed pertinent to a consideration of the writer and her work. Aside from a few minor alterations made for the sake of greater coherence or accommodation of the material into an interview format, the questions and answers are reproduced as originally written.

Joe David Bellamy: What are your writing habits? What times of day do you like to write? How many pages do you average— if there is an average? How do you manage to write so much? Is this simply natural facility, or have you cultivated it in some unusual way?

Joyce Carol Oates: I don't have any formal writing habits. Most of the time I do nothing, and the fact of time passing so relentlessly is a source of anguish to me. There are not enough hours in the day. Yet I waste most of my time, in daydreaming, in drawing faces on pieces of paper (I have a compulsion to draw faces; I've drawn several million faces in my life, and I'm doomed to carry this peculiar habit with me to the grave). We live on the Detroit River, and I spend a lot of time looking at the river. Everything is flowing away, flowing by. When I'm with people I often fall into a kind of waking sleep, a daydreaming about the people, the strangers, who are to be the "characters" in a story or a novel I will be writing. I can't do much about this habit. At times my head seems crowded; there is a kind of pressure inside it, almost a frightening physical sense of confusion, fullness, dizziness. Strange people appear in my thoughts, and define themselves slowly to me: first their faces, then their personalities and quirks and personal histories, then their relationships with other people, who very slowly appear; and a kind of "plot" then becomes clear to me, as I figure out how all these people come together and what they are doing. I can see them at times very closely, and indeed I "am" them—my personality merges with theirs. At other times I can see them from a distance; the general shape of their lives, which will be transformed into a novel, becomes clear to me; so I try to put this all together, working very slowly, never hurrying the process. I can't hurry it any more than I can prevent it. When the story is more or less coherent and has emerged from the underground, then I can begin to write quite quickly. In *Wonderland* (published in October, 1971) I did about the same number of pages on certain days; in fact last summer, working in a kind of trance, elated and exhausted, for many hours at a time. I wasn't creating a story but simply recording it, remembering it. This is true for all of my writing; I have never "made up" a story while sitting at the typewriter. But then, of course, there is revision.

JDB: What are you working on now?

JCO: I am putting together a group of short stories called *Marriages and Infidelities*, which include stories that are re-imaginings of famous stories (for instance, "The Dead," "The Lady with the Pet Dog," "The Metamorphosis," "Where I Lived and What I Lived For," "The Turn of the Screw"); and my thoughts are much with this book, when I am able to get them free of *Wonderland*. ("The Dead"—retitled by the editors of *McCall's*—was published in the July issue of that magazine. "The Turn of the Screw" will be out soon in *Iowa Review*.) These stories are meant to be autonomous stories, yet they are also testaments of my love and extreme devotion to these other writers; I imagine a kind of spiritual "marriage" between myself and them, or let's say our "daimons" in the Yeatsian sense—exactly in the Yeatsian sense, which is so exasperating and irrational!

Now I am in a state of spiritual exhaustion, I think, from the last novel I did, *Wonderland*, a novel about brains—the human brain—which was my most ambitious novel and almost did me in. I had to read a great deal about the human brain, particularly the pathology of the brain; I don't recommend it for anyone. Just going through the galleys brought back to me in a flash all the excitement and dread and exhaustion of those long days last summer when I wrote the novel. I couldn't do it again. It might be my last novel, at least my last large, ambitious novel, where I try to re-create a man's soul, absorb myself into his consciousness and co-exist with him. In my ordinary daily life I am a very conventional person, I think—I hope; but while writing *Wonderland* I found it difficult to keep up the barriers, to keep myself going as Joyce Smith, a professor of English, a wife, a woman, with certain friends, certain duties. It is sometimes such a *duty* to remain sane and accountable. Any study of the human brain leads one again and again to the most despairing, unanswerable questions . . . there is no way out of the physical fact of the brain, no way *out* of this confinement. Yet it can't be measured or adequately explained, at least not the relationship between the brain and the "mind" it somehow generates. It has been months since I've finished *Wonderland*, but I can't seem to get free of it. I keep reliving parts of it, not in the way I still relive *them* (I was very fond of Jules Wendall, the hero of *them*), but in another way. It's like a bad dream that never came to a completion. It's the first novel I have written that doesn't end in violence, that doesn't liberate the hero through violence, and therefore there is still a sickish, despairing, confusing atmosphere about it. . . .

JDB: *Wonderland* sounds most intriguing. I was interested in what you said about the ending, how there seems to be a connection between its coming back to haunt you and the fact that it *doesn't* end in violence, doesn't "liberate the hero through violence." Do you have any idea why this is so? Or, for that matter, why violence in general characterizes so much of your work?

Related to this, more specific situations occur to me too—for example, a situation in your work where a man is following a woman or where a woman fears or imagines or even possibly hopes a man is following her (but is at the same time repelled); or a situation where a character might be thinking impulsively of suicide. Why do such situations tend to recur? They are inherently dramatic, obviously. Maybe this is a question you don't care to think about, to become conscious about, I'm asking you to do the critic's job really—or even the psychoanalyst's job—on your own work. That's probably not fair. But I do tend to be curious about it.

JCO: I can't do justice to your question about violence; I can't add much to my fiction on this subject. I don't know. Am I personally haunted by the fear of violence, the need for violence, or do I reflect everyone else's feelings about it? I sense it around me, both the fear and the desire, and perhaps I simply have appropriated it from other people. My own life is quiet, very ordinary and conservative; on a scale of 1 to 10 my own energies (id or otherwise) must be around 2, hovering feebly. I sometimes think of how strange it must be to be a man, burdened with biologically determined energies that no one in his right mind would choose. . . . This is the era of Women's Liberation, but I really must say that I think men have a far more difficult time, simply living, existing, trying to measure up to the absurd standards of "masculinity" in our culture and in nature itself, which is so cruel.

JDB: Coincidentally, I did read your story after "The Dead" in the July *McCall's*. I did catch the Joyce echo, at the end especially, with the snow falling. It is a strong, intriguing, impressive story. (Since Ilena is a writer and so many of the peripheral details of her life seem similar to your own, I did seem somewhat troubled [actually "embalmed" comes to mind] to learn about her weariness in answering questions about her "writing habits.")

Also, the whole atmosphere of autobiographical confusion, that is, of the mixture of fiction with details that suggested some autobiographical accuracy, was constantly frustrating and amazing and oddly gratifying to my imagination. I suppose it's inevitable that readers develop a sense of curiosity about the personal lives of writers they admire (what else is biography for?). (The question I want to ask here is not, I think, ultimately embarrassing.) Some writers, once they become famous enough (Norman Mailer comes to mind), learn to make good dramatic use of characters similar to or possibly identical to, or even quite different from (but apparently similar to—the reader never knows), themselves. Do you think you were doing something of that sort in this story? (I hope that's a fair question.)

JCO: Some of the details in the story are authentic, some slightly invented, but the general tone of busyness is real enough; except I haven't the aloneness of the character in the story, her freedom to simply be alone once in a while, even if only to think dark thoughts and recall with amazement simpler times.

My use of myself in stories—well, it has always been there, the use of emotions I've felt. I should be a rational, contained person, I guess, but really I am very emotional—I believe that the storm of emotion constitutes our human tragedy, if anything does. It's our constant battle with nature (Nature), trying to subdue chaos outside and inside ourselves, occasionally winning small victories, then being swept along by some cataclysmic event of our own making. I feel an enormous sympathy with people who've gone under, who haven't won even the small victories. . . .

JDB: Questions about writing habits *are* probably futile. The implication behind the questions is usually: "Tell me your secret. If I know how you do it, maybe I will be able to do it." All of this preliminary is unnecessary. I want to ask you a few more simple-minded, possibly boring questions about your writing habits, and then I won't bring up the subject again. (a) Do you drink coffee before or while working? If so, how much? (b) Do you sleep well? How many hours a night on the average? Do you remember your dreams well—your nighttime dreams, I mean? (c) Have you ever tried amphetamines or other sorts of stimulants to help you work better? (I'm thinking of Ilena in the *McCall's* story, and also of John Barth, who said he sometimes uses a very mild form of speed to help him work better).

JCO: [This is] a very normal question, which you needn't apologize for, [about] the use of drinks, drugs, coffee, and so on. I don't take drugs of any kind, or even drink, or smoke (I'm so dull—see Alfred Kazin's essay on me in the August *Harper's*), or even drink coffee; it's just the way I happened to grow up, nothing essentially puritanical and certainly not moral about it. I am addicted to work, which is to say the expulsion of built-up ideas and formless forms, the need to get rid of little stories that crowd my head. Alfred Kazin was quite right in saying that I sometimes write as if to relieve my mind of things that haunt it, not to create literature that will live. (But I don't think many writers really work consciously to create literature that will "live"—that will be monumental, like *Ulysses*. I think most writers write out of an interior compulsion, hoping that it will add up to an artistic statement of some worth.) . . . About my dreams: I seem to be always dreaming, awake or asleep, though when I'm awake I know I'm awake. I wonder if this is normal . . . ? My husband evidently doesn't experience this. Asleep, I dream about anything, just like anyone else; but I have terrible nights of insomnia, when my mind is galloping along and I feel a strange eerie nervousness, absolutely inexplicable. What a nuisance! Or, maybe it isn't a nuisance? An ideal insomnia allows for a lot of reading. When the house is dark and quiet and the entire world turned off for the night, it's a marvelous feeling to be there, alone, with a book, or a blank piece of paper, or even a blank mind, just sitting there alone. Such moments of solitude redeem all the rushing hours, the daylight confusion of people and duties. I like to write, but I really love to read: that must be the greatest pleasure of civilization.

JDB: What *do* you read?

JCO: I read constantly, in three areas—the rereading of old works (I'm now going through *Ulysses* again), the reading of an avalanche of literary quarterlies, magazines, reviews, and so on, that come into our home steadily (some magazines are not read but devoured: *New American Review, Tri-Quarterly*, for instance, incredibly good magazines), and new novels. There is a vigor and an excitement in contemporary writing that I think is remarkable. I have only to reach out for any current magazine—let's say *New American Review*, which is handy, issue #10—to discover at least one story that is striking, maybe even a masterpiece. In this issue of *NAR* it is Philip Roth's "On the Air," Kafka and Lenny Bruce and pure Rothian genius, very hard, bitter, terrifying stuff.

JDB: What about the future of fiction in general? Do you think the novel may be dead or dying?

JCO: The novel can't be dead or even close to dying if an American publisher can bring out one good novel a year, just one: let's say Bellow's *Mr. Sammler's Planet* last year and Doctorow's *The Book of Daniel* this year. We would hope for more, and we usually do get more.

JDB: What sort of possibilities do you see for those fiction writers who are trying to break out of the conventions of the so-called realistic tradition? Are you one of these writers?

JCO: Fiction writers have broken out of the "conventions of the so-called realistic tradition" years ago, decades ago; it's a commonplace of critical thought to point all the way back to *Tristram Shandy* as a convention-breaking work, but even (even!) *Tom Jones* is rather iconoclastic. There has never been a novel so fantastic as *Remembrance of Things Past*. It is all things, a complete life, an extended thought, an arrangement and rearrangement of reality that is much more believable than the reality of most lives lived daily, at least in my part of the world. July 10, 1971, was Proust's one hundredth birthday, and he is very much alive. Another iconoclastic novel is *Dr. Faustus*. What an accomplishment! I am always rereading Mann in utter admiration, in love. Ah, to be able to write like Thomas Mann . . . or even to write a novel that Mann might approve of, even mildly . . . . When I write a story or a novel I don't feel that I am any particular person, with a particular ego. I seem to share, however vaguely, in the "tradition"—the tradition of literature, of all that has been done that I know about and love. Each story has a form and a style that is best suited for it, and all I do is wait around until these things come together—the people in my imagination, who are to be the "characters" in the formal work, the form, the style, the language, the setting (which is another character), the mood, the year. So I don't think of myself as "one of those writers who is trying to break free of conventions." There aren't any conventions really. And if *Middlemarch* is a conventional novel, how wonderful it would be if contemporary novelists could write anything comparable! There are no conventions or traditions, only personalities.

JDB: Your statement "There are no conventions or traditions, only personalities" I find very liberating and helpful. But I still worry about that question. Of course, fiction writers broke away from the conventions of the so-called realistic tradition years ago; and, of course, the history of the novel can be seen as a series of rebellions against previously "established" forms all the way back to the very beginning. But aren't those rebellions still going on? And if it isn't one writer rebelling against a "tradition," maybe it's a personality rebelling against another personality; or simply any writer working to find something new to keep from boring herself or himself to death.

Maybe what I should have asked was, What sort of presently occurring formal innovations interest you the most? Or, wouldn't you agree that the electric media, for example, have had various sorts of unprecedented influences on contemporary writing? I mean something beyond bothersome prophecies of its demise—formal influences, time-and-space influences? And haven't these affected you? In your own work there seems to be a greater interest in formal experimentation. "The Turn of the Screw" might be one example. In *The Wheel of Love*, stories such as "How I Contemplated the World" and "Matter and Energy," or even "The Wheel of Love" or "Unmailed, Unwritten Letters" (which is much more than a simple epistolary story), seem more formally innovative to me than any of the earlier stories, say, in *By the North Gate*. Why is this?

JCO: I am interested in formal experimentation, yes, but generally this grows out of a certain plot. The form and the style seem naturally suited to the story that has to be told; as in "Matter and Energy" (a story I feel very close to), where the young girl's present life is entirely conditioned by what happened in the past, and her love for a man entirely conditioned—ruined—by her love for her mother, a rotten, hopeless love. Think of the horror, of existing always with the memory of such a mother, committed to an insane asylum—while "you" are free, evidently, to walk around and act normal, to try to love, to act out a certain role. One always thinks of a few other people day after day; there's no escape. A father, a mother, a few beloved people—that is the extent of the universe, emotionally. And if something has gone wrong inside this small universe, then nothing can ever be made right. (This story is based on the anguished recollections of a student of mine, whose mother is in an asylum and who tried to kill him, many years ago. He is now an adult, an earnest and intelligent young man, but at the same time he is *still* that child; he is still coming home to that mother, to that event.) So the form of the story grew naturally out of its subject matter. In "The Turn of the Screw," the use of journals is a kind of Victorian cliché; among other things, I wanted to suggest how interior lives touch upon one another in odd, jagged, oblique ways, without communicating any essential truth, in fact without communicating truth. In "Unmailed, Unwritten Letters" (which is perhaps my favorite story, at least emotionally), the epistolary form is a way the heroine has of sending out cries for help, not meant to be heard; simply a way of articulating a private bewilderment. Not that I want to dwell upon this story, but it seems to have touched some common chord in people—I've received a number of letters from other writers/critics/men of letters of a type, who seem to like it. What does this mean about our American marriages . . . ?

JDB: What is your concept of characterization? Or what are your ideas about characterization? This is overly general perhaps (and maybe less coherent than one might hope for). How about this: Do you think "hardened" character such as the kind in Victorian novels is real or valid?

JCO: Your questions about characterization are quite coherent questions, yet I can't answer them because—as you might gather from what I have already said—I don't write the way other people evidently write, or at least I can't make sense of what they say about their writing. My characters really dictate themselves to me. I am not free of them, really, and I can't force them into situations they haven't themselves willed. They have the autonomy of characters in a dream. In fact, when I glance through what I have tried to say to you, it occurs to me that I am really transcribing dreams, giving them a certain civilized, extended shape, clearing a few things up, adding daytime details, subtracting fantastic details, and so on, in order to make the story or the novel a work of art. Private dreams have no interest for other people; the dream must be made public, by using one's wit.

People say that I write a great deal, and they are usually curious about when I "find time." But the odd thing is that I waste most of my time. I don't think I am especially productive, but perhaps other writers are less productive. In the past, however, writers like Henry James, Edith Wharton, Dickens (of course), and so on and so forth, wrote a great deal, wrote innumerable volumes, because they were professional writers and writers write. Today, it seems something of an oddity that a writer actually writes, and some writers or critics who don't spend much time writing seem to resent more productive writers. Someone said that John Updike publishes books as often as John O'Hara did, but thankfully his books weren't quite as long as O'Hara's. . . . This is an attitude I can't understand. Any book by Updike is a happy event. The more, the better. If any critic

imagines that he is tired of Updike, then he should not read the
next Updike novel and he certainly should not review it.

. . . I don't know that the above will strike you as good enough,
or that I have answered your questions. I know one thing,
though: I would never have thought of some of these things in a
person-to-person interview. The whole *social* aspect of such
interviewing gets in the way of ideas.

You are kind in the many things you say about my writing and
about me (you probably do know me quite well, because I've told
you things that acquaintances and social friends of mine would
never be told, not in dozens of years)—it may be that I am
mysterious, in a way; certainly there are things about myself that
don't make sense to me and are therefore mysterious, to me; but
the main thing about me is that I am enormously interested in
other people, other lives, and that with the least provocation (a
few hints of your personal life, let's say, your appearance, your
house and setting), I could "go into" your personality and try to
imagine it, try to find a way of dramatizing it. I am fascinated by
people I meet, or don't meet, people I only correspond with, or
read about; and I hope my interest in them isn't vampiristic,
because I don't want to take life from them, but only to honor the
life in them, to give some permanent form to their personalities.
It seems to me that there are so many people who are inarticulate,
but who suffer and doubt and love, nobly, who need to be
immortalized or at least explained.

Here in Windsor, life is filling up with people: parents coming
to visit, trunks to be packed, last-minute arrangements to be made,
a dozen, a hundred chores, such as what to serve for dinner
tonight. But thank God for trivial events! They keep us from
spinning completely off into the dark, into the abstract universe.

I hope these answers make some kind of sense to you. Much
of this I haven't thought out, until now; it sounds bizarre but is
very honest.

Joyce Carol Oates: Love and Violence

Walter Clemons

Originally appeared in *Newsweek*, 1972. Reprinted by permission.

She is a tall, pale young woman with enormous eyes and a timid, little-girl voice who rather plaintively assures interviewers, "I'm not that interesting." If you met her at a literary party and failed to catch her name, it might be hard to imagine her reading, much less writing, the unflinching fiction that has made Joyce Carol Oates perhaps the most significant novelist to have emerged in the United States in the last decade.

At 34, her sweeping vision of America as a delusive wonderland of colliding forces, where love as often as hate leads to violence, has established Miss Oates as a major—and controversial—figure in American writing. Her frailness is deceptive. In less than ten years she has published five powerfully disquieting novels—*With Shuddering Fall, A Garden of Earthly Delights, Expensive People, them,* for which she won the National Book Award in 1970, and *Wonderland.* There were also four collections of stories, two books of poems, a collection of essays on tragedy and a couple of hundred book reviews and stories not yet collected in book form. Three plays have been produced off-Broadway, and she has finished a fourth. During this same period she produced two other novels she kept around her house for a while and finally put out with the garbage. "I thought I might die and someone might find them," she says cheerfully. "I don't miss them."

Each of Joyce Carol Oates's books has been a different technical and intellectual experiment, gradually building up a fictional world that is recognizably her own. It is a world of such violence that Oates has often been called "Gothic": 16-year-old Loretta Wendall, early in *them*, wakes up to find her lover dead beside her, shot by her brother, and she is shortly thereafter raped by the policeman who agrees to remove the body to the alley; the brilliant opening section of *Wonderland* ends with a boy's escape from a murderous father who has wiped out the other members of his family.

But Oates is non-Gothic, and original, in her tenacious adherence to the humble ordinariness that surrounds violence. Her people blot out that they can't deal with. "They do not understand that they have been 'destroyed,'" she says. They go on, as dully and inarticulately as before, and as a result some have found her accounts of them all too full of verisimilitude. "Events do not build toward a climax, or accumulate tension and meaning," critic Elizabeth Dalton complained of *them*. They "simply seem to happen in the random and insignificant way of real life." But this is the problem that Oates shares with every American writer today—how to bring order to that extremity. As Philip Roth has put it: "The American writer in the middle of the twentieth century has his hands full in trying to understand, and then describe, and then make *credible*, much of the American reality. It stupefies, it sickens . . . and finally it is even a kind of embarrassment to one's own meager imagination."

What Joyce Carol Oates has done is to take the novel back to its root meaning—"news"—in a period when some of the best of her contemporaries have frankly explored fiction as artifice or turned from fiction to the New Journalism or to the "nonfiction novel" of Mailer or Capote. She is nineteenth century in her patient faith that the novel can show us *The Way We Live Now*, as Trollope called one of his best books. "I have a laughably Balzacian ambition to get the whole world into a book," she said when she saw *them* for the first time in page proofs and was disappointed that it was only 500 pages. "It was 700 pages in manuscript," mused Oates. "Well, next time."

It is this urgent desire to tell the whole truth about the way we live that makes Joyce Carol Oates seem so shockproof about today's shocking world. "It seems that I write about things that are violent and extreme," she says, "but it is always against a background of something deep and imperishable. I feel I can wade in blood, I can endure the 10,000 evil visions because there is this absolutely imperishable reality behind it."

"Her sweetly brutal sense of what American experience is really like," as Alfred Kazin has called it, has its source in a period she cannot remember, though she returns to it regularly in her fiction. The Depression was almost over when she was born in 1938 in the town of Lockport in upstate New York, but she feels its effect on her parents' lives.

"I'm from a part of the world and an economic background where people don't even graduate from high school. My father probably went to about the seventh grade—he had to get out and work when he was 11 or 12, and his whole life has been colored by that, the Depression. And my mother, the same way. But if I have any artistic talent, I think I inherited it from them. My father has always been able to play the violin and the piano—*instinctively*. Where did that come from? And my mother has a domestic artistic talent: what she does with flowers, what she does with the house, her life is an artistic life. If either of them could have gone to college, who knows? But at that point in our economic history, that was out of the question. They were out working, not yet even teenagers. It was a grim, a very grim world."

The world of her childhood—on her maternal grandparents' farm—was grim domestically as well, though she resolutely refuses to go into detail: "Very, very terrible things, that were not sudden but lasted for years, involving long and lingering deaths, cancer . . . and other problems, too. But my mother was a radiant personality, she always was, and I think she's gotten even more so." She put her parents into *Wonderland*; the hero, whose life is shaped by his narrow escape from a murderous father, drives out toward Buffalo and stops near an old cider mill, where he sees a couple and their little girl. "That's my parents and me," Joyce Carol Oates says. "I'm about 4 or 5 years old. There's a snapshot of us in this old swing we had. I thought I'd put us right in the novel, because that's the way I remember my childhood. My father looks out into the lane at this stranger and moves as if to guard and protect his family."

She has always insisted that, except for small details like this, her fiction isn't autobiographical. "I don't really care to write about my own life, because I've already experienced it." But she is emphatic about the importance of her rural childhood. "The thing about me—if—" and she pauses, to put in her customary, embarrassed disclaimer: "I don't feel I'm that important or interesting." Then she adds: "The real clue to me is that I'm like certain people who are not really understood—Jung and Heidegger are good examples—people of peasant stock, from the country, who then come into a world of literature or philosophy. Part of us is very intellectual, wanting to read all the books in the library—or even wanting to *write* all the books in the library. Then there's the other side of us, which is sheer silence, inarticulate— the silence of nature, of the sky, of pure being."

She was 17 when she entered Syracuse University on a scholarship in 1956, the first member of her family to go to college. Nevertheless, Joyce experienced little cultural shock. "There were many 'farm girls,' as they called us, at Syracuse and I made friends with girls very much like myself, and then on the vacations I brought books back home—my parents were introduced to a world of books, and excitement, through me, simply because they'd sent me there."

Yet one of her most moving early stories, "Archways," describes the plight of students in a remedial-reading course in a state university, "educated now into knowing their unworth." These were "desperate, doomed young people, many of them from the country, remote incidental rural sections of the state," bewildered by the university "so available to them (they, with their high school diplomas) and yet, as it turned out, so forbidden to them, its great machinery even now working, perhaps, to process cards, grades, symbols that would send them back to their families and the lives they supposed they had escaped."

The defeat that oppresses Joyce Carol Oates's imagination in this story, however, bears no resemblance to her own career at Syracuse. "She was the most brilliant student we've ever had here," says Donald A. Dike, professor of English and Creative Writing at Syracuse, to whom *With Shuddering Fall* is dedicated. He remembers that she wrote mostly short stories, "but about once a term she'd drop a 400-page novel on my desk and I'd read that, too. She had some conscience problems about her writing in those days; she was afraid it was 'not nice' and might offend her parents, and I tried to reassure her."

There is a good-girl, honor-student earnestness about Joyce Carol Oates to this day that baffles and irritates some observers.

But there is no doubting her sincerity when she says, "I absolutely don't believe there is very much originality. I just see myself as standing in a very strong tradition and my debt to other writers is very obvious. I couldn't exist without them. I don't have much autonomous existence, nor does anyone. We are interconnected— it seems we are individual and separate, whereas in fact we're not." Her lack of ego amounts almost to an absentmindedness about her own existence. "My own life just seems to be what I'm doing at the present. If I'm working on a book, that seems to be the book, and I can't remember how I did other things."

Her daily life, in fact, bears little resemblance to the turbulent world of her imagination. She and her husband, Raymond Smith, met as graduate students at the University of Wisconsin in 1961 ("at a faculty tea," she remembers, "and we were married three months later—it was very romantic"). Both now teach in the English department of the University of Windsor, right across the river from Detroit. Detroit—"so transparent, you can hear it ticking," where she taught from 1962 to 1967, the year of the riots recorded in *them*—is visible from the Smiths' riverside back lawn, but they seldom visit it.

She loves teaching and is good at it. "I wish it would never end," says one student of her course in contemporary literature. Though Joyce Carol Oates has never written a novel about university life, it is the subject of some of her best stories.

One of these is "The Dead," an electrifying study of a red-haired, pill-popping teacher-novelist whose marriage disintegrates as she becomes a literary celebrity. Ilena Williams, lecturing to audiences who "could not see the colorless glop she vomited up in motel bathrooms," says things Joyce Carol Oates has said; Ilena reads from her latest work, "a series of short stories in honor of certain dead writers with whom she felt a kinship." And "The Dead" itself is, of course, a homage to, and re-invention of, James Joyce's famous story of the same title. Ilena is an alternate self, Joyce Carol Oates says, "a way I could have gone. Sometimes a crossroad appears and one can go one direction or the other. Sometimes just writing a story about it, mapping out these directions, saves one from doing it, and maybe in reading it someone else may be saved from it, too."

At home, her electric typewriter is in the bedroom; her husband works in a study just off the living room. One oddity of their quiet life together puzzles an outsider: Ray Smith doesn't read his wife's fiction. "He read *Wonderland*," Joyce Carol Oates says, "and he seemed to like it. He sometimes says, 'Should I read this, honey?' and I usually would rather he didn't. I think I would place such a great, exaggerated value on his word that even a slight twist of an eyebrow—I know him so well—would hurt me and I might feel resentment. I give him things to read, book reviews mostly, impersonal things, and he'll tell me that he likes them. But then I feel, does he really? 'Do you *really* like it?' 'Yes.' 'But do you *really*?' 'Well, yes, but this one sentence, maybe, could be fixed.' And I usually fix it. But I think in a close situation like a marriage it's asking for trouble."

"It's a matter of respecting her privacy," says Smith. "I wouldn't want to inhibit her in her choice of subject matter or in any way. I don't want to stand over her shoulder." It works for them. *A Garden of Earthly Delights*, *them* and the volume of poems titled *Love and Its Derangements* are dedicated "to my husband, Raymond."

Oates's work habits are as unique as everything else about her. She writes incessantly, wherever she is—while waiting for her luggage on trips, between takes of a *Newsweek* cover-photo session. Though she writes so rapidly that she sometimes finishes a story in a single evening, she thinks of herself as a slow worker, meaning that she proceeds by periods of "daydreaming" that may last for months before she's ready to sit down at the typewriter. "The novel I'm just about to write now," she says, "I've been working on for a very long time. I've lived through it in my imagination. I know the ending, I know the last paragraph, I know what's going through this person's mind. But I have to find the words to get into it. I woke up this morning with another first paragraph in my head—I've written about five of them. When I get that right . . ." She smiles and snaps her fingers.

Joyce Carol Oates's productivity has aroused irrelevant wonder and impertinent criticism. Her real claim to attention is quite different: the power of her imagination to project her into lives quite different from her own and the fidelity with which she responds to its pressures. The rough world of stock-car racers in

With Shuddering Fall was convincingly created by a young woman who had never seen such a race and dislikes even riding in cars. "You start from what you know about speed," she said, "and go on from there. I read a couple of issues of car magazines. And I remembered fairgrounds. I liked walking around them in the winter, when there was nobody around."

The opening scene of *A Garden of Earthly Delights*, in which a group of migrant workers stand in the rain beside a wrecked truck while a woman gives birth, stays in the reader's mind years afterward and doesn't diminish with rereading. In the preface to *them*, her best book, Oates tried to explain how the family recollections of one of her students at the University of Detroit led to the writing of the novel: "For me, as a witness, so much material had the effect of temporarily blocking out my own reality, my personal life and substituting for it the various nightmare adventures of the Wendalls. Their lives pressed upon mine eerily, so that I began to dream about them instead of about myself, dreaming and redreaming their lives. Because their world was so remote from me it entered me with tremendous power, and in a sense the novel wrote itself."

Unlike the macho male tradition of Hemingway and Mailer— the writer as hunter or athlete of experience—Oates belongs to the tradition of insight and imagination. "I guess I experience things in ways I don't understand," she says. "I think I have a vulnerability to a vibrating field of other people's experiences. I lived through the '60s in the United States, I was aware of hatreds and powerful feelings all around me."

She admires Mailer's personal approach. "Mailer has tried to get right out there into the thick of things: he's sought the centers of action, he's put himself physically in the presence of dangers that maybe he glories in. Yet he also wants an intellectual and imaginative distance and I think he's achieved it. I feel these things going on even though I'm not out there physically, and I feel I have to transcribe them—the 10,000 horrible visions you go through to reach the 10,000 beautiful visions. So in a strange way I would compare the attempt—just the attempt—of what I'm doing with Mailer's, though he and I are totally different, totally antithetical, I'm sure, in personality."

Intensely feminine, Joyce Carol Oates is not a doctrinaire feminist; she is a writer first of all, whose sex is neither an issue nor a weapon. Her utter lack of malice and her generosity to fellow authors contrast with the snobbish attitude that many sleek Eastern writers adopt toward her—an attitude summed up by one big female literary name with the dismissive comment: "She's not our sort." One outspoken admirer, however, is Joan Didion (*Play It as It Lays*), a National Book Award judge for 1971 who staunchly supported *Wonderland* for the fiction prize. "I thought it was an extraordinary book," Didion says. "It fascinated me as a writer. The question we all founder on, whether personality has any meaning—instead of theorizing, she just plunged in and dramatized it. She tried for so much more than the other books we were considering."

The first half of *Wonderland*, from the December day on which Jesse Vogel survives the slaughter of his whole family to his escape from a foster-father as grotesque as his real father, is probably the most impressive fiction Joyce Carol Oates has written, inexorable and nightmarishly precise. But the book gave her more trouble, she says, than any of her others. "It was very painful to write. I was able to dramatize the situation in *Wonderland*, but I couldn't resolve the moral questions it raised and that failure distresses me."

As she talks, one realizes that the "moral failure" that is worrying her is the one that has tormented writers before her, most notably Tolstoy: what use is art if it doesn't help people live better? "With *Wonderland* I came to the end of a phase of my life, though I didn't know it," Joyce Carol Oates reflects. "I want to move toward a more articulate moral position, not just dramatizing nightmarish problems but trying to show possible ways of transcending them."

Her recent book of stories, *Marriages and Infidelities*, was intended as a first step in that direction. She once told an interviewer that love was the subject of all her work, and she now says: "I believe we achieve our salvation, or our ruin, by the marriages we contract. I conceived of a book of marriages. Some are conventional marriages of men and women, others are marriages in another sense—with a phase of art, with something that transcends the limitations of the ego. But because people are mortal, most of the marriages they go into are mistakes of some kind, misreadings of themselves. I thought by putting together a sequence of marriages, one might see how this one succeeds and that one fails. And how *this* one leads to some meaning beyond the self."

For all her wading in blood, her unblinking perception of despair in so many lives today, Oates is an optimist. "Blake, Whitman, Lawrence and others have had a vision of a trans-formation of the human spirit. I agree with it strongly myself. I think it's coming. I don't think it's as close as Charles Reich thinks in *The Greening of America*. He seems to think it's imminent—or even that it's already arrived at Yale. I don't think I'll live to see it. But I want to do what little I can to bring it nearer."

In the decade since Philip Roth observed that the violence, vulgarity and unreality of American life baffled any effort to write credible realistic fiction about it, Roth himself has abandoned the effort and resorted to his own highly individual variants: comic monologue, political burlesque and sexual phantasmagoria. And in that same period Norman Mailer has—at least temporarily—committed himself more to nonfiction than to the novel. Impatiently, often brilliantly, writers of the '60s—John Barth, Donald Barthelme, Thomas Pynchon, Robert Coover, Thomas McGuane and John Gardner—have resorted to parodistic reinventions of the novel, to Borgesian miniaturization, to freeze-dried black comedy as replacements for the realistic narrative that no longer seems feasible to them.

On this fictional scene, Joyce Carol Oates is singular. Though she is as aware as anyone of the possibilities of experimentation and as haunted and oppressed as any of her contemporaries by feelings that American life may be "too much," too crazed, too accelerated to be captured in a novel, she hasn't lost confidence in the power of narrative fiction to give coherence to jumbled experience and to bring about a change of heart. "Let us consider," she recently wrote, "the conclusion of Saul Bellow's *Mister Sammler's Planet*, which is so powerful that it forces us to immediately reread the entire novel, because we have been *altered in the process of reading it* and are now, at its conclusion, ready to begin reading it."

In a letter to *The New York Times Book Review* last summer, she replied with some asperity to a critic who had suggested that she "slow down": "Since critics are constantly telling me to 'slow down,' I must say gently, very gently, that everything I have done so far is only preliminary to my most serious work . . . Every harsh review of my books begins with the routine assessment of my 'output,' in the usual consumer terms. It would be kinder to begin with a recitation of all I have not done . . . owing to our usual human weakness of not expecting enough of ourselves."

She is 34. She has energy, dedication, and a stubborn integrity. Like the most important modern writers—Joyce, Proust, Mann—she has an absolute identification with her material: the spirit of a society at a crucial point in its history. She may not produce an American *Ulysses, Remembrance of Things Past* or *The Magic Mountain*; perhaps no writer ever again will, or can, make so huge an act of imaginative appropriation. But in her eagerness to give everything, to absorb everything, "to get the whole world into a book," Joyce Carol Oates belongs to that small group of writers who keep alive the central ambitions and energies of literature.

Transformation of Self: An Interview with Joyce Carol Oates

Originally appeared in *The Ohio Review*, 1973. Reprinted by permission.

Ohio Review: Your fame is as a writer of fiction; therefore the inevitable question is: how do you view the relationship between your novels and stories and your poetry?

Joyce Carol Oates: Everything is related. If it wouldn't alarm me, I'd someday go back through all my writing and note how the obsessions come and go, horizontally (a single psychological "plot" worked out in a story, a play, poems, parts of novels). Because these things come so directly out of my head, they go into whatever form is handy at the moment. The poems are nearly all lyric expressions of larger, dramatic, emotional predicaments, and they belong to fully-developed fictional characters who "exist" elsewhere. The poems are therefore shorthand, instantaneous, accounts of a state of mind that might have been treated in a 400-page work. I've always had a blindness for, a real inability to appreciate, the purely "lyric"—it seems so faceless, so blank and strangely inhuman, like a few bars of a Mozart symphony, perhaps the most beautiful part of the symphony but . . . but one yearns for more, to *know* more. My heroes are people like Yeats and Lawrence, who, when you read their poetry, you know you are in immediate contact with an immense emotional reality. All of Yeats's poems, at least after *The Green Helmet*, are part of his life story—his personality—the Collected Works which is Yeats. They can be read separately, but not truly understood. And Lawrence, of course, was always writing about himself, his changing moods and ideas, so that poems like his New Mexican series relate beautifully to stories like "The Princess" or "The Woman Who Rode Away"; the poem "One Woman to all Women" might well be spoken by Ursula of *Women in Love*, after her experience of the "glorious equilibrium" of love.

A poem of mine in *Love and Its Derangements*, called "You/Your," was written out of exactly the same maniacal stupor as certain parts of *them*; but it is from the woman's point of view, her befuddlement at her dependence upon a man, upon a man's loving *her*, from which she will get whatever identity she possesses. The woman is Jules' mistress, Nadine, who later tries to kill him. And why not? But when I wrote this part of *them* I felt Nadine to be an enemy, since I was obviously on Jules' side. In fact, many poems in *Derangements* are similar to this one—not that they belong to Nadine; they belong rather to certain experiences that gave me the material for Nadine.

OR: Is this true of the title poem too?

JCO: Yes. "Love and Its Derangements" is a paranoid expression of this same state of mind; it very obviously belongs to the same emotional experience as the short stories of mine "Unmailed, Unwritten Letters," "I Was in Love," sections in *Wonderland* dealing with Jesse's wife, Helene, a play I wrote recently called *Ontological Proof of My Existence*, and so forth, and so forth. This bizarre paranoia isn't anything to cultivate, but I evidently needed to write about it. Then, seeing these things externalized, out of my own imagination, they seemed to be totally foreign, freakish . . . but, like old snapshots that distort and don't flatter and yet are obviously of yourself, they must be claimed.

OR: Would you, then, call this "externalization" process an aesthetic goal?

JCO: Well, here is my theory of "art," at least my temporary theory: any work can be expanded nearly to infinity, or contracted back to almost nothing. And any "work," any artistic experience, can be translated back and forth into various forms—music, painting, literature. This is possible simply because all art is dream-like, springs from the dreaming mind, and is handled either gingerly or enthusiastically by the conscious mind. You experience a certain fantasy, you can't manage it, can't comprehend it; it's a mystery; so, if you are talented in some way, you realize that you might as well try to externalize it to see if anyone else recognizes it. Art is communication. It's always communication, even if you, the artist, are the only one who experiences it: it's the effort of the Ego to communicate with a deeper self. Art is magnificent, divine, because it records the struggles of exceptional men to order their fantasies, their doubts, even their certainties, into an external structure that celebrates the life force itself, the energy of life, as well as the simple fact that someone created it—and especially the fact that you, the audience, are sharing it. These things are obvious, and yet profoundly important. When the work of art is tremendously effective, as *Crime and Punishment* is, it becomes to the careful reader an absolute—no, a superior—experience of its "plot," in this case the committing of two murders. You never need to commit murder if you read that novel sympathetically. The redemption, the conclusion, are absolutely unconvincing; it's the committing of the murders that is important—the exorcism of "evil."

OR: Well, if you could single out a particular artistic intent for your work—poetry and/or fiction—what would it be?

JCO: What I would like to do, always, in my writing is create an obvious and yet perhaps audacious feat: I would like to create the psychological and emotional equivalent of an experience, so completely and in such exhaustive detail, that anyone who reads it sympathetically will have *experienced* that event in his mind (which is where we live anyway). Much of our mental life is, of course, memory. Well, I would like to have absorbed into my system certain "fictional" events so that they are as powerful as memory: so I never need to wonder, as Emma Bovary did, whether I am making a mistake or whether this is maybe a good thing. . . . I will *remember* Emma's experience and I will have learned from it. I don't really believe in "art for art's sake." All art is moral, educational, illustrative. It instructs. If it's working well, it communicates to you exactly what you'd feel if you, like Raskolnikov, had made a mistake. If it works only fitfully, feebly, it can at least tell you how boring it must be to be Samuel Beckett, and it will help you steer yourself in another direction. Even minimal art, like Kline's and Rothko's and—this is probably a terrible thing to say—Berryman's most personal poems, will make you realize how deathly, how suicidal, a certain kind of art is, this obsession with repeating a static announcement about one's own Self. My own writing is very obviously the recording of various states of mind, some of them extreme, and even a dark depressing novel like *Wonderland* can be argued to possess a certain human value: it shows you how to survive. It shows you that someone managed to get through.

OR: Yes. But how do these hopes relate to the impulse toward poetry?

JCO: I believe that any truly felt lyric poem (not simply some Midwestern professor's attempt to write a Poem, to add to his bibliography for the Head of the English Department) can be expanded outward into a story—a novel—anything. Also, I believe that at any point in a lengthy work, poems can be written to very sharply illustrate what is happening, without the occasional tedium of "he walked to the door" "he said" "he smiled and wept." You do really feel a need, in a big novel—I just finished a 700-page novel yesterday—to get out from under the demands of realistic fiction, to say sharply and even bluntly what you are doing. This can be solved of course, by going into a character's head and creating a kind of poetic-prose, using images rather than regular syntactical statements, which I do all the time.

Since the artistic impulse leaps from the unconscious mind, the form it takes in the real, shared, civilized world is really a matter of the artist's skill, his taste, his patience with his own material, and his good luck. The difference between any novel of Beckett's and any work of Chekhov's is not emotional or psychological (since their personalities are obviously similar), but a matter of the degree of formalization, of externalization, of an interior vision. Beckett gives us his thought processes on so primary a level that they are simply language; Chekhov allows his fantasy more room, more time, chooses images in the "real," historical world to illustrate his fantasy, and therefore creates an art much more engaging than Beckett's. Beckett is deathly and boring, but not boring *because* deathly—the Death Trip can be very exciting. He's deathly because he is boring. What is the difference between Henry James and Genet? Probably not much, primarily. If we could truly see into James' head! You can see this sort of thing beautifully in Kafka—long, sometimes-exploratory, unfinished novels; the shorter, very neat stories; the dream-fantasies he jotted down but never bothered to work up into fiction. I find the recording of the "creative process" in its bare, unadorned form less and less interesting. The dynamics of Jackson Pollock, for instance, vs. the formalized visions of Picasso, let's say some of his dancing figures. All minimal art, like Cage's music, like pop art, like the atrocious Id-pouring of much contemporary poetry, just does not interest me at all; it's only intellectual, it's sterile. "When I paint smoke," Picasso said, "I want you to be able to drive a nail in it." Exactly.

OR: Your poems raise, essentially, the same issues as your fiction, but with the exception of early poems such as "Five Confessions" or "Three Dances of Death," they tend to raise those issues (bad word) in terms of you rather than in terms of a character. Is your poetry, then, your more "personal" medium?

JCO: Much of the poetry is indeed personal, but, then, much of the fiction is personal also; but distorted a little, made into fiction. What excites me about writing is the uses I can make of myself, of various small adventures, errors, miscalculations, stunning discoveries, near-disasters, and occasional reversals of everything, but so worked into a fictional structure that no one could guess how autobiographical it all is. Also, I like to combine myself with another person—I mean a real person—in fact, you must be cautious or I will get into you—and synthesize selves, probable experiences, etc., to make a third person, a "fictional" person. The weirdest thing I have ever done is to take a direct experience *as I was experiencing it*, second by second, and write it down, record it. This turned out to be the short story "Plot," which was published in *Paris Review* and will be in my new book of stories, *Marriages & Infidelities* (Fall 1972). The young man in the story thinks he is cracking up, totally disintegrating, and he keeps telling his readers how he feels, the pressures inside his skull, the paranoia, the half-jokes/half-pleas, and all that, and though the man is totally fiction (though based on someone I know, who had been on drugs but did recover) most of what he says I really meant. Now, when I read that story, coming across it in the library at the University of London, not expecting to see it out so soon, now, reading it is really a triumph for me, because here is this months-old self of mine, really frightened at going under, and *yet* thinking, imagining, that it might be just a romantic doom, and yet rather panicked by it. . . . And I did write it, I did record it, there it is. And here I am, a survivor. So I feel that literature is wonderfully optimistic, instructive, because it so often demonstrates how human beings get through things, maneuver themselves through chaos, and then *write about it*. I'm struck by the incredible inventive energy and craziness of someone like Bob Dylan who, in a few years, went from poverty, obscurity, maybe even ineptness, to being incredibly successful and talented, obviously a genius—a demonic genius—who then came close to total annihilation, and who *then* actually had an accident that nearly killed him, and who *then* recovered, kept going, has a family and appears to be, judging from the photographs, a totally different person. What is this? How are such bizarre things possible? Dylan went through so many transformations, emotionally and musically and *even physically*, that he must be a fictional character. But he exists, he's real. And just to exist, sometimes, can be a real triumph.

OR: Is there some special attraction that the "demonic" genius holds for you?

JCO: I identify very strongly with certain highly energetic people, like Dylan, also like Mozart, Picasso, Lawrence, Dostoyevsky, Roethke, Dickey, etc.—not because I really think I am one of them—nor do I want to patronize Dylan by this remark, because he isn't Mozart; he is much wealthier than Mozart ever was, for one thing—so far as achievement goes, but I feel a spiritual kinship. The thing about such artists is that they are so violently driven, so excited, that *what* they create is not at all important to them. Of course critics think so; critics linger lovingly over every image, every punctuation mark. But these artists are celebrating art itself, creativity itself, as it flows through their particular egos. This isn't egotism at all; it's the opposite. Picasso says somewhere that God Himself is really only "another artist." He has no fixed style but keeps "inventing" odd things, like the giraffe, the cat, the elephant, etc. He's experimental, exploratory. So this kind of artist, like "God," let's say the creative process itself, just keeps going, picking up and exploiting and discarding all kinds of things, imitating, borrowing, stealing, synthesizing, moving on. . . . By the time his critics figure out one thing he has done, he's jumped far ahead; he has no real interest in much of what they say; he just keeps going. Mozart had a supernatural energy, of course (and he could paint, draw, make up stories, he was marvelously talented), but he worked within a social framework, he accepted a framework, that in a way betrayed him—even though he is the greatest composer (!). Picasso, of course, broke everything down, sheer untrammeled Id combined with a shrewd, tough Ego, the makings of a real criminal or military man, and he got to be the archetype for the Artist. What he says about Art is so true that no one can really add to it: "Painting isn't an aesthetic operation, it's a form of magic designed as a mediator between the strange, hostile world and us, a way of seizing the power by giving form to our terrors as well as our desires."

That's why the whole experience is so dangerous, so alarming, when a particular self—let's say Joyce Carol Oates, of whom you are asking these questions—gets confused with the rather impersonal, inhuman flow of energy, which has nothing to do with an individual ego at all. It takes a great deal of contemplation, of near-disasters and confusions, before one realizes, as Picasso evidently did, early in his life, that there are two selves not really related, though symbiotic. All human beings are susceptible to being "used," if you want to call it that, by Nature—Nature only wants to reproduce itself. In the past a young woman like myself would simply have baby after baby, would be, simply, helplessly, a kind of machine to manufacture babies; she would have to recognize this other "self," this impersonal and rather inhuman self, that exists only to keep the species going. The artist endures some of the same perplexities. But, if he is intelligent enough, he tries to direct the fantasies, the hyperactivity, the visions and disjunctions, into external forms that can be of some aid to others; at the very least they might earn him a living. Every utterance of a private vision is a kind of achievement—even a child's finger-painting—so the utterance of a lengthy, sustained, humanly communicating work like a novel, has got to be a real triumph. And a work of art is better than no work of art, just as something is better than nothing. Whoever said that the greatest happiness is not to have been begotten is absolutely wrong: anything is better than nothing.

OR: Certainly one of the crucial differences between *Anonymous Sins* and *Love and Its Derangements* is the sense of total unity of the latter. Your first book of poems (and this is not meant in any way as a judgment), like most first books, was a collection of things, of "sins" if you will, with a mixture of temperaments and tones. And, as your title suggests, the points of view were often "anonymous." In *Love*, however, it seems to me that you've created a suite of poems, with a single tone, and a voice at once more pure and more personal, womanly. They're like the classical sonnet sequence, dedication and all, various in their dramatic and metaphoric particulars but unified in the general thrust.

JCO: *Anonymous Sins* was written over a lengthy period of time, but *Love and Its Derangements* was written during a period of intense concentration, so that it is like a novella, the asides of a novella. However, it can't be said that the book is unified, because it is a very schizophrenic book, or one might say, less politely, it is hypocritical. It represents two different selves, two warring selves, but within one book, as if they really went together . . . but there isn't much sense of their being joined, because the one poem, the poem that brought both parts together, was of course the poem I could never write. All this sounds shadowy, unclear. But my objective, statistical, structured, "socially" integrated self is hypocritical. This doesn't ordinarily bother me, because I don't think any way of living is perfect—to surrender totally to one's real self, like Rimbaud?— to deny one's self, like Henry James?—to compromise, as most people do? But it bothers me slightly in this case, because I believe in utter honesty in my writing (and in my teaching) and this doesn't quite make it. It's as if someone excitedly confessed to a crime, elaborately describing it, and then remarked in a footnote that the whole thing is fiction; of course; it had better be. But, perhaps, the book is of some value because it does describe how a person can evidently get along in two quite warring and distinct ways, with only a few suggestions of total disintegration (as in "Jigsaw Puzzle") but having enough wit and caution to end with a very womanly, very gentle acquiescence.

OR: Your two books of poems do share, however, the preoccupation with "the imagination of pain," the metaphysics of pain. Pain seems to be the test of authenticity of your emotion. Do you agree?

JCO: Most of my writing is preoccupied with "the imagination of pain," and this is simply because people need help with pain, never with joy. There's no need to write about happy people, happy problems; there's only the moral need to instruct readers concerning the direction to take, in order to achieve happiness (or whatever: maybe they don't want happiness, only confusion). So I feel the moral imperative to chart the psychological processes of someone, usually a hero, but sometimes a heroine, who has gone through suffering of one kind or another, but who survives it (or almost survives). I was very deeply into, very obsessed with, a certain small group of people a few years ago; they became the "Wendall" family of *them*. Well, some of these people are "real," and some fictionalized, of course, but the fact about them—which reviewers seemed never to mention, though the book was widely reviewed—is that they all survived. Critics for magazines like *Look* and *The New Yorker* dwelled on the characters' sufferings, their miseries (*them* is about poverty, in America), but what excited me about the Wendalls and what really excited them, what made them quite pleased with themselves, was how well they did. Now, of course, a well-educated, liberal, handsomely paid New York reviewer might think that the small grubby successes of the poor all across America are depressing—and of course they would be, to such a person; but to any of the millions of "Wendalls" in the United States, these accomplishments are marvelous. My young heroine stole someone else's husband; my young hero got out of Detroit by way of a fluke, a federally funded poverty program, and he made it to the West Coast. These are bitter little ironic successes, to us, but not to them. It takes education, money, and a lot of spare time to develop the ironic sense, the habit of irony.

Everyone experiences "pain" of one kind or another. It might be momentary, only an idea. But there's a terrible need to suppress it, to hide it, to deny it. Therefore, we all smile at one another and assure one another that things are fine. Like Sylvia

Plath near the end of her life, with what Alvarez called her "bright cheerfulness," a really American kind of hypocrisy. And it does you in, ultimately, this hypocrisy, because it cuts you off from other people who are feeling this kind of pain . . . people who might comfort you, might even save you. Therefore, unless confessional poetry is truly self-pitying and maudlin and sterile (like an academic exercise), it is quite instructive. Lowell says in the introduction to *Notebook* that there were, of course, good times for him during those combative years; but happiness somehow gets omitted. Yes, it does. It must be hinted at, however: it must be at least mentioned. When a writer fails to do this, his writing can be dangerous in proportion as it is good. Kafka is an example of this: Kafka is murderous. That's why I am so excited about Janouch's *Conversations with Kafka*, because here is the Kafka totally left out of the fiction, the letters, and the diaries. *Here* is the other half of a human being. Reading that book has been a truly exhilarating experience for me, an almost religious experience. You discover that Kafka is not murderous after all; Kafka is a saint.

As for pain in itself, however, I think it's a dead end; I think it has got to point beyond itself. In my most miserable, self-obsessed stories and poems, many of which are my best things, I attempted to get beyond the pain, somehow, simply by stating the terrible, obvious fact that in the midst of miseries, people are very often, irrationally, quite happy. This is what is so strange. You believe you can pity someone—antiseptically, safely—like a well-to-do northern liberal "pitying" the southern blacks—then you discover to your amazement and perhaps your embarrassment that these people aren't so wretched after all, but you rather thought they were, hoped they were, precisely so that you could pity them. I won't defend *Wonderland*, which is probably an immoral novel, and which I won't ever reread, myself (though I have revised the ending), but other works of mine are simply not so dark, so depressing, so joyless as some people think. It always amazes me, truly astonishes me, that critics can't see how essentially cheerful my characters are, even the vicious ones. But criminals have a right to happiness, just as much as staunch, well-educated, tax-paying reviewers and academics.

OR: I wish you'd talk for a minute about some of the "formal" differences between your two volumes of poetry. Your last book feels "freer," more metaphorically aware.

JCO: The poems in *Love and Its Derangements* were worked over endlessly—revised, savagely cut, discarded and pulled back again. Each of the poems is a blur to me, a continuously shifting and changing emotional event, which in my frustration I somehow declared permanent. It was too much, the compulsion to keep rewriting, revising. And I didn't think I was aiming for "perfection," either, since I don't believe in perfection, and would be bored by it; instead, I felt that the poem would change each time I wrote it, and therefore I *must* keep rewriting it endlessly. It was as if a thousand versions of one poem clamored and demanded to be given equal utterance, equal consideration. The only thing to do, the only sane, pragmatic thing, was to force the poems into some kind of publication, in the forms that seemed to work best; so there they are. My fiction comes out quite differently—it is mostly pre-imagined, pre-experienced, and I only have to record it. But the poems were not pre-existing. They had to be given a vocabulary, they had to be experienced. A third collection of my poems, *Angel Fire*, bothered me in much the same way. I think that the writing of poetry might be too direct for me, too troubling and explosive; I can handle fiction better, with less after-effects. Sometimes I believe that art is cathartic, and rids you of evils; at other times I believe it cultivates its own tensions, and is perhaps dangerous. It's like having to paint those canvases of Pollock's: *of course* you're going to be destroyed. Do you create troubling works because you are troubled, or are you made troubled by creating these works, which might be faddish, fashionable, in their morbidity? This seems to me a very interesting question. I know that I will never write another "tragic" work, not just because it is something of a betrayal of humanity, but because it is just too dangerous for me to live through. I feel that I touched bottom, in ways, in *Wonderland*, and in some of the poems; I can glance back and say, yes, that was it, that is going to be it; the way you might look back over a dangerous mountain road you've traveled, rather proud at getting through it, but really shaken, knowing you will never do it again.

OR: In both your fiction and poetry, you see love as a violent, even destructive, experience. At one point in *Love* you speak of being "rubbed raw with the skin / of men." Another time, in a poem called "The Grave Dwellers," you say "we must be . . . inspired / to an infinite love / in a series of boxes." Poe speaks of love similarly—loving as a kind of dying. Am I reading too much into your work? Love, to you, seems the most *self-conscious* of experiences, as we must *know* it to *have* it.

JCO: "Love" is really two things, perhaps more. There is the sensible, comradely, species-loving love, in which I recognize in you and others a humanity, a sympathetic personality, an *otherness* that is sacred—you can even feel this in strangers, glancing at strangers riding by on a bus (just a meeting of eyes, thank God, and then they're gone). Then there is the totally irrational, possessive, ego-destroying love, which can't be controlled and is, perhaps, a pathological condition of the soul. These two emotions have nothing in common; except, perhaps, the first can grow out of the second, as when people fall in love, become acquainted and then marry. And hope it will endure. I can't begin to explain the second kind of "love." It is truly bizarre, mysterious, anti-social. It is even in a way anti-natural, anti-species, because it sometimes generates in one person (usually the man) a desire to kill the beloved, if the beloved can't be captured. What can one do, how can one escape this? It's like a free-floating germ, a kind of virus for which there is no cure. I just finished a long novel, called *Do With Me What You Will*, which is mainly about the experience of this kind of love, how it is endured, and finally shaped into something civilized— "marriage"—but at great cost to the lovers and to other people. It is so essentially murderous, that someone must be a victim; if not the lovers, then innocent bystanders. But what solution is there? Bad as it is to fall hopelessly in love with someone unattainable (one could at least write infinite variations on a love poem, like Yeats to Maud Gonne), it is far worse to be the innocent object of someone's (unattainable) love. Then you feel yourself hunted, boxed-up, continually *thought about*; you realize that you are part of someone's fantasy, uncontrollable by himself or by you, and this is truly terrifying. But if the woman, the "beloved object," halfway shares in the obsession, then she enters a hellish experience in which she struggles to be free and/but also to perpetuate the delusion, which is so pleasant. It is a kind of madness, obviously, in which both lovers are very energetic and creative—in the artistic sense, really—because they create together a kind of manic fiction, prose or poetry, that they may have to abandon sooner or later, but which they will never forget. And to have gone through it, this is quite an accomplishment also; this is not exactly a negligible feat.

Correspondence with Miss Joyce Carol Oates

Dale Boesky

Originally appeared in the *International Review of Psychoanalysis* (1975) 2: 481-86. Reprinted by permission.

The fascination and profound respect with which Freud approached his psychoanalytic studies of literature was echoed in the enthusiastic response of many serious writers to issues of mutual interest to psychoanalysts and the creative artist. The subsequent history of applied psychoanalysis has unfortunately been sometimes turbulent because of important misunderstandings of psychoanalytic issues on the part of writers and literary critics but also because of some facile and clumsy perceptions of serious literary work on the part of psychoanalysis.

After a recent opportunity to hear the noted American writer, Joyce Carol Oates, discussing some of these issues, I wrote to her about certain questions which relate to the methodology of applied psychoanalysis and literature and found her responses to be so stimulating that I concluded they should be brought to the attention of the psychoanalytic community. In the interests of increasing the coherence of certain passages in these two remarkable letters I have included the relevant excerpts from my own rather lengthy letters which will clarify the context of her responses.

21 September 1973

Dear Miss Oates,

I think a good point at which to begin your reactions and comments about issues relating to literature and psychoanalysis would be to reexamine an assumption which was initially novel but has become widely accepted. I refer to the notion that it is valid for a psychoanalyst to approach an understanding of a literary character just as though the character were 'real'. This assumption implies that one can make certain inferences from the character's behaviour about his concealed motivations but that one can also make other inferences about things that happened to this character before the chronological events of the novel or short story even began, just as one would in attempting to understand a living personality. All of that seems to be old hat in our present times, at least to a writer like yourself who is familiar with psychoanalysis and sympathetic to the psychoanalytic point of view. But there are many ambiguous areas, questions and misconceptions in this assumption that we can treat a fictitious character as we would a real person in our efforts to understand him and it occurred to me that dealing with this question could be approached in more concrete terms by using one of your own novels to illustrate my question.

[In the remainder of this letter I attempted to use Miss Oates' novel *them* as the basis for illustrating a variety of issues and questions to which I asked her reactions.]

Yours sincerely,
Dale Boesky

30 September 1973

Dear Dr. Boesky,

Your letter is filled with stimulating and challenging questions, and I have read it several times, and allowed it to settle in my mind, before even attempting a reply. It has caused me to rethink a part of my past (the time of the writing of *them*) and to formulate, however tentatively, a kind of hypothesis dealing with what you call the 'interplay between fiction and reality'. Though I am familiar with some of Freud's writings, especially those in which he deals with literature, I have only a very generalized idea of Freudian or psychoanalytic theory, and for all I know practicing analysts today work far more freely and improvise more, when dealing with individual patients, than the layman can guess. It is my personal opinion—as it was Whitman's—that extraordinary human beings, especially those who would attempt to 'heal' others, effect their cures not by what they say, verbally, but by the example of their personalities. In this, the psychoanalyst is an artist: he creates or helps to create that most fascinating and elusive of art-works, the human personality. And then he releases it to the world, without further claim.

It is certainly appropriate for a psychoanalyst to approach a 'fictional' character as if he were real, for a serious author deals only with 'real' experiences and 'real' emotions, though they are usually assigned to people with fictitious names. I can't believe, frankly, that anyone could—or would want to—write about experiences the emotional equivalents of which he has not experienced personally. Writing is a far more conscious form of dreaming, and no one dreams dreams that are of no interest to him, however trivial and absurd they may appear to someone else. Thus the recurring 'theme' or 'plot' in a writer's work must have the analogous function of the recurring dream: something demands to be raised to consciousness, to be comprehended by the ego, but for some reason the ego resists or refuses to understand. And so he is fated to dream and re-dream the same paradoxical problem, and he can't be freed of it until he 'solves' it. Since I am a novelist in the tradition, let us say, of Dickens and Dostoyevsky and Stendhal rather than that of Virginia Woolf or Samuel Beckett, I am always concerned with the larger social/political/moral implications of my characters' experiences. In other words, I could not take the time to write about a group of people who did not represent, in their various struggles, fantasies, unusual experiences, hopes, etc., our society in miniature. But of course I may have a heretical or unusual theory of the 'neuroses'—I don't believe in them at all, but see them (in my friends and students, as well as in my fictional characters) as symptoms of restlessness, a normal and desirable straining against the too-close confines of a personality now outgrown, or a social 'role' too restrictive. Therefore, in my fiction, the troubled people are precisely those who yearn for a higher life—those in whom the life-form itself is stirring. By singling out individuals who are representative of our society and who, as people, interest me very much, I attempt to submerge myself in that foreign personality and see *how* and *why* and *to what end* the behavior that people call 'anti-social' or 'neurotic' is actually functioning. And it is always my discovery that these people are genuinely superior to the role in life, the social station, the economic level, the marriage, the job, the philosophical beliefs, etc., in which they find themselves. They must have liberation, room to grow in. If they don't get it, they become violent or self-destructive or apathetic, and sink back to an earlier level of existence. They are not sick, but normal—it is normal to grow, and to continue to grow, and a society that does not allow for this fact of life will always be plagued by neuroses. On the other hand, the apparently well-adapted human being, who is content with whatever he has in life, with his job, his marriage, his prospects, is a person who has come to the end of his personal development, and will not have to struggle any longer (unless something happens to upset him). So, it is the restless who interest me, as a novelist, for only out of restlessness can higher personalities emerge, just as, in a social context, it is only out of occasional surprises and upheavals that new ways of life can emerge. In working closely with my creative writing students and with my teaching assistants (whom I'm supposed to 'help' learn to teach—an impossible ideal) I get them to work with and explore their areas of conflict, to see these conflicts as special gifts or doorways unique to them, and it is always the case that this works well . . . so far, of course, as one can judge in such casual settings. Thus, by getting a highly nervous student to redefine his neurotic terror of teaching in terms of its being ordinary excitement, shared by all good teachers, one can see a gradual change, if not always in the personality itself, at least in behavior.

In dealing with the turbulent world of American life, however, such direct and intuitive methods rarely work; immediately we are faced with the reality of political and economic structures, which will not go away no matter how their effects are redefined. So, in *them*, I chose to deal with what I see to be the natural and inevitable consequences of poverty in an affluent society. And the novel's epigraph, from Webster, is one of the keys to the novel: *'Because we are poor, shall we be vicious?'* 'Shall' in Webster's context had the force of 'must'—*must we be forced to be vicious?*—but I like the poetic ambiguity of its modern usage. For some individuals, poverty does not necessitate viciousness, but for many Americans—especially black Americans, whose story I don't feel capable of telling, for obvious reasons—it seems to predicate behavior that, to those on a higher economic level, seems 'antisocial'. *Them* is about 'them', those who are disqualified from American citizenship for various reasons, and who make up the great majority of mental patients, convicts, welfare clients, the great army of the helpless and impotent, who become a burden on others and are therefore resented as 'them'.

Your questions about Chapter 15, Maureen's dream, are very interesting. I meant Maureen's dream to have symbolic meanings far beyond her own personal condition. Dreaming of 'money' would mean any number of things to a girl in her situation: for it seems the key, the *very* forbidden secret, the way out of a deathly predicament. You are quite right in seeing that her mother is provoking her into promiscuous behavior, and is using her (quite unconsciously, of course) as a kind of attraction, in order to keep her husband at home. It is a roundabout kind of seduction, all the more sinister in that the daughter cannot ever accuse her mother of anything, or even think coherently about what is happening. Perhaps this claustrophobic situation or similar situations have occurred in the past of patients under therapy . . . ? But since the past is hopelessly past and there is no way of checking the patient's memory against 'reality', the psychoanalyst is obviously at a disadvantage. . . . In Maureen's case, her integrity as an individual is being completely violated by her mother's attempt to 'use' her, and she sees no way out except—naively—the way her brother seems to have gone, by acquiring money, somehow, anyhow, as if 'money' were the key to freedom.

. . . which of course it is, at least in part.

Maureen will associate sexual contact only with money, with getting something from someone else, so she is doomed (at least for a long while) to be frigid in her relationships with men, even with her husband, whom she seems to love. Her normal love-impulses or sexual impulses are completely blocked. Not only does that seem to me valid in terms of a girl's character, but it must be seen in a symbolic sense as a symptom of illness in a 'competitive culture'. For we are instructed in various ways that the highest ideal of life is to achieve economic superiority—and if we want that ideal, we must compete furiously with others who seem to want it also. We can't be friendly, we can't admit a natural brotherly love. (President Nixon, for instance, made a personal congratulatory telephone call to the first woman athlete to earn over $100,000 a year—which, apart from being sadly comic, points out the value some of our leaders assign to money, sheer money. He did not telephone her because she was a good athlete, after all.) What is unfortunate about the plight of the poor people in *them*, and poor people generally, is that they never do learn the obvious lessons the affluent learn—that money might mean freedom of one kind or another, but certainly doesn't guarantee happiness.

In terms of the dream, and Maureen's tense relationship with her stepfather, it seems to me only natural that a girl of her age, in close confinement with a man, however physically unappealing (though in fact he isn't ugly—just rather coarse) might begin to associate him with her own sexual urges. It might be quite commonplace for girls to have fantasies about men near them, teachers, ministers, older men generally, but if these fantasies should ever be confronted with reality, it would be disastrous for the girls' development. I believe firmly that all kinds of fantasies are normal—if not normal, why would they arise?—but that a definite line must be drawn between the interior and the 'exterior'. Most people draw this line quite readily. Indeed, it very often happens that the daydreamer does not really *want* his or her fantasy to come true; he wants it only as fantasy, for reasons he can't explain. Or it may be that a young girl (perhaps a young man also . . . ?) desires the appropriation of certain qualities in an older man—his freedom, evident wisdom, his knowledge and wider experience—rather than the man himself in any physical sense. My characters generally fall in love with people who will unlock a 'higher' self in them—as I think we all do, in fact. The love-object of an individual will determine his or her development, obviously, and if the love-object is somehow beneath one's own personality (a good example in literature is Proust's Swann and his intolerable Odette) or, in Maureen's case, *used* only as a means of her escaping an intolerable, confined life, the natural growth of the personality is damaged. How easy to see such things, and how difficult to apply them consistently to real life!—for it is precisely the stubbornness of the obsession or the neurosis that is the character's or patient's problem, and with which the writer/analyst must do battle. And it soon becomes clear that rational instruction does no good, or little good; there is a positively gleeful stubbornness in the Unconscious, at times, which thwarts all attempts at dislodging it. In such cases . . . and I try to deal with them now and then in my fiction, though usually off in a corner, in minor characters . . . in such cases it is well to see that the individual is probably a victim of some insoluble, larger problem, which no amount of local effort can deal with. (Examples might be the 'paranoia' of single women in large cities, the 'paranoia' (which certainly allowed many people longer lives) of sensitive people in the formative stages of Hitler's Germany, the 'catatonia' or 'hysteria' of those who, if cured, will only be sent back to families or social environments that caused their problems in the first case. I am personally familiar with people who could—maybe they already have!—literally drive others crazy, in ways so subtle as to elude direct confrontation, and since these people appear to be quite normal, sane, and agreeable themselves, it is extremely hard for younger people or those with relatively weak egos to assert themselves against them. Novelists almost invariably deal with people who, though burdened with what used to be called 'original sin', yet have a fair chance at being freed from it; the gloom general to Faulkner's writing arises, as Faulkner tells us so many times, from the impossible racial situation in the South, and the 'sin', in Faulkner's eyes unforgivable, of slavery. I deal with subjects similar to Faulkner's in that I do see a historical 'guilt' in America, lately compounded by our involvement in Vietnam, but I cannot share his general pessimism—always, in the interstices of history, during the various plagues and Hundred Years Wars and Inquisitions, the life-force does continue, and probably always will. So I identify with those who seek it out and attempt to kindle it, to give it room to grow—those in medicine, in psychology and its various branches, and others—and I believe it is these people who, having taken over many of the difficult burdens of religious leaders of the past, help to determine in ways impossible to gauge the psychological well-being of a society, which may have to force its way along, in opposition to or independent of the ostensible ego-ideals of the society (money, 'success', status, etc., etc.).

. . . But, without meaning to sound dramatic, I do feel, instinctively, that psychiatrists and psychoanalysts and, to a somewhat lesser extent, medical doctors themselves, work in areas extremely dangerous to their own well-being; as a novelist I sometimes suffer along with my characters, in my attempt to honor their emotional miseries, but I do know, always, that they are *characters in a work of art* . . . however representative of real life their agonies are. Yet the 'healer' knows very well that his patients are real, quite real. So he puts himself in the position of being always engaged in that reclamation work of which Freud spoke (in rather confident terms—unusually confident for him)—sometimes clearly against the patient's buried wishes (for don't troubled people very much 'enjoy' their difficulties, which help give them an identity?)—and he, in a saintly capacity indeed, must, if he is to be successful at all, assimilate into himself the neurotic's problems, his consciousness . . . ? For such work the ego must certainly be set aside, as it is in writing; but the important difference must be that the conscious artist, the professional writer, always determines the course of the 'therapy' and can show the way to a 'cure', step-by-step, quite literally demonstrating a way out, while the therapist, who deals with a number of individuals simultaneously, cannot be certain ahead of time what will happen . . . ? Perhaps I am simply in awe of people who deal in areas in which I probably couldn't function . . . There may actually be a great deal written on the subject. But one of man's basic myths is that of the savior who, in taking the sins of others upon himself, must die in his ego, must perhaps die in reality—out of his own generosity, always, and his idealistic miscalculation of what man's will or conscious mind can endure. This myth seems so basic to the human race, it must have its practical roots.

All you have said about Maureen's dream is true, and such nuggets of truth help to illuminate private areas of 'neurosis'. Yet the problem is this: what shall the therapist do if, in interpreting correctly a symptom of some intolerable conflict beyond the individual's ability to change, he allows the patient to see that the 'neurosis' is inherent in his culture? . . . Teachers, incidentally, run into this problem constantly. So we must allow some margin of detachment, some area of personal ego-growth quite exclusive of what the culture seems to offer in its extroverted sense. In *them* I deal in utter seriousness with the possibility of the transformation of our culture by eastern religion—at least the 'mysticism' of the Indian saint who teaches, contrary to what America teaches Maureen and Jules, that 'we are all members of a single family'. If people are miserable today it must be that they identify far too deeply with their historical roles. So in my fiction I try to show that the local, the private, the family-determined, the political, the accidental, is to be transcended through an identification with the ahistorical. (Many American writers do this, I believe—the transcendence is usually through a union or interest in nature, sometimes through political activity, sometimes a directly 'religious' identification. . . . Since I interpret most activities that take the individual out of his claustrophobic ego-role as 'religious', I suppose I am in some vague way a 'religious' writer, though not in any conventional sense. And I want not at all to be called a 'religious writer'!) I really do believe that, in ways quite beyond my understanding, there will be a gradual transformation of consciousness in the West and that, as is perhaps often the case with neurotics, the 'problem' will never be solved but simply outgrown and forgotten. And new problems will arise—since it is our privilege to live melodramatically.

I have allowed my thoughts to wander and hope the various digressions are illuminating rather than detracting. I use as my basic methodology the technique of Debussy and other impressionists, who allow thoughts to arise and flower and fade and reappear, but who direct all movement eventually toward a few primary statements . . . a technique not suited for fiction or poetry, but sometimes helpful in a kind of conversational, informal setting, which invites one to reveal rather than conceal or carefully organize.

Sincerely,
Joyce Carol Oates

27 October 1973

Dear Miss Oates,

In the event that you feel psychoanalysis can contribute to a study of the issue of recurrent themes in an author's work, do you have any literary cautions, safeguards, instructions—or a caveat to the analyst which might occur to you? A warning to the 'analyst' who reduces serious works of art to the 'discovery' of an oedipal complex would be one obvious example. Do you find yourself irked by any particular recurrent psychoanalytic errors as applied to literary works?

I thought I detected an implicit comparison that you drew between the analyst attempting to reconstruct the fictitious past of his real patient and the novelist creating a 'real' past for the 'fictitious' character. Am I correct in hoping that you have some ideas about how the novelist goes about 'reconstructing' the past of his character?

Do you share the view that certain writers fail in their creative attempt to bring a character to life because of a disturbance in the special balance between submerging oneself in the character to a depth where one can get an authentic 'feel' of the character and yet being able to step back and observe? Do you think there are examples you could give of fictitious characters who bear the deformity of a creative birth marred by failures in the artist's empathy? Subtle failures would be so much more interesting than gross monstrosities. . . .

Sincerely,
Dale Boesky

5 November 1973

Dear Dr. Boesky,

Writers, like everyone else, represent various stages of consciousness, of maturity. A psychoanalytical approach to a writer like Strindberg would be quite reasonable (though of course Strindberg's anger and confusions and prejudices also had their analogues in his society, in his civilization); with

Dostoyevsky, it takes us only partway. Freud, of course, dealt mainly with the murder of the father, as if Mitya were the novel's hero, and not Alyosha/Father Zossima (who represent a very high spiritual consciousness), in the work I consider probably the world's outstanding novel, *The Brothers Karamazov*. The psychoanalytical critic who limits himself to psychopathology limits his appeal and value to a larger public, for we need to know how we can transcend the small, private, evidently 'isolated' neuroses that, taken as a whole, become an entire culture. . . . Of course this takes you far afield. The writer, having no ostensible limitations to his 'practice', can deal with—for instance—the monomania of a Captain Ahab (in Melville's *Moby Dick*, our Great American novel) and examine it allegorically, from the point of view of a dispassionate and intelligent narrator, Ishmael, and pronounce judgment upon the entire American 'way' of life—free enterprise, ruthless exploitation of nature and of human beings, the Faustian and self-serving ethics of the competitive culture. But, presumably, if Ahab were to show up in one's waiting room—a comic possibility, indeed—the analyst would surely have to treat him as an individual. Therefore, in answer to your questions about warnings to analysts who approach literature, I want to emphasize the fact that only a very, very few writers write only of themselves, or of extremely claustrophobic, limited worlds. For one thing, works of this nature rarely get published. (As an occasional editor myself, I see them—and they are never or rarely mature enough to qualify as art, in any way.) Even Jean Genet's writing (which I find myself unable to appreciate quite as much as others do, though his playwriting abilities are considerable) is more than simply pathology. The merely pathological just does not get published. So the analyst should proceed with the fairly certain assumption that the work before him is a critique of society, of religion, culture, philosophy, or something quite beyond its subject matter. The Karamazov family is all of Russia. Raskolnikov, in *Crime and Punishment*, is the victim of what Dostoyevsky saw to be pernicious 'Western'-atheistic ideas, as well as the murderer of two women. The many-leveled approach not only brings us closer to the writer's actual imagination, but is infinitely more valuable as criticism to be read by other people.

What you say about the distinction between sympathy and empathy is very interesting. You are certainly right—maudlin pity is the antithesis of a therapeutic empathy, and may be in its own way a form of extravagant self-indulgence. The writer, like the analyst, must *never* be so deeply involved with any of his characters, especially his heroes or heroines, that he cannot also see them objectively. And we must, of course, see ourselves objectively. I don't value the 'ego', for instance, quite so much as I did when I was younger—the private selfness of the self, the privately named and owned ego, while it is of course the guide or medium for all experiences, simply cannot take itself very seriously, in the long run. So I exist both inside and outside my characters, as in fact I exist both inside and outside myself, to the extent to which I am capable of doing so. (Admittedly, the emotions draw us back 'into' ourselves all too often—but we have the advantage, if we are interested in the workings of our minds, of knowing that the emotional pull is always temporary; we do not mistake moods for permanent facts of life.) The writer's and the analyst's approach to his people must be similar to D. H. Lawrence's—as he said, you don't cure the diseased by helping them complain of their illnesses or by catching the illnesses, in order to share their suffering. This sympathetic 'catching of illness' is a real danger for the writer, and I could go on at great length listing artists who, in objectifying their demonic obsessions, somehow fell in love with them and continued to work with them, again and again and again, until they were hypnotized not by the Unconscious (as most people are, I suppose) but by their own seemingly objective art. Sylvia Plath, John Berryman, Eugene O'Neill, Malcolm Lowry, Shelley, Byron (though not to the degree to which the others succumbed), the painters Jackson Pollock, Rothko, the Dadaists (very nearly all of them; many committed suicide or went insane) . . . Faulkner, although evidently an alcoholic, managed to battle his way out of the cocoon of his private, bitter pessimism, by which he exorcized his depression over the death of his only daughter by linking it to the larger, and surely justified, 'depression' an intelligent Southerner might feel in the American South. Faulkner must have seized the cultural issue as a kind of life-line, and indeed it did work for him—since he spent the later years of his life as a kind of literary emissary, did a great deal of traveling, gave lectures, speeches, etc., and wrote novels (*Intruder in the Dust: A Fable*) which, while not so aesthetically compelling as his earlier works, spoke to larger world-issues and might have been written by another man, another personality. . . . The salvation of the writer is, perhaps, determined by the degree to which he can seek out, in the objective world, an adequate expression of his private dismay or disappointment or trauma. If he succeeds with the first work in exorcizing the past, he is on his way to being a healthy artist. (This is why so many first novels are rawly auto-biographical.) Joyce's *Dubliners* and *A Portrait of an Artist* are works of joyous liberation, though their subject matter is fairly grim, since it deals with an extremely repressed, even pathologically repressed, world.

Very frankly, I am not a writer compelled by past disap-pointments or very much anger at the world. If I am 'angry' at all it's because, through unfortunate economic circumstances (among them the Depression of the 30s), my extremely intelligent and sensitive and creative parents were denied the possibility of developing their talents. But this 'anger' cannot be maintained in the face of the realization that very few human beings who have ever lived on earth have been allowed to fulfill themselves. . . . So I am probably one of the few American writers writing today who is overwhelmingly grateful for the very fact of *existing*, let alone being allowed to write, to give a form to my thoughts. . . . I never compare contemporary society to a Platonic ideal, which is, I believe, the error some people make, causing them to become alienated and cynical, as most of our 'black humorists' have become. Perhaps it is a sense that civilization must be preserved and nurtured, rather than angrily assaulted, that underlies all my fiction, for it seems to me that a civilization cannot endure unless it knows the very worst, the most dangerous things about itself.

'Fictitious characters who bare the deformity . . .' of the artist might include nearly all female voices or characters in T. S. Eliot's poetry; Sylvia Plath's 'men' (I put quotes around the word deliberately); nearly all the 'Americans' in Nabokov's work.

I've left for last your question about how the novelist goes about creating character (which is the same thing as reconstructing a character's past, since we *are* partly the total of our experiences). Here I find myself not quite knowing what to say. I never rationally, logically, step-by-step create anything, not even plots or sequences of events, since whenever I've tried to do this I soon lose interest in the work and the work isn't very good. In fact, I quite deliberately forced the first ending of my novel *Wonderland*, wanting it to conform to a preordained structure, a kind of American tragedy of the isolated ego. I sensed that it was not the true ending, but wrote it anyway. And that was the only novel of mine which, after publication, caused me distress—I kept thinking about it, was nagged by it, and halfway through my next novel (about entirely different, far more free and happy people) had to go back to write the true ending of the other. . . . When I say I *had to* I am not exaggerating. I felt that I had unleashed a kind of perverted, misrepresentative horror upon the world. In the past it might not have bothered me, since I had the idea that very few people read my work. Now, however, I receive letters every day—sometimes 8 or 10 in a single morning (!!!)—and the nature of the letters concerning *Wonderland* was such that I could see very clearly the direct, moral connections we have with one another, to present the truth, at least, not to willfully distort anything. So I believe I am more aware of the psychological connections between people than others are, who don't receive actual written documentation of their effect upon a public. This has the effect of making me feel that I must never distort in any rational or 'aesthetic' manner what I write; it must be a sincere expression of my deeper self, no matter that it might seem strange or distasteful to the ego. . . . But *how* does the artist go about creating his art? It remains a mystery. We can't know ourselves—how our hearts beat or why, why our blood agrees to coagulate if we're scratched, why oxygen keeps us going so nicely, so inexpensively. The explanations artists give of their creativity are always disappointing, if not unbelievable. Because we don't ultimately know why, out of the myriad possibilities of personality, a certain personality dominates, certain qualities rise to the surface and are activated. (The impulse toward 'healing' I believe to be the highest of all human impulses, probably the first really human impulse in our species—which accounts for my interest in doctors, 'doctoring' in various ways, religious leaders, mystics, etc.) I write because I'm fascinated by the world, and when you write of it you experience it doubly—first through the senses, then on paper. And of course you can take the world a step or two beyond its present condition—attempting to prophesize the future, a little. I make the attempt, very rarely a successful one, not to resist disturbing elements or characters in my dreams; whatever remains of my 'ego' when I sleep tries to retain the knowledge that I am sleeping, and *must* not run away from the dream-figures presented by the Unconscious. I believe we must not elude or deny such images, since they arise only to help us somehow. But of course when one is sleeping it is difficult to keep such principles in mind. . . . Immediately upon waking, however, I review the dreams and try to re-experience them, even the occasionally unpleasant ones. (I have very few nightmares, thankfully.) So in my writing I proceed in exactly the same way. Nothing must be denied or softened or feared; all must be accepted. By a constant deflation of the Unconscious, with an awareness that the Unconscious is wiser, older, more dangerous, more idiosyncratic, more generous and more therapeutic than the ego, the ideal artist hopes to synthesize the ostensible contradictions of life and experience it as a seamless unity.

Sincerely,
Joyce Carol Oates

Joyce Carol Oates: The Art of Fiction

Robert Phillips

Originally appeared in The Paris Review, 1978. Reprinted by permission.

Joyce Carol Oates is the rarest of commodities, an author modest about her work, though there is such a quantity of it that she has three publishers—one for fiction, one for poetry, and a "small press" for more experimental work, limited editions and books her other publishers simply cannot schedule.

In the fall of 1978, Ms. Oates and her professor-husband, Raymond Smith, moved from the University of Windsor in Canada, to New Jersey, where she assumed duties as writer-in-residence at Princeton University. Despite the demands of her students and writing, she continues to devote much energy to *The Ontario Review*, a literary journal which her husband edits and which she serves as a contributing editor.

Ms. Oates is striking looking, slender with straight dark hair and large, inquiring eyes. A highly attractive woman, she is not photogenic; no photo has ever done justice to her appearance, which conveys grace and high intelligence. If her manner is taken for aloofness—as it sometimes has been—it is, in fact, a shyness which the publication of thirty-three books, the production of three plays, and the winning of the National Book Award for her novel *them*, has not displaced.

Anyone who has known her for a long time, however, is likely to point out how less shy she is than formerly. As an undergraduate at Syracuse University, where she was valedictorian of a class of over 2,000—receiving an "A" in all subjects but physical education—she was too timid to read her papers aloud when called upon in class. Professors read them for her.

This interview began at the Windsor home in the summer of 1976. When interviewed, her speaking voice was, as always, soft and reflective. One receives the impression she never speaks in anything but perfectly formed sentences. Ms. Oates answered all questions openly, while curled with her Persian cats upon a sofa. (She is a confirmed cat-lover and recently took in two more kittens at the Princeton house.) Talk continued during a stroll by the bank of the Detroit river where she confessed to having sat for hours, watching the horizon, the boats, and dreaming her characters into existence. She sets these dreams physically onto paper on a writing table in one corner of the master bedroom.

Additional questions were asked in New York during the 1976 Christmas season when Ms. Oates and her husband attended a seminar on her work which was part of that year's Modern Language Association convention. Many of the questions in this interview were answered via correspondence. She felt only by writing out her replies could she say precisely what she wished to, without possibility of misunderstanding or misquotation.

Robert Phillips: We may as well get this one over with first: You're frequently charged with producing too much.

Joyce Carol Oates: Productivity is a relative matter. And it's really insignificant: What is ultimately important is a writer's strongest books. It may be the case that we all must write many books in order to achieve a few lasting ones—just as a young poet might have to write hundreds of poems before writing his first significant one. Each book as it is written, however, is a completely absorbing experience, and feels always as if it were *the* work I was born to write. Afterward, of course, as the years pass, it's possible to become more detached, more critical.

I really don't know what to say. I note and can to some extent sympathize with the objurgatory tone of certain critics who feel that I write too much because, quite wrongly, they believe they ought to have read most of my books before attempting to criticize a recently published one. (At least I *think* that's why they react a bit irritably.) Yet each book is a world unto itself, and must stand alone and it should not matter whether a book is a writer's first, or tenth, or fiftieth.

RP: About your critics—do you read them, usually? Have you ever learned anything from a book review or an essay on your work?

JCO: Sometimes I read reviews, and without exception I will read critical essays that are sent to me. The critical essays are interesting on their own terms. Of course it's a pleasure simply to discover that someone has read and responded to one's work; being understood, and being praised, is beyond expectation most of the time. . . . The average review is a quickly written piece not meant to be definitive. So it would be misguided for a writer to read such reviews attentively. All writers without exception find themselves clapperclawed from time to time; I think the experience (provided one survives it) is wonderfully liberating. After the first death there is no other. . . . A writer who has published as many books as I have, has developed, of necessity, a hide like a rhino's, while inside there dwells a frail, hopeful butterfly of a spirit.

RP: Returning to the matter of your "productivity": Have you ever dictated into a machine?

JCO: No, oddly enough I've written my last several novels in long-hand first. I had an enormous, rather frightening stack of pages and notes for *The Assassins*, probably 800 pages—or was it closer to 1000? It alarms me to remember. *Childwold* needed to be written in long-hand, of course. And now everything finds its initial expression in long-hand and the typewriter has become a rather alien thing—a thing of formality and impersonality. My first novels were all written on a typewriter: first draft straight through, then revisions, then final draft. But I can't do that any longer.

The thought of dictating into a machine doesn't appeal to me at all. Henry James's later works would have been better had he resisted that curious sort of self-indulgence, dictating to a secretary. The roaming garrulousness of ordinary speech is usually corrected when it's transcribed into written prose.

RP: Do you ever worry—considering the vast body of your work—if you haven't written a particular scene before, or had characters say the same lines?

JCO: Evidently there are writers (John Cheever, Mavis Gallant come immediately to mind) who never reread their work, and there are others who reread constantly. I suspect I am somewhere in the middle. If I thought I *had* written a scene before, or written the same lines before, I would simply look it up.

RP: What kind of work schedule do you follow?

JCO: I haven't any formal schedule, but I love to write in the morning before breakfast. Sometimes the writing goes so smoothly that I don't take a break for many hours—and consequently have breakfast at two or three in the afternoon on good days. On school days, days that I teach, I usually write for an hour or forty-five minutes in the morning, before my first class. But I don't have any formal schedule and at the moment I am feeling rather melancholy, or derailed, or simply lost, because I completed a novel some weeks ago and haven't begun another . . . except in scattered, stray notes.

RP: Do you find emotional stability is necessary in order to write? Or can you get to work whatever your state of mind? Is your mood reflected in what you write? How do you describe that perfect state in which you can write from early morning into the afternoon?

JCO: One must be pitiless about this matter of 'mood.' In a sense the writing will *create* the mood. If art is, as I believe it to be, a genuinely transcendental function—a means by which we rise out of limited, parochial states of mind—then it should not matter very much what states of mind or emotion we are in. Generally I've found this to be true: I have forced myself to begin writing when I've been utterly exhausted, when I've felt my soul as thin as a playing card, when nothing has seemed worth enduring for another five minutes . . . and somehow the activity of writing changes everything. Or appears to do so. Joyce said of the underlying structure of *Ulysses*—the Odyssean parallel and parody—that he really didn't care whether it was plausible, so long as it served as a bridge to get his 'soldiers' across. Once they were across, what does it matter if the bridge collapses? One might say the same thing about the use of one's self as a means for the writing to get written. Once the soldiers are across the stream. . . .

RP: What does happen when you finish a novel? Is the next project one that has been waiting in line? Or is the choice more spontaneous?

JCO: When I complete a novel I set it aside, and begin work on short stories, and eventually another long work. When I complete *that* novel I return to the earlier novel and rewrite much of it. In the meantime the second novel lies in a desk drawer. Sometimes I work on two novels simultaneously, though one usually forces the other into the background. The rhythm of writing, revising, writing, revising, etc., seems to suit me. I am inclined to think that as I grow older I will come to be infatuated with the art of revision, and there may come a time when I will dread giving up a novel at all. My next novel, *Unholy Loves*, was written around the time of *Childwold*, for instance, and revised after the completion of that novel, and again revised this past spring and summer. My reputation for writing quickly and effortlessly notwithstanding, I am strongly in favor of intelligent, even fastidious revision, which is, or certainly should be, an art in itself.

RP: Do you keep a diary?

JCO: I began keeping a formal journal several years ago. It resembles a sort of ongoing letter to myself, mainly about literary matters. What interests me in the process of my own experience is the wide range of my feelings. For instance, after I finish a novel I tend to think of the experience of having written it as being largely pleasant and challenging. But in fact (for I keep careful records) the experience is various: I do suffer temporary bouts of frustration and inertia and depression. There are pages in recent novels that I've rewritten as many as 17 times, and a story, "The Widows," which I revised both before and after publication in *The Hudson Review*, and then revised slightly again before I included it in my next collection of stories—a fastidiousness that could go on into infinity.

Afterward, however, I simply forget. My feelings crystallize (or are mythologized) into something much less complex. All of us who keep journals do so for different reasons I suppose, but we must have in common a fascination with the surprising patterns that emerge over the years—a sort of arabesque in which certain elements appear and reappear, like the designs in a well-wrought novel. The voice of my journal is very much like the one I find myself using in these replies to you: the voice in which I think or meditate when I'm not writing fiction.

RP: Besides writing and teaching, what daily special activities are important to you? Travel, jogging, music? I hear you're an excellent pianist?

JCO: We travel a great deal, usually by car. We've driven slowly across the continent several times, and we've explored the South and New England and of course New York State with loving thoroughness. As a pianist I've defined myself as an "enthusiastic amateur," which is about the most merciful thing that can be said. I like to draw; I like to listen to music, and I spend an inordinate amount of time doing nothing. I don't even think it can be called daydreaming.

I also enjoy that much-maligned occupation of housewifery, but hardly dare say so, things being what they are today. I like to cook, to tend plants, to garden (minimally), to do simple domestic things, to stroll around the shopping malls and observe the qualities of people, overhearing snatches of conversations, noting people's appearances, their clothes, and so forth. Walking and driving a car are part of my life as a writer, really. I can't imagine myself apart from these activities.

RP: Despite critical and financial success, you continue to teach. Why?

JCO: I teach a full load at the University of Windsor, which means three courses. One is creative writing, one is the graduate seminar (in the Modern Period), the third is an oversized (115 students) undergraduate course that is lively and stimulating but really too swollen to be satisfying to me. There is, generally, a closeness between students and faculty at Windsor that is very rewarding, however. Anyone who teaches knows that you don't really experience a text until you've taught it, in loving detail, with an intelligent and responsive class. At the present time I'm going through Joyce's work with nine graduate students and each seminar meeting is very exciting (and draining) and I can't think, frankly, of anything else I would rather do.

RP: It is a sometimes-publicized fact that your professor-husband does not read most of your work. Is there any practical reason for this?

JCO: Ray has such a busy life of his own, preparing classes, editing *The Ontario Review* and so forth, that he really hasn't time to read my work. I do, occasionally, show him reviews and he makes brief comments on them. I would have liked, I think, to have established an easy-going relationship with some other writers, but somehow that never came about. Two or three of us at Windsor do read one another's poems, but criticism as such is minimal. I've never been able to respond very fully to criticism, frankly, because I've usually been absorbed in another work by the time the criticism is available to me. Also, critics sometimes appear to be addressing themselves to works other than those I remember writing.

RP: Do you feel in any way an expatriate or an exile, living in Canada?

JCO: We are certainly exiles of a sort. But we would be, I think, exiles if we lived in Detroit as well. Fortunately, Windsor is really an international, cosmopolitan community and our Canadian colleagues are not intensely and narrowly nationalistic.

But I wonder—doesn't everyone feel rather exiled? When I return home to Millersport, New York, and visit nearby Lockport, the extraordinary changes that have taken place make me feel like a stranger; the mere passage of time makes us all exiles. The situation is a comic one, perhaps, since it affirms the power of the evolving community over the individual, but I think we tend to feel it as tragic. Windsor is a relatively stable community, and my husband and I have come to feel, oddly, more at home here than we probably would anywhere else.

RP: Have you ever consciously changed your life style to help your work as a writer?

JCO: Not really. My nature is orderly and observant and scrupulous, and deeply introverted, so life wherever I attempt it turns out to be claustral. *Live like the bourgeois*, Flaubert suggested, but I was living like that long before I came across Flaubert's remark.

RP: You wrote *Do With Me What You Will* during your year living in London. While there you met many writers such as Doris Lessing, Margaret Drabble, Colin Wilson, Iris Murdoch— writers you respect, as your reviews of their work indicate. Would you make any observations on the role of the writer in society in England versus that which you experience here?

JCO: The English novelist is almost without exception an observer of society. (I suppose I mean "society" in its most immediate, limited sense.) Apart from writers like Lawrence (who doesn't seem altogether *English*, in fact) there hasn't been an intense interest in subjectivity, in the psychology of living, breathing human beings. Of course there have been marvelous novels. And there is Doris Lessing, who writes books that can no longer be categorized: fictional parable, autobiography, allegory . . . ? And John Fowles. And Iris Murdoch.

But there is a feel to the American novel that is radically different. We are willing to risk being called "formless" by people whose ideas of form are rigidly limited, and we are wilder, more exploratory, more ambitious, perhaps less easily shamed, less easily discouraged. The intellectual life as such we tend to keep out of our novels, fearing the sort of highly readable but ultimately disappointing cerebral quality of Huxley's work . . . or, on a somewhat lower level, C. P. Snow's.

RP: The English edition of *Wonderland* has a different ending from the American. Why? Do you often rewrite published work?

JCO: I was forced to rewrite the ending of that particular novel because it struck me that the first ending was not the correct one. I have not rewritten any other published work (except of course for short stories, which sometimes get rewritten before inclusion in a book) and don't intend to if I can possibly help it.

RP: You've written novels on highly specialized fields, such as brain surgery. How do you research such backgrounds?

JCO: A great deal of reading, mainly. Some years ago I developed a few odd symptoms that necessitated my seeing a doctor, and since there was for a time talk of my being sent to a neurologist, I nervously and superstitiously began reading the relevant journals. What I came upon so chilled me that I must have gotten well as a result . . .

RP: In addition to the novel about medicine, you've written one each on law, politics, religion, spectator sports: Are you consciously filling out a "program" of novels about American life?

JCO: Not really consciously. The great concern with "medicine" really grew out of an experience of some duration that brought me into contact with certain thoughts of mortality: of hospitals, illnesses, doctors, the world of death and dying and our human defenses against such phenomena. (A member of my family to whom I was very close died rather slowly of cancer.) I attempted to deal with my own very inchoate feelings about these matters by dramatizing what I saw to be contemporary responses to "mortality." My effort to wed myself with a fictional character and our synthesis in turn with a larger, almost allegorical condition resulted in a novel that was difficult to write and also, I suspect, difficult to read.

A concern with law seemed to spring naturally out of the thinking many of us were doing in the '60s: what is the relationship between "law" and civilization, what hope has civilization without "law," and yet what hope has civilization with law as it has developed in our tradition? More personal matters blended with the larger issues of "crime" and "guilt" so that I felt I was able to transcend a purely private and purely local drama that might have had emotional significance for me, but very little beyond that; quite by accident I found myself writing about a woman conditioned to be unnaturally "passive" in a world of hearty masculine combat—an issue that became topical even as the novel *Do With Me What You Will* was published and is topical still, to some extent.

The "political" novel, *The Assassins*, grew out of two experiences I had some years ago, at high-level conferences involving politicians, academic specialists, lawyers, and a scattering—no, hardly that—of literary people. (I won't be more specific at the moment.) A certain vertiginous fascination with work which I noted in my own nature I was able to objectify (and, I think, exaggerate) in terms of the various characters' fanaticism involving their own "work"—most obviously in Andrew Petrie's obsession with "transforming the consciousness of America." *The Assassins* is about megalomania and its inevitable consequences and it seemed necessary that the assassins be involved in politics, given the peculiar conditions of our era.

The new "religious" novel, *Son of the Morning*, is rather painfully autobiographical, in part; but only in part. The religion it explores is not institutional but rather subjective, intensely personal, so as a novel it is perhaps not like the earlier three I have mentioned, or the racing novel, *With Shuddering Fall*. Rather, *Son of the Morning* is a novel that begins with wide ambitions and ends very, very humbly.

RP: Somewhere in print you called *The Assassins* the favorite of your novels. It received very mixed reviews. I've often thought that book was misread. For instance, I think the "martyr" in that novel arranged for his own assassination, true? And that his wife was never really attacked outside the country house; she never left it. Her maiming was all confined within her head.

JCO: What a fine surprise! You read the scene exactly as it was meant to be read. Even well-intentioned reviewers missed the point; so far as I know, only two or three people read Yvonne's scene as I had intended it to be read. Yet the hallucinatory nature of the "dismemberment" scene is explicit. And Andrew Petrie did, of course, arrange for his own assassination, as the novel makes clear in the concluding pages.

The novel has been misread, of course, partly because it's rather long and I think reviewers, who are usually pressed for time, simply treated it in a perfunctory way. I'm not certain that it is my favorite novel. But it is, or was, my most ambitious. It involved a great deal of effort, the collating of passages (and memories) that differ from or contradict one another. One becomes attached to such perverse, maddening ugly ducklings, but I can't really blame reviewers for being impatient with the novel. As my novels grow in complexity they please me more and please the "literary world" hardly at all—a sad situation, but not a paralyzing one.

RP: It's not merely a matter of complexity. One feels that your fiction has become more and more urgent, more subjective and less concerned with the outward details of this world—especially in *Childwold*. Was that novel a deliberate attempt to write a "poetic novel"? Or is it a long poem?

JCO: I don't see that *Childwold* is not concerned with the outward details of the world. In fact it's made up almost entirely of visual details—of the natural world, of the farm the Bartletts own, and of the small city they gravitate to. But you are right, certainly, in suggesting that it is a "poetic novel." I had wanted to create a prose poem in the form of a novel, or a novel in the form of a prose poem: the exciting thing for me was to deal with the tension that arose between the image-centered structure of poetry and the narrative-centered and linear structure of the interplay of persons that constitutes a novel. In other words, poetry focuses upon the image, the particular thing, or emotion, or feeling; while prose fiction focuses upon motion through time and space. The one impulse is toward stasis, the other toward movement. Between the two impulses there arose a certain tension that made the writing of the novel quite challenging. I suppose it is an experimental work but I shy away from thinking of my work in those terms: it seems to me there is a certain self-consciousness about anyone who sets himself up as an 'experimental' writer. All writing is experimental.

But experimentation for its own sake doesn't much interest me; it seems to belong to the early '60s, when Dadaism was being rediscovered. In a sense we are all post-*Wake* writers and it's Joyce, and only Joyce, who casts a long terrifying shadow. . . . The problem is that virtuoso writing appeals to the intellect and tends to leave one's emotions untouched. When I read aloud to my students the last few pages of *Finnegan's Wake*, and come to that glorious, and heartbreaking, final section ("But you're changing, accolsha, you're changing from me, I can feel.") I think I'm able to communicate the almost overwhelmingly beautiful emotion behind it, and the experience certainly leaves me shaken, but it would be foolish to think that the average reader, even the average intelligent reader, would be willing to labor at the *Wake*, through those hundreds of dense pages, in order to attain an emotional and spiritual sense of the work's wholeness, as well as its genius. Joyce's *Ulysses* appeals to me more: the graceful synthesis of the "naturalistic" and the "symbolic" suits my temperament also. . . . I try to write books that can be read in one way by a literal-minded reader, and in quite another way by a reader alert to symbolic abbreviation and parodistic elements. And yet, it's the same book—or nearly. A trompe l'oeil, a work of "as if."

RP: Very little has been made of the humor in your work, the parody. Some of your books, like *Expensive People, The Hungry Ghosts*, and parts of *Wonderland* seem almost Pinteresque in their absurd humor. Is Pinter an influence? Do you consider yourself a comedic writer?

JCO: There's been humor of a sort in my writing from the first; but it's understated, or deadpan. Pinter has never struck me as very funny. Doesn't he really write tragedy?

I liked Ionesco at one time. And Kafka. And Dickens (from whom Kafka learned certain effects, though he uses them, of course, for different ends). I respond to English satire, as I mentioned earlier. Absurdist or "dark" or "black" or whatever: what isn't tragic belongs to the comic spirit. The novel is nourished by both and swallows both up greedily.

RP: What have you learned from Kafka?

JCO: To make a jest of the horror. To take myself less seriously.

RP: John Updike has been accused of a lack of violence in his work. You're often accused of portraying too much. What is the function of violence in your work?

JCO: Given the number of pages I have written, and the "violent" incidents dispersed throughout them, I rather doubt that I am a violent writer in any meaningful sense of the word. Certainly the violence is minimal in a novel like *them*, which purported to be a naturalistic work set in Detroit in the '60's; real life is much more chaotic.

RP: Which of your books gave you the greatest trouble to write? And which gave the greatest pleasure or pride?

JCO: Both *Wonderland* and *The Assassins* were difficult to write. *Expensive People* was the least difficult. I am personally very fond of *Childwold* since it represents, in a kind of diffracted way, a complete world made of money and imagination, a blending-together of different times. It always surprises me that other people find that novel admirable because, to me, it seems very private . . . the sort of thing a writer can do only once.

Aside from that, *Do With Me What You Will* gives me a fair amount of pleasure, and of course, I am closest to the novel I finished most recently, *Son of the Morning*. (In general, I think we are always fondest of the books we've just completed, aren't we? For obvious reasons.) But when I think of Jules and Maureen and Loretta of *them*, I wonder if perhaps that isn't my favorite novel, after all.

RP: For whom do you write—yourself, your friends, your "public"? Do you imagine an ideal reader for your work?

JCO: Well, there are certain stories, like those in *The Hungry Ghosts*, which I have written for an academic community and, in some cases, for specific people. But in general the writing writes itself—I mean a character determines his or her "voice" and I must follow along. Had I my own way the first section of *The Assassins* would be much abbreviated. But it was impossible to shut Hugh Petrie up once he got going and, long and painful and unwieldy as his section is, it's nevertheless been shortened. The problem with creating such highly conscious and intuitive characters is that they tend to perceive the contours of the literary landscape in which they dwell and, like Kasch of *Childwold*, try to guide or even to take over the direction of the narrative. Hugh did not want to die, and so his section went on and on, and it isn't an exaggeration to say that I felt real dismay in dealing with him.

Son of the Morning is a first-person narration by a man who is addressing himself throughout to God. Hence the whole novel is a prayer. Hence the ideal reader is, then, God. Everyone else, myself included, is secondary.

RP: Do you consider yourself religious? Do you feel there is a firm religious basis to your work?

JCO: I wish I knew how to answer this. Having completed a novel that is saturated with what Jung calls the God-experience, I find that I know less than ever about myself and my own beliefs. I have beliefs, of course, like everyone—but I don't always believe in them. Faith comes and goes. God diffracts into a bewildering plenitude of elements—the environment, love, friends and family, career, profession, "fate," biochemical harmony or disharmony, whether the sky is slate-gray or a bright mesmerizing blue. These elements then coalesce again into something seemingly unified. But it's a human predilection, isn't it?—our tendency to see, and to wish to see, what we've projected outward upon the universe from our own souls? I hope to continue to write about religious experience, but at the moment I feel quite drained, quite depleted. And as baffled as ever.

RP: You mention Jung. Is Freud also an influence? Laing?

JCO: Freud I have always found rather limited and biased; Jung and Laing I've read only in recent years. As an undergraduate at Syracuse University I discovered Nietzsche and it may be the Nietzschean influence (which is certainly far more provocative than Freud's) that characterizes some of my work. I don't really know, consciously. For me, stories usually begin—or began, since I write so few of them now—out of some magical association between characters and their settings. There are some stories (I won't say which ones) which evolved almost entirely out of their settings, usually rural.

RP: Your earliest stories and novels seem influenced by Faulkner and by Flannery O'Connor. Are these influences you acknowledge? Are there others?

JCO: I've been reading for so many years, and my influences must be so vast—it would be very difficult to answer. An influence I rarely mention is Thoreau, whom I read at a very impressionable age (my early teens), and Henry James, O'Connor and Faulkner, certainly, Katherine Anne Porter, and Dostoyevsky. An odd mixture.

RP: The title *Wonderland*, and frequent other allusions in your work, point toward a knowledge of, if not an affinity for, Lewis Carroll. What is the connection, and is it an important one?

JCO: Lewis Carroll's *Alice in Wonderland* and *Through the Looking-glass* were my very first books. Carroll's wonderful blend of illogic and humor and horror and justice has always appealed to me, and I had a marvelous time teaching the books last year in my undergraduate course.

RP: Was there anything you were particularly afraid of, as a child?

JCO: Like most children, I was probably afraid of a variety of things. The unknown? The possibility of those queer fortuitous metamorphoses that seem to overtake certain of Carroll's characters? Physical pain? Getting lost? . . . My proclivity for the irreverent and the nonsensical was either inspired by Carroll, or confirmed by him. I was always, and continue to be, an essentially mischievous child. This is one of my best-kept secrets.

RP: You began writing at a very early age. Was it encouraged by your family? Was yours a family of artistic ambitions?

JCO: In later years my parents have become "artistic," but when they were younger, and their children were younger, they had no time for anything much except work. I was always encouraged by my parents, my grandmother, and my teachers, to be creative. I can't remember when I first began to tell stories—by drawing, it was then—but I must have been very young. It was an instinct I followed quite naturally.

RP: Much of your work is set in the 1930s, a period during which you were merely an infant at best. Why is that decade so important to your work or vision?

JCO: Since I was born in 1938, the decade is of great significance to me. This was the world of my parents, who were young adults at the time, the world I was born into. The '30s seem in an odd way still "living" to me, partly in terms of my parents' and grandparents' memories, and partly in terms of its treatment in books and films. But the '20s is too remote—lost to me entirely! I simply haven't had the imaginative power to get that far back.

I identify very closely with my parents in ways I can't satisfactorily explain. The lives they lived before I was born seem somehow accessible to me. Not directly, of course, but imaginatively. A memory belonging to my mother or father seems almost to "belong" to me. In studying old photographs I am struck sometimes by a sense of my being contemporary with my parents—as if I'd known them when they were, let's say, only teenagers. Is this odd? I wonder. I rather suspect others share in their family's experiences and memories without knowing quite how.

RP: When we were undergraduates together at Syracuse, you already were something of a legend. It was rumored you'd finish a novel, turn it over, and immediately begin writing another on the backside. When both sides were covered, you'd throw it all out, and reach for clean paper. Was it at Syracuse you first became aware you were going to be a writer?

JCO: I began writing in high school, consciously training myself by writing novel after novel and always throwing them out when I completed them. I remember a 300-page book of interrelated stories that must have been modeled on Hemingway's *In Our Time* (I hadn't yet read *Dubliners*), though the subject matter was much more romantic than Hemingway's. I remember a bloated trifurcated novel that had as its vague model *The Sound and the Fury* . . . Fortunately these experiments were thrown away and I haven't remembered them until this moment.

Syracuse was a very exciting place academically and intellectually for me. I doubt that I missed more than half a dozen classes in my four years there; and none of them in English.

RP: I remember you were in a sorority. It is incredible to contemplate you as a "sorority girl."

JCO: My experience in a sorority wasn't disastrous, but merely despairing. (I tried to resign but found out that upon joining I had signed some sort of legal contract.) However, I did make some close friends in the sorority, so the experience wasn't a total loss. I would never do it again, certainly. In fact, it's one of the three or four things in my entire life I would never do again.

RP: Why was life in a Syracuse sorority so despairing? Have you written about it?

JCO: The racial and religious bigotry; the asininity of 'secret ceremonies'; the moronic emphasis upon 'activities' totally unrelated to—in fact antithetical to—intellectual exploration; the bullying of the presumably weak by the presumably strong; the deliberate pursuit of an attractive 'image' for the group as a whole, no matter how cynical the individuals might have been; the aping of the worst American traits—boosterism, God-fearing-ism, smug ignorance, a craven worship of conformity; the sheer mess of the place once one got beyond the downstairs. . . . I tried to escape in my junior year but a connection between sororities and the Dean of Women and the university housing office made escape all but impossible, and it seemed that, in my freshman naiveté, I had actually signed some sort of contract that had 'legal' status . . . all of which quite cowed me. I remember a powdered and perfumed alum explaining the sorority's exclusion of Jews and blacks: "You see, we have conferences at the Lake Placid Club, and wouldn't it be a shame if all our members couldn't attend. . . . Why, it would be embarrassing for them, wouldn't it?"

I was valedictorian of my class, the class of 1960. I fantasized beginning my address by saying: "I managed to do well academically at Syracuse despite the concerted efforts of my sorority to prevent me. . . ."

I haven't written about it, and never will. It's simply too stupid and trivial a subject. To even care about such adolescent nonsense one would have to have the sensitivity of a John O'Hara, who seems to have taken it all seriously.

RP: I recall you won the poetry contest at Syracuse in your senior year. But your books of poetry appeared relatively later than your fiction. Were you always writing poetry?

JCO: No, I really began to write poetry later. The poetry still comes with difficulty, I must admit. Tiny lyric asides, droll wry enigmatic statements: they aren't easy, are they? I'm assembling a book which I think will be my last—of poems, I mean. No one wants to read a novelist's poetry. It's enough—too much, in fact— to deal with the novels. Strangely enough my fellow poets have been magnanimous indeed in accepting me as a poet. I would not have been surprised had they ignored me, but, in fact, they've been wonderfully supportive and encouraging. Which contradicts the general notion that poets are highly competitive and jealous of one another's accomplishments . . .

RP: You say no one wants to read a novelist's poetry. What about Robert Penn Warren? John Updike? Erica Jong? I suppose Allen Tate and James Dickey are poets who happened to write novels . . .

JCO: I suppose I was thinking only of hypothetical reactions to my own poetry. Robert Penn Warren aside, however, there is a tendency on the part of critics to want very much to categorize writers. Hence one is either a writer of prose or of poetry. If Lawrence hadn't written those novels he would have been far more readily acclaimed as one of the greatest poets in the language. As it is, however, his poetry has been neglected. (At least until recently.)

RP: *By the North Gate*, your first book, is a collection of short stories, and you continue to publish them. Is the short story your greatest love? Do you hold with the old adage that it is more difficult to write a good story than a novel?

JCO: Brief subjects require brief statements. There is *nothing* so difficult as a novel, as anyone knows who has attempted one; a short story is bliss to write set beside a novel of even ordinary proportions.

But in recent years I haven't been writing much short fiction. I don't quite know why. All my energies seem to be drawn into longer works. It's probably the case that my period of greatest productivity is behind me, and I'm becoming more interested in focusing upon a single work, usually a novel, and trying to "perfect" it section by section and page by page.

RP: Nevertheless, you've published more short stories, perhaps, than any other serious writer in America today. I remember that when you chose the 21 stories to compose *The Wheel of Love*, you picked from some ninety which had been in magazines the two years since your previous collection. What will become of the seventy or so stories you didn't include in that collection? Were some added to later collections? Will you ever go back and pick up uncollected work?

JCO: If I'm serious about a story I preserve it in book form; otherwise I intend it to be forgotten. This is true, of course, for poems and reviews and essays as well. I went back and selected a number of stories that for thematic reasons were not included in *The Wheel of Love*, and put them into a collection called *The Seduction and Other Stories*. Each of the story collections is organized around a central theme and is meant to be read as a whole—the arrangement of the stories being a rigorous one, not at all haphazard.

RP: You don't drink. Have you tried any consciousness-expanding drugs?

JCO: No. Even tea (because of caffeine) is too strong for me. I must have been born with a rather sensitive constitution.

RP: Earlier you mentioned Hugh Petrie in *The Assassins*. He is but one of many deranged characters in your books. Have you known any genuine madmen?

JCO: Unfortunately, I have been acquainted with a small number of persons who might be considered mentally disturbed. And others, strangers, are sometimes drawn my way; I don't know why.

Last week when I went to the university, I wasn't allowed to teach my large lecture class because, during the night, one of my graduate students had received a telephone call from a very angry, distraught man who announced that he intended to kill me. So I had to spend several hours sequestered away with the head of our department and the head of security at the university and two special investigators from the Windsor City Police. The situation was more embarrassing than disturbing. It's the first time anyone has so explicitly and publicly threatened my life—there have been shy, indirect threats made in the past, which I've known enough not to take seriously.

(The man who called my student is a stranger to us all, not even a resident of Windsor. I have no idea why he's so angry with me. But does a disturbed person really need a reason . . . ?)

RP: How about the less threatening, but nonetheless hurtful, reactions of friends and relatives—any reactions to conscious or unconscious portraits in your work?

JCO: My parents (and I, as a child) appear very briefly in *Wonderland*, glimpsed by the harassed young hero on his way to, or from, Buffalo. Otherwise there are no portraits of family or relatives in my writing. My mother and father both respond (rather touchingly at times) to the setting of my stories and novels, which they recognize. But since there is nothing of a personal nature in the writing, I have not experienced any difficulties along those lines.

RP: Aside from the singular incident at the university, what are the disadvantages of being famous?

JCO: I'm not aware of being famous, especially here in Windsor, where the two major bookstores, Coles', don't even stock my books. The number of people who are 'aware' of me, let alone who read my writing, is very small. Consequently I enjoy a certain degree of invisibility and anonymity at the university, which I might not have at an American university—which is one of the reasons I am so much at home here.

RP: Are you aware of any personal limitations?

JCO: Shyness has prevented me from doing many things; also the amount of work and responsibility I have here at Windsor.

RP: Do you feel you have any conspicuous or secret flaw as a writer?

JCO: My most conspicuous flaw is . . . well, it's so conspicuous that anyone could discern it. And my secret flaw is happily secret.

RP: What are the advantages of being a woman writer?

JCO: Advantages! Too many to enumerate, probably. Since, being a woman, I can't be taken altogether seriously by the sort of male critics who rank writers 1, 2, 3 in the public press, I am free, I suppose, to do as I like. I haven't much sense of, or interest in, competition; I can't even grasp what Hemingway and the epigonic Mailer mean by battling it out with other talent in the ring. A work of art has never, to my knowledge, displaced another work of art. The living are no more in competition with the dead than they are with the living. . . . Being a woman allows me a certain invisibility. Like Ellison's *Invisible Man*. (My long journal, which must be several hundred pages by now, has the title *Invisible Woman*. Because a woman, being so mechanically judged by her appearance, has the advantage of hiding within it—of being absolutely whatever she knows herself to be, in contrast with what others imagine her to be, I feel no connection at all with my physical appearance and have often wondered whether this was a freedom any man—writer or not—might enjoy.)

RP: Do you find it difficult to write from the point of view of the male?

JCO: Absolutely not. I am as sympathetic with any of my male characters as I am with any of my female characters. In many respects I am closest in temperament to certain of my male characters—Nathan Vickery of *Son of the Morning*, for instance—and feel an absolute kinship with them. "The Kingdom of God is within."

RP: Can you tell the sex of a writer from the prose?

JCO: Never.

RP: What male writers have been especially effective, do you think, in their depiction of women?

JCO: Tolstoy, Lawrence, Shakespeare, Flaubert. . . . Very few, really. But then very few women have been effective in their depiction of them.

RP: Do you enjoy writing?

JCO: I do enjoy writing, yes. A great deal. And I feel somewhat at a loss, aimless and foolishly sentimental, and disconnected, when I've finished one work and haven't yet become absorbed in another. All of us who write work out of a conviction that we are participating in some sort of communal activity. Whether my role is writing, or reading and responding, might not be very important. I take seriously Flaubert's statement that we must love one another in our art as the mystics love one another in God. By honoring another's creation we honor something that deeply connects us all, and goes beyond us.

Of course writing is only one activity out of a vast number of activities that constitute our lives. It seems to be the one that some of us have concentrated on, as if we were fated for it. Since I have a great deal of faith in the process and the wisdom of the unconscious, and have learned from experience to take lightly the judgments of the ego, and its inevitable doubts, I never find myself constrained to answer such questions. Life is energy, and energy is creativity. And even when we as individuals pass on, the energy is retained in the work of art, locked in it and awaiting release if only someone will take the time and the care to unlock it . . .

The Emergence of Joyce Carol Oates

Lucinda Franks

From *The New York Times Magazine*. © 1980 The New York Times Co. Reprinted by permission.

In a trance Raphael stretched out upon his raft. . . . The pond had made itself manifest to him. It took him into its depth, it embraced him, whispered . . . "Come here, come here to me, I will take you in. I will give you new life."

The undersized child with . . . that furtive expression tinged with a melancholy irony . . . was seen less and less frequently that summer until, finally, one morning, it was discovered that he had simply vanished . . . "Raphael," they called. . . . "Where are you hiding?" . . . They went in search of him to Mink Pond, of course. . . . But where was Mink Pond? It seemed, oddly, that Mink Pond, too, had vanished.

—from Bellefleur by Joyce Carol Oates

She slides back the glass doors, steps out onto her stone terrace and invites you, for a short time, to enter her world. A hawk dips down through the trees, a cat and dog face off with hisses and growls. You recognize all of them: a gallery of misplaced characters. The bird belongs not here in Joyce Carol Oates's backyard on the outskirts of Princeton, N. J., but elsewhere and you half expect it to swoop down and ferry you to Bellefleur Castle; the rainbow-colored cat, the holly, the dragonflies, all are escapees from the author's 35th and latest book.

Beyond the terrace, a familiar body of water, choked with rushes and water iris, stretches languidly before you.

"Yes, it's Mink Pond," says the author. "That, like many things in the land of the Bellefleurs, is a symbol. No! Raphael did not die. The pond is an emblem of his imagination—a more hospitable place for him—and that, in the end, is where he returned."

And, in the end, all the raw pieces of reality—the people, places, bits of gossip, confession—that touch the life of Joyce Carol

Oates are, like Raphael, swallowed up in her imagination, transformed, compressed, cut and set like diamonds in her fiction.

The cat, Misty, oblivious of the fact that he has been re-created in his mistress's literature as the dazzling Mahalaleel—an aristocratic stray who as the *grand-chat* of Bellefleur Castle is more iridescent, much silkier and infinitely more commanding than the original—lurks beneath the garden chairs waiting to pounce on one of his brothers, all of whom had been rescued by the author, who is childless, from a roadside abandonment.

She sits casually, but she is tall and erect as a signal tower, fading in and out each time a blue jay or cat intercepts her attention. She looks somehow lost in time, as though she has emerged from the Gothic porticos of her own *Bellefleur*. If her face is dramatically arresting, she seems to dress it down with the ordinary. At first impression—dainty hairstyle, rosebud lips, Middle Western drawl—she looks as if a frilly apron or wrist flower would suit her. But then, there are the eyes: intense, brown, shining; twice as big and taking in twice as much as you might expect.

She speaks almost below her breath, as though there were someone in the next room who she didn't want to overhear her. It is hard to believe that this is the voice directing the stories that tell of sons who murder their mothers, of religious leaders who gouge out their own eyes, of medical students who cannibalize cadavers.

She reminds you of a magician's sleeve, from which a chain of connected handkerchiefs is pulled; it doesn't seem possible (the sleeve is not very wide), but the material keeps coming and coming until it fills the stage. There are many worlds, you realize, belonging to Joyce Carol Oates, beyond the one which you are being permitted to visit.

Winner of the National Book Award for fiction in 1970 for her novel *them*, frequent recipient of an O. Henry Award, a member of the American Academy and Institute of Arts and Letters, Joyce Carol Oates is regarded as one of the nation's preeminent fiction writers. Nevertheless, at age 42, she has not received the popular recognition accorded her equals, largely because in the past she herself has chosen obscurity, refusing interviews and talk-show invitations. In the last 17 years, she has produced 12 novels, 11 collections of short stories, eight volumes of poetry, three books of literary criticism, one play, and hundreds of book reviews. That is an average of about two books a year, a record of prolificacy that has earned not only the awe but also the suspicion of many critics, who accuse her of "automatic writing." She has always, however, enjoyed a rather rarefied audience, with a group of only about 20,000 faithful buying her books in hard cover.

Now, however, with the publication of *Bellefleur*, hopes abound that this state of affairs will change. Unlike her other books, which are fixed in time and place and usually deal with a specific genre group, *Bellefleur* spans six generations of an American family, beginning with one Jean-Pierre Bellefleur who, having been banished from France, builds in 1802 a castle in the valleys of a place that sounds very much like the Adirondacks. It is a Gothic saga, a tableau of the real and the surreal, rich with magic, whimsy, tragedy and humor and just the right number of unforgettable characters (some of whom turn into animals from time to time) to fit the prescription for a commercial success. The heads of her publishers are alive with fantasies that she will become the book publishing world's next queen-for-a-day, with her hefty backlist turning into coffers of gold. Fawcett books, the paperback house that has issued all of her novels, has apparently decided this might happen; it has put in a floor bid of $200,000 —$50,000 higher than it has ever paid for a Joyce Carol Oates book—for the as yet unscheduled paperback auction of *Bellefleur*.

Their high hopes may be realized. In last Sunday's *New York Times Book Review*, John Gardner said that "whatever its faults, *Bellefleur* is simply brilliant," and he called Miss Oates "one of the great writers of our time."

She walked past the front steps, her hair blowing helplessly across her face. . . . Why was everything so raw, so open? It was like walking along the beach, narrowing her eyes slightly against the wind. She felt a certainty, an excitement, that something would happen very shortly, and that her life would begin.

—from *Do With Me What You Will*

* * *

Deep in the leafy, lazy Princeton street, carpenters are banging, sawing, lifting shovelfuls of earth, building a new wing on the home of Miss Oates and her husband, Raymond Smith, a professor of 18th-century literature. The butterflies fluttering about the terrace seem like metaphors for the feeling of expansion, of something taking flight, for the sides of the house are made of glass.

"I'm so glad you did not come when it was raining," Miss Oates says, bringing out tea, water and soda pop at intervals. "It's so gloomy in a glass house on a dark day."

And more exposed, perhaps, than an earlier self ever would have wished. There was a time when she and her husband lived in an apartment so small that she had to write in her bedroom on a card table. The bookstore in the Canadian town where she taught until two years ago—at the University of Windsor—did not even carry her books. To the New York literary community, she seemed like one step away from J. D. Salinger in her upcountry isolation. She liked it just fine that way. It gave her the liberty to be what she wanted to be, free of the pressure of spotlights and literary fashions. It protected her from the terror of being paraded about, examined—a bug on a pin beneath hot lights.

A frequent reviewer for *The New York Times Book Review*, she has refused to read reviews of her own work. In the past, she has instructed her agent not to inform her of any public reaction to her work. And she has never let the person dearest to her in the world—her husband—read the body of her work. Although he reads the occasional book review she writes, virtually all of the rest of her work is off-limits because, she says, "it would be like living with a constant condemnation if he didn't like it." He will escort her to a speech or a reading but then will wait out in the hall. "If she makes a mistake," he reasons, "the mistake dies there. If I am present, it lives on."

"He would like to read my work," she says, "but it is not a burning issue between us. There is no pressure on him, or me, and it makes life easier."

Although frail, Miss Oates has an extraordinary physical presence (its impact is as startling as coming upon a deer in the middle of a wood), and the secret of that may rest in her solemnity, her reserve, a kind of power of concealment. So emotion-bound does she become in anything that she is writing that life itself is often too strenuous. She does not smoke or drink, and even tea is too strong for her. Highly sensitive and receptive, she is a kind and generous friend to young writers. Yet there is an aloofness as she appraises people from behind rose-tinted glasses, a guardedness that makes it difficult for anyone to get to know her.

Nevertheless, there is a second Joyce Carol Oates taking form and it is as though she were becoming, in a certain sense, not unlike one of her own characters. She creates people who isolate themselves from the complexity of their worlds, who cast about in states of narcissism and hubris, trying to impose their own single-visioned reality on the chaos of life, or who retreat altogether into cataleptic states of denial. Almost always, these characters find redemption and survival by accepting the natural order of the universe, by resigning themselves to the fact that there is no one answer, no deliverance, by rejoining and flowing with the society around them.

In an external sense, Miss Oates has embarked on a kind of reunion of her own. For the first time, she has expressed an interest in knowing the details of advance sales bids and promotional data on her new novel. Eager to debunk the assumption that she is a recluse writing in "a fever possessed," she brings out the notes and drafts of Bellefleur, staggering beneath a pile that contains plot charts, maps and the *Bellefleur* family trees.

This spring, another precedent was broken. She and her husband went to Western and Eastern Europe, a six-week tour that included attending literary symposiums and giving speeches. It was her first time on an airplane since she left college.

The shift began, friends say, when she accepted a position of visiting professor of creative writing at Princeton University in 1978. Until then, she had clung to a tightly circumscribed life. Born in the five-house town of Millersport, on the shoulders of the Erie Canal, Joyce Carol Oates went to Syracuse University on a scholarship and got her M. A. in English from the University of Wisconsin, where she met and married Smith. She settled down to teach, first at the University of Detroit, then across the river in Ontario at the University of Windsor.

"She grew up in a small place, taught in a small place all her life and now she has undergone a life change," says Evelyn Shrifte, her editor at Vanguard Press, her first publisher. "She has gotten bolder."

This fall will be her third year at Princeton, and there is evidence that she plans to stay permanently. In addition to buying, and even expanding, a house, she and her husband have recently started in their home a small book-publishing press, an off-shoot of *The Ontario Review*, a literary journal which the couple founded in 1974 and which Smith edits.

Even more significant, in December 1978, Joyce Carol Oates changed publishers. Breaking with Vanguard, which had published all of her fiction since her first book in 1963, she signed on with the much larger house of E. P. Dutton, which will promote her books on a much grander scale.

"She has broken a kind of isolation," says her long-time friend and literary agent Blanche Gregory. "She is among professors of great prestige—Princeton was the watering ground of Fitzgerald, you know—and she goes to parties and hops on a train to New York and sees [Donald] Barthelme or John Updike or a dozen others." Miss Oates herself says, "It's a wonderful new experience, being part of a literary community."

She teaches only two writing workshops a week, as opposed to a full course load at Windsor. Whereas the academic world at Windsor was "cold and stark," she says she finds her Princeton students more exciting and exacting.

I, too, drift into sleep and am rewarded with astonishing, unspeakable sights. In fact, I have grown to fear sleep, at the very edge of sleep my entire body jerks, waking me. But the visions are not always nightmares. They can be sweet, soothing, hypnotic. I think they are the dreams of others, former occupants of this rented bed. Surely they are not my own.
                                                              —from *Son of the Morning*

Joyce Carol Oates chops shrimp in her pin-neat kitchen, the counters so clear you could somersault the length of them.

Humming, she sets the shellfish afloat in a tart and airy yogurt soup. Smith, large, handsome and bashful, emerges from his study. He looks like a man who has lost something. A glance at his wife doing the cooking, and he smiles longingly.

The living room seems oddly untouched: the glass dining table glints with sun; perfectly placed about the room are shiny ashtrays, hanging plants, a collection of old clocks, stacked records. One wonders whether the couple has rearranged both the room and themselves—halted the motion, stopped everything in time—on account of the invasion by this stranger with a note pad. Whatever the reason, they move delicately, as though they were traveling down narrow aisles in a china shop, watched by a crowd of window shoppers with their noses pressed to the glass.

"Some cheese, honey?" she asks, straightening her husband's collar. Smith cuts himself tiny squares of cheese, arranges them on a plate and studies them. He talks—very softly, but as distinctly as if he were addressing a Dictaphone—about putting out *The Ontario Review*. She boasts about how hard he works at it. Their voices drift like a melody above the contrapuntal movements of their hands— hers, reedlike, do a series of arabesques as she lifts spoon to lip; his simply glide about the air—a pas de deux of two spirits that have danced well together for a very long time.

One cannot imagine either of them tearing through the house to catch a train, or throwing an ashtray in exasperation, or even raising their voices.

Instead, they take long bicycle trips, drive about in their car, walk and poke into lost corners of Manhattan. "I also spend an inordinate amount of time," Miss Oates confesses, "doing absolutely nothing."

It is clear, however, that whatever she does, including "nothing," she is a writer who spends sometimes 24 hours a day writing. She once went to bed and dreamed an entire new ending for an already published book, *Wonderland*, which was incorporated in subsequent editions.

"If you are a writer," she says, "you locate yourself behind a wall of silence and no matter what you are doing, driving a car or walking or doing housework, which I love, you can still be writing because you have that space."

Often during the evening, she will curl up on the couch with her pad and pencil and scrawl, like a little girl making up a story. Then, before she goes to bed, she will read over the pages she has written and the notes she has made that day. Where most writers must battle the currents of self-doubt to get to the reverse magnet that is their typewriter, Joyce Carol Oates can hardly resist the pull.

Her study is spare: a large desk with just a few papers scattered about, a file cabinet, a bulletin board tacked with chapter headings, a small settee. "I usually work from about 8:30 A.M. to 1 P.M.; then in the afternoon I'll make telephone calls, or teach, or go to New York. Then I'll make dinner and then, from about 8 until 11:30, I'll work again."

That adds up to anywhere from one to ten pages a day, but usually about five, unless she is writing a short story, when she will do a draft in one day. "As I get older, I find I can't write as fast, and I have to rewrite again and again, sometimes as much as seventeen times."

Her characters, she says, are composites of real people, but her husband never appears in her books. "He is a loving, tender, kind, wonderful man who does not belong in a novel. People like him are the backbone of the earth, no doubt, but he is not melodramatic or intrusive."

She is currently writing a book about betrayal—the betrayal of the American people by such politicians as Nixon and Kissinger—and about personal disappointment. "I've had friends who have been betrayed by their husbands. It haunts me. That kind of betrayal is the worst. It comes like a sword; to wake up one day and find everything you thought was true is false. You just can't absorb it into your reality."

"If it happened to me, I don't think I could survive it."

Gradually she began to see the blood on him. . . . Across the side of his head, shyly turned from her, a stream of blood was moving and soaking into the pillow. . . . She did not move. She could smell his blood. Words came to her again, like an incantation, My brother is to blame, that bastard.

—from *them*

* * *

Whether describing the bloodshed of the slums of Detroit, as she did in *them*, or the clinical butchery inside a hospital, as she did in *Wonderland* (there, a student cuts out a uterus from a cadaver, broils it and eats it), Joyce Carol Oates has been criticized for an excess of exquisitely detailed gore.

She reacts archly to this: "I did not create the streets of Detroit. When I write about a man who murders or commits suicide, where do I get the idea from? From a hundred different sources, from the violence and cynicism that is part of our national character.

"People don't criticize journalists for writing too much about the slaughter in Cambodia. Why should a novelist be singled out for writing about what she sees?"

She often plots her stories from newspaper headlines and she views her writing as a reflection of American life. If Norman Mailer resorts to nonfiction to novelize America (his account of the life of Gary Gilmore in *The Executioner's Song* is called a "truelife novel"), then Joyce Carol Oates only attempts her own reproduction of the nation's larger-than-life characters and events.

"When people say there is too much violence in Oates," she says, "what they are saying is there is too much reality in life."

She does admit, however, that even she finds her material rough to write. "If I have to write a particularly gory part, I distance myself. I forget I am me and enter the scene through the narrator. I simply become a vessel for him."

The gallery floor shines, it is so highly polished. . . . You step close to the photographs, you peer anxiously at them. . . . Sunrise, trees, mountains, the remarkable delicacy of light, the blossoming of light in leaves. . . . You want to cry out in amazement that you have not seen anything before; you have never seen the mountains before, though you stare out that bedroom window every day of your life.

—from *Childwold*

When Joyce Carol Oates was just 25, she went to New York for the first time. "Oh, her eyes were as wide as an ocean!" says Evelyn Shrifte, her former editor. The young author had come to the big city for the publication by Vanguard of her first book, a short-story collection. "I can see her now. The bells were ringing at St. Pat's and it was magic for her.

"Vanguard had taken a chance on her. She was fresh out of school, and I thought she was a genius," says Miss Shrifte, who still mentions the names of Miss Oates's characters as if they were old friends. "She and Ray stayed at my house. They didn't have much money then and we would sit around at night and I would read and they would read and then, at 11 P.M., we would have Tab and a cookie.

"I am very sad that we lost her and I can't help but think that some of the promotion she's getting is ghastly," Miss Shrifte adds. "We always tried to treat her with dignity. Our ads simply mentioned the name Joyce Carol Oates, as you might mention Beethoven, no explanation needed.

"I never edited her. We didn't care about a best seller, we just cared about her being herself. Well, maybe she can be promoted. Maybe that's what she likes now. Maybe it's what she deserves."

Dutton has persuaded Miss Oates to take a royalty rate cut to enable a 558-page book to be retailed at a price accessible to a wider public. The publishing house plans to spend upward of $35,000 on promotion, much more than Vanguard ever spent, and it took the unusual step of distributing 1,000 copies free to booksellers at the American Booksellers Association Convention last June. Most of Miss Oates's previous books have had only etchings or photographs on their covers, but Dutton commissioned an original oil painting for the cover of *Bellefleur*. Trade-journal advertisements proclaim the book as "a breakthrough work . . . the mythic culmination of Joyce Carol Oates's ongoing portrait of American life."

"She's going to get a second kind of reader: ordinary people who might not follow serious literature, but who like a good read," says Karen Braziller, her editor at Dutton. "And what author could be unhappy at selling a few more books?"

Month followed month and she failed, she failed to conceive, and it was this word she insisted upon—fail, failed—this word Gideon had to endure.

But now. . . . Now the woman was so wonderfully, so arrogantly pregnant . . . nothing was so real to her now as certain flashes of sensation

—tastes, colors, even odors, vague impulses and premonitions—which she interpreted as the baby's continuous dreaming, deep in her body.
                                                    —from *Bellefleur*

"For years, I had wanted to write *Bellefleur*," Miss Oates says. "I would collect images along the way—a clavichord I saw, a snatch of conversation I heard—but I never could find the right voice. I would just throw the pages away; I was blocked."

The novel began in her mind with a sudden image of a woman sitting beside a baby in a cradle in a shabby but lushly overgrown walled garden. "'Oh! I'd love to be there,' I thought. It was a warm, penetrating, nostalgic image," and from there, Oates yearned and dreamed right into the book. She worked intensely from the summer of 1978, when she arrived in Princeton, until the following May, to finish it.

The theme threading through the story of the Bellefleurs is the tragedy of greed, the megalomania in the American character that ultimately leads to self-destruction.

Bellefleur, more than any other Oates novel, took possession of her. "It was very peculiar. It was a puzzle haranguing me. I'd hurry to my desk in the morning and sometimes it would take hours to get going, but I would try to do a chapter a day. I was in a very tense and excited state."

She calls *Bellefleur* her "vampire" novel. "Even talking about it still drains me," she says, looking all at once as though she had left the room. "I've had many such psychic vampire experiences in the past.

"I developed some theories about 19th-century Gothicism while writing the book. Using the werewolf, for instance, is a way of writing about an emotional obsession turning into a kind of animal.

"It seemed a race against time. I guess writers always have this feeling that they will die before they complete their work."

When she finished the last page, a feeling of deep melancholia came over her. "There was nothing to make your heart beat fast, nothing to make you afraid . . . I felt very homesick, like loving a place you know you will never go back to."

How fierce the Hawker Tempest . . . fierce and urgent and combative and never playful, like the other planes. . . . Such an airplane must be freed from the spell of gravity, it must be taken into the air as often as possible. . . .

There were so many Bellefleurs, people said, but perhaps most of them had never existed. . . . Though Gideon, of course, certainly existed. At least until the day he committed suicide by diving his airplane into Bellefleur Manor.

—from *Bellefleur*

When Joyce Carol Oates was a child in Erie County—which has been re-created as the Eden County of many of her books, including *Bellefleur*—she remembers how her father, a tool-and-die designer, loved to fly small airplanes. "It scared my mother and me to death.

"It was a big sport in Millersport. My father loved to get into this little chair with wings; he loved the feel of the wind, like being in a hang glider. It became obsessive with him.

"The youngish men would do stunts, flying low over the house, seeing how close they could get. There were a lot of accidents and I was afraid my father would crash, which he didn't."

But the character Gideon Bellefleur, who also became addicted to the thrill of small planes, did. A lingering childhood fear realized finally in her novel? Thus, perhaps, is the creative mind fueled by a need to unconsciously resolve the wishes and fears of the past.

A harsh note to the children's play. Someone is drunk and angry and someone else is frightened and angry and the others are laughing . . . the others stand about laughing, rude jocular hearty, good-natured, the girl is saying, "Stop, stop! Goddam you, stop!"

—from *Childwold*

Joyce Carol Oates was a slight, skinny girl. The boys all looked very tall to her. She went to a one-room schoolhouse and then local junior and senior high schools, and going on the school bus every day was a journey of intimidation and violence.

"It was so rural and everybody intermarried," she says. "There were a lot of mentally retarded kids and the older ones would bully the smaller.

"They were rough and ignorant boys and they quit school usually at 16. They appear in my books now and then. It was exhausting. A continual daily scramble for existence."

As chaos swirled outside, inside the Oates farmhouse it was warm, safe, a watering ground. Her family, Roman Catholic, was multitiered and close-knit. She was attached to her younger brother and sister and the grandparents who lived with them. Her paternal grandmother, who appears often in her work, bought her her first typewriter when she was 14.

"She influenced me greatly," she says, wistful. "I listened to her stories and then I began to pretend to write them; I simulated handwriting before I knew letters. And sometimes I just drew symbols—butterflies, cats, trees."

If there was much that was terrible about where she grew up as a child, there was something attractive about the roughness of that world, the little hamlet, the old graveyard, her friends' ramshackle houses full of children. As she takes her place before the typewriter now, she is drawn again and again back to an earlier self.

"When I remember, I remember sometimes even the time before I was born, when my parents were young," she sighs, looking out through the glass toward her pond. "Childhood is the province of the imagination and when I immerse myself in it, I re-create it as it was, as it could have been, as I wanted—and didn't want—it to be."

Speaking About Short Fiction: An Interview with Joyce Carol Oates

Sanford Pinsker

Originally appeared in *Studies in Short Fiction*, 1981. Reprinted by permission.

Joyce Carol Oates needs no special introduction to readers of contemporary American fiction. Since the publication of *By the North Gate* in 1963, collections of her stories have appeared regularly. She is, as well, a frequent reviewer of other people's short fiction. To both efforts Miss Oates brings unusual amounts of energy and intelligence.

On March 10, 1980, she spent an exhausting day on the Franklin & Marshall campus—visiting classes, answering students' questions (including one that packed a naïve, unintentional wallop: "Did your childhood affect you much?") and, of course, reading from her work. Somewhere between the end of lunch and the start of a classroom visit, I broached the subject of an interview. I promised not to ask her any autobiographical questions, either about her childhood or about her present situation. She accepted. Then I offered to record our conversation about aspects of the short story and to edit the tape later. This she declined, preferring instead to conduct the conversation by mail.

So, for the next few months I sent questions and she responded— always promptly and always with the same intensity she had radiated during her visit. Some of my questions did not stimulate, did not inspire. In one postcard she complained of being "overwhelmed with interviews." Nonetheless, she persisted, and the results follow:

Sanford Pinsker: I. B. Singer once told me that he thought some subjects were more appropriate to the short story than to longer forms. A dybbuk, for example, could not be the protagonist of a family novel. As far as I know, there are no dybbuks in *your* canon, but would you agree with Singer's general premise—namely, that some subjects are, by definition, appropriate or congenial to the short story?

Joyce Carol Oates: I cannot agree that some subjects are by definition appropriate or inappropriate to the short story. The "short story" is a highly elastic term, after all. A brief enigmatic dream-tale by Kafka . . . a dense, meditative, slow-moving story by Henry James . . . a spare exchange of dialogue by Hemingway: all can be considered "stories" yet each differs radically from the others. Surely there is a novelist somewhere who *could* write a family novel with a dybbuk as the protagonist? (In fact I may have done this myself, in a manner of speaking, in my new novel *Bellefleur*.)

SP: Not only has criticism of individual short stories or of writers who work principally in this genre been rather sparse, but one gets the feeling that theoretical speculation about short fiction has been almost completely dormant. Am I right about these suspicions? Or put another way: Is there anything new to say about the American short story that Edgar Allan Poe hasn't already said in his famous remarks about Hawthorne's short stories?

JCO: Poe's remarks are inappropriate to our time, and in fact to the marvelous modern tradition of the story that begins with Chekhov, Joyce, Conrad, and James. Speculation about short fiction should probably remain minimal since "speculation" about most works of art is usually a waste of time. Those of us who love the practice of an art often hate theorizing because it is always theorizing based upon past models: as such, it must inevitably decline toward the conservative, the reactionary, the exhortative, the school of *should* and *should not*. Genuine artists create their own modes of art and nothing interests them except the free play of the imagination. Poe's and Hawthorne's impulses in fiction were bound up with the allegorical, the static, and the highly romantic (which is to say, the impersonal). How can one draw a reasonably sober line between Hawthorne, James, Stephen Crane, Faulkner, and Hubert Selby, Jr. . . . ? Where would Beckett or Flannery O'Connor or Saul Bellow fit in? It isn't even true that short stories are necessarily *short*.

SP: One of the continuing myths about you is that you write many of your short stories in a single, long burst of creative energy—often nearly all night—and that in the morning there is a manuscript of yet another Oates story. Is this a fact about how you often work, or, rather, yet another version of the romantic artist that simply isn't true?

JCO: I would be interested in seeing the story or interview that claimed I wrote all night long—since in fact I have never done so. While it is true that my first drafts are almost always written out—often in longhand—in a single long (and draining) burst of what might be called energy, it is always the case that the subsequent drafts are much longer and are often spread out over a period of time. There are always "first drafts" of stories among my worksheets, waiting for their formalization, their re-imagining. What prompts me to begin work on them at a certain time, on a certain day—I can't know. I have never in my life written anything straight out, not even a five-line poem. I have always revised and edited.

SP: Would it be fair to say that you find satirical short stories—especially the ones placed in an academic setting—more congenial than the prospect of a long academic novel? I guess what I mean is this: I can see you writing versions of the stories in *Hungry Ghosts*, but not a book like Mary McCarthy's *Groves of Academe*. (I realize that *Expensive People* has something of this flavor perhaps, but I don't see it primarily as an academic satire.)

JCO: My most recent novel, *Unholy Loves* (1979), is an academic comedy set at an upstate New York university larger than Bennington, smaller than Cornell, prestigious yet not quite competitive with Harvard, Princeton, and Yale.

SP: Some of your stories strike me as thoroughly conventional in technique, some as dazzlingly experimental. Nonetheless, one doesn't normally associate your stories with the work of Barthelme, Sukenick, Sorrentino or others of the Post-Modernist school. Could you comment about the whole matter of "experimentation" with regard to short fiction?

JCO: "Experimentation" for its own sake has never interested me, but if a story's content—if its protagonist—is "post-modernist" in sensibility, then the style of the story will probably reflect this predilection. As time passes and I become more and more comfortable with telling a linear story and populating it with characters, I inevitably become more and more interested in the structures into which fiction can be put, and the kinds of language used to evoke them. But the degree of sophistication of my protagonist usually dictates the degree of sophistication of the story. I admit to a current fascination with the phenomenon of *time*—I seem to want to tell a story as if it were sheer lyric, all its components present simultaneously. The only "stories" that interest me at the present time are long ones—very long. I am fascinated too with the concept of a "novel" shaped out of a sequence of closely related and intertwined "short stories." (My use of quotation marks indicates my skepticism about literary terms.)

SP: Let's pursue your fascination with "sheer lyric" just a bit. I often have the sense that your fiction begins with a powerful, haunting image (e.g. the pack of wild dogs in *Son of the Morning*) that may have surfaced first in a poem (as I *think* was the case with the dogs) or a short story. Do you generally move from shorter units of the imagination to longer ones, or do other considerations bring an image into its proper structure? In this regard, do you work like a painter, going through a series of "studies" in a subject until you find the one that fulfills the image's potential?

JCO: This is very difficult to answer. I think yes, yes I do begin with an image; then again I think—well, no, I obviously begin with an "idea" (the "idea" of trying to create in words a "religious consciousness" set in a recognizable United States, in the era of Born-Again politicians and other hazards to one's mental health). The haunting image of the walled garden in *Bellefleur* was one point of departure for that novel; then again, the hope to create a microcosm of America—imperialist, exploitative, yet tirelessly optimistic—was certainly another. I suppose in some queer way the two evolve together: the image, the idea: and create somehow an adequate structure which can do justice to them both.

SP: Perhaps we can move our discussion of the creative process from the writing desk to the lectern. A good many people who teach poetry workshops grumble that their students are unacquainted with poetry generally, that they don't *read* enough. Indeed, the complaint might also be leveled at those who have more manuscripts of their own to submit than they do individual volumes of poetry on their bookshelves. Do short story writers face similar problems in the classroom? And if so, do they matter as much? At all?

JCO: Prose fiction is probably more generally, because more easily, read. In any case I require an anthology of short stories in my workshops, and we spend a fair amount of time analyzing and discussing other writers. This is not only enormously rewarding in itself—my Princeton students are avid readers, and quite enthusiastic—but, as one might imagine, instructive for all.

SP: We are told constantly that Formalism's heyday is over, that critics have moved beyond the close-reading of texts to larger, more theoretical speculations (Structuralism, Post-Structuralism and the like). At the same time, though, there is still a decided preference for the "teachable" short story when one makes choices for a syllabus in, say, an Introduction to Fiction class. From your point of view, what ought teachers to do? (I realize that this is broadly put, but what I'm angling for is nothing less than this—Are there any advices you might care to give?)

JCO: Teachers follow their instincts—their likes and dislikes—like everyone else. I can't imagine prescribing for anyone else.

SP: I'm sure you've heard the assorted dissatisfactions people have with anthologies, but I wonder if you might comment on one in particular—namely, that anthologies encourage the sad reality of a writer becoming known—and thus labeled—by two or three stories some editor has chosen. Does that fact of publishing life bother you? Would you prefer an anthology—of the sort that sometimes happen in collections of poetry—where the writers, rather than an editor, pick their respective favorites?

JCO: This is certainly an excellent idea; I know we would all welcome it. But, to my knowledge, it hasn't been done—or at least I have not been involved. (Perhaps you know someone who would enjoy editing such a book.)

SP: Because your short stories appear in such a wide range of magazines and journals, could you give us some indication of how many short stories you have circulating to editors at any given moment? And I'm sure that readers, especially those who are struggling, beginning writers, would be interested in knowing if the pains of rejection slips ever go away completely. Robert Lowell once said something to the effect that when he began writing poetry, it seemed as if he could not get any of his poems published. Later, however, he discovered an even greater, more vexing problem when he could get all of them accepted. Has that, roughly, been your situation? And if not, why do you think that that's the case?

JCO: Strange as it might sound, I have been writing very few short stories in recent years. All my energies are going into long—very long—works. A "short story" will appear in *Kenyon Review* sometime soon—but it is more than 60 pages long. The novel exerts a powerful fascination for me at the present time—large, ambitious, audacious, playful, "allegorical" structures—which have space enough for variations upon themes, counterpoint, parody, contrasts, historical and social and economic peculiarities, etc.! So I have barely a handful of stories, and perhaps the same number of poems. (In any case, the vagaries of acceptances and rejections are blessedly peripheral to me—dealt with entirely by my agent.)

SP: To conclude, can we go back to some matters of technique you touched on earlier? Am I right in thinking that presenting all the components of a story simultaneously is something of what you are doing in *Childwold*? And if so, could you talk a bit about the technical differences between that book, that texture of writing, and your earliest stories about Eden County. By that I mean, similarities of people and place still persist, but the effect has altered radically. This, I take it, is a function of style, but what else? And too: Do you think that the phenomenon of time is a narrative problem exclusively, or a matter of a protagonist's apprehension of psychological reality, or both?

JCO: Well—the components of a story, unlike those, say, of a painting, cannot be presented simultaneously. And though *Childwold* is frequently image-centered, it quite clearly unfolds in time, and tells a coherent story: indeed, it is meant to point beyond its narrative conclusion to a "future" beyond the closing paragraph. (That is, Laney's "future" as an independent and even educated young woman—free of Kasch's imagination.) *Bellefleur* is more obviously a "classical," even clockwork, sort of structure, in which the narrative voice (i.e. the author) is serenely experimental, within my own terms of reference.

An Interview with Joyce Carol Oates

Leif Sjoberg

Originally appeared in *Contemporary Literature*, Summer 1982. © 1982 University of Wisconsin Press. Reprinted by permission.

This interview, which originally appeared in the Stockholm magazine, *Artes*, began at Princeton, where Joyce Carol Oates is a professor in the Creative Writing program. It was conducted over a period of several weeks in 1980, and continued through letters and telephone conversations.

Leif Sjoberg: Among all the poetry readings at the 92nd Street "Y" that I have attended, yours was the only one in which the writer held the manuscript up to the audience so that they could see its length. You wanted to "give warning," as you said, and to prepare your listeners "for the length of the poem" and the need for "concentration" for the duration of the poem. It was as if you established an agreement with your listeners about this particular poem, and when it was read we all relaxed, and you talked a little about it, quite informally. Have you done this at other readings, too?

Joyce Carol Oates: I make it a practice to suggest to the audience the relative length of a poem. This is important, but we take it for granted when we read the printed page, since we absorb the length unconsciously. Of course, my audience at the "Y" was too large for the necessary sort of intimacy. At smaller gatherings, or when meeting with university students, I make certain that they can see the size of the poem, so to speak.

LS: In one piece that you read, "Leave-taking," there seemed to be a strong personal element. What was your central purpose in that poem?

JCO: I had wanted to give voice to the uncanny, and rather beautiful, "presence of absence" we sometimes experience when we see the familiar world emptied of ourselves. So many people have commented on this poem in which the house, emptied of furniture, belongings, and its tenants, has a future and a past, but no present! I was very pleased with the number of personal responses from listeners.

LS: Did I miss something you said in that context about existential matters: doubting one's existence at certain moments, or the like?

JCO: We *believe* we exist in terms of other people, our surroundings, our activities, or our environment. If these are altered or denied—what then? Is there a personality that is, to quote Dickinson, a "zero at the bone?" Or is personality nearly all cultural—external trappings? These are questions some of my poems address themselves to.

LS: At this same reading, you mentioned that you had extracted a large portion of a one-thousand page novel manuscript and made prose poems of it. How can that be done without getting the genres all mixed up?

JCO: My new long novel is a series of interlocking tales, many of them mountain legends, fairy tales, and fabricated history. A typical mountain legend would lend itself easily to the narrative poem structure. The novel itself consists, in part, of prose poem sections. I chose deliberately to bring together the lyric, the epic, and the dramatic in a single experimental form.

LS: What do you want to achieve with your poetry?

JCO: I hope to achieve with my poetry whatever I hope to achieve with my fiction.

LS: And that is?

JCO: It is a kind of homage or worship, very difficult to explain.

LS: Is inventiveness enough in poetry/art? How important is the corollary, observation, or "discovery," as Stevens put it?

JCO: I am not a didactic person and cannot feel comfortable prescribing any general rules for poetry. I tend to feel that the practice of poetry is all—the theorizing is often a feeble attempt to justify the practice. I think that, if Stevens could have written as powerfully as Whitman, along Whitman's lines, no doubt he would have. But he could not—so his aesthetic theories differ. The same is true for Eliot, who often teaches cultural prejudices in the guise of poetry.

Remember that poetry is a great, great art—an enormous art—it can accommodate a great multitude of individuals!

LS: O.K. Let's hear what you think of some of them. "The time for Beauty is over," said Pound, and continued, "Mankind may return to it but it has no use for it at present. The more art develops the more scientific it will be, just as science will become artistic." Do you think we are likely to get more poems closer to science and the methods it employs?

JCO: I believe that the science most humanists reject is bad science, devoid of human subtlety and imagination. Though I have not the training to appreciate it, I feel fairly certain that higher mathematics and physics can be as beautiful as poetry. Perhaps the inevitable tragedy of our complex civilization is that we must be specialists in our fields—and our fields have become increasingly difficult, so that communication is nearly impossible.

LS: To return to Pound: he must have been of two minds in his views on "learned" poetry, on the one hand, and pure emotional poetry, on the other, since in "A Retrospect" he suggests that "Only emotion endures," and feels it is better to recall those particularly beautiful lines that ring in a person's head rather than locating them and accounting for their source and meaning, as scholars tend to do. What are some of the lines of poetry that have been especially haunting, meaningful, or beautiful to you?

JCO: Many lines of poetry!—many indeed. Lines from Whitman, Yeats, Frost, Lawrence, Stevens ("Sunday Morning"), Eliot (*Four Quartets* above all), Keats . . . and, of course, Shakespeare, Donne, Wordsworth, Chaucer. For brevity, there is no one quite so uncanny as Emily Dickinson:

After great pain, a formal feeling comes—
The Nerves sit ceremonious, like Tombs—
The stiff Heart questions was it He, that bore,
And Yesterday, or Centuries before?

. . .

This is the Hour of Lead—
Remembered, if outlived,
As Freezing persons, recollect the Snow—
First—Chill—then Stupor—then the letting go—

LS: What about Pound?

JCO: I am quite ambivalent about Pound. Much of his poetry, it seems to me, is shrill and indefensible—as poetry and as wisdom.

LS: I sense that you are not too keen on influences?

JCO: As a student and teacher of English and American literature I have read literally thousands of poems, by both the classic poets and relatively unknown poets. No doubt there have been innumerable influences, but they are diffuse.

Most American poets have been influenced by Walt Whitman, our most "American" poet, and, to a lesser extent, Emily Dickinson. But I think Dickinson is so unique a voice that it is almost impossible to be influenced by her. Many of us writing now have been influenced—perhaps far in the past—by William Carlos Williams, who is, of course, related to Whitman, too.

LS: I recall a poem you dedicated to the short story writer Flannery O'Connor; is there a connection there?

JCO: My dedication in that instance indicates a thematic concern rather than any indebtedness to her writing. I was interested in O'Connor's apocalyptic imagination and what I take to be an excessive Puritanism in her—a punitive inclination which I do not share.

LS: Do you have a convenient definition of poetry?

JCO: Poetry is a rite involving language—at its very highest a sacred rite in that it transcends the personality of the poet and communicates its vision, whether explicitly or by indirection, to others. Many poems speak of the almost impersonal nature of the art when it is most pure and inspired.

LS: I would like to ask what poem satisfies you the most among your own works?

JCO: Always the most recent work; that is, a long poem in *The Atlantic* called "The Present Tense."

LS: If I am not mistaken, you have published nine major novels, ten collections of short stories, five collections of poetry, two books of essays, plays, and anthologies, and at present you are working on a major novel while teaching. Creativity seems to be your proper element, but the rest of us do not create a great deal, or at least not much of permanent value. Do you feel that you are unusually prolific?

JCO: I believe I have a reputation for writing a great deal only because the older, healthy tradition of the writer as an extremely hard-working and persistent craftsman is no longer fashionable. It appears that I am somewhat unusual, but measured against Balzac, Dickens, Henry James, Edith Wharton, Dostoyevsky, and many others, among the serious writers, I am certainly not unusual. I find solace in their example and would place myself— I hope not immodestly, but one must have ideals—in their tradition.

LS: Do you write every day?

JCO: Yes, usually for many hours. I write and write and write, and rewrite, and even if I retain only a single page from a full day's work, it *is* a single page, and these pages add up. As a result I have acquired the reputation over the years of being prolific when in fact I am measured against people who simply don't work as hard or as long.

LS: Do you find this unfair?

JCO: That goes without saying, but I have learned to be amused rather than hurt or antagonized by certain charges. I take with absolute seriousness Flaubert's claim that "we must love one another in our art as the mystics love one another in God"— and so my dedication to literature springs from a conviction that it is a "mystical" affirmation of our common human bond.

Writing and, of course, reading are quite simply, for me, the most transcendent of experiences. Even ostensibly violent or despairing literature, like Beckett's, for instance, or much of Faulkner's, I interpret in James Joyce's words as underscoring the eternal affirmation of the human spirit. I am somewhat embarrassed to be speaking in such terms, but those are my beliefs. That I am so passionately committed is probably evidenced by my presumed proliferousness! But even so mandarin a writer as Nabokov—whom I admire, but with qualifications—manages to be prolific, when his total oeuvre is examined.

LS: Coming back to the question of your own creativity. Is there a compulsive element in all this activity . . . ?

JCO: I assure you, there is very little that is compulsive about my life, either in my writing or otherwise. I believe that the creative impulse is natural in all human beings, and that it is particularly powerful in children unless it is suppressed. Consequently, one is behaving normally and instinctively and healthily when one is creating—literature, art, music, or whatever. An excellent cook is also creative! I am disturbed that a natural human inclination should, by some Freudian turn of phrase, be considered compulsive—perhaps even pathological. To me this is a complete misreading of the human enterprise. One should also enjoy one's work, and look forward to it daily.

Surprisingly enough, over the years I have come to be more certain of these beliefs. I am possibly more dedicated to teaching now than I was in my early twenties, and the same is true about my feelings toward literature. In the past twenty years I have seen my ideals affirmed rather than eroded. Of course I have difficult days with my writing, but in general all that I have just said is true for every hour of my life.

LS: Swedish literature is, of course, far from lacking in violence, but it has tended to emphasize sex rather than violence, while American literature—and TV—tend to be more violent. What is your rationale for employing the theme of violence so often in your books?

JCO: I don't accept charges that I am unduly violent in my writing. Most of my novels and stories are explorations of the contemporary world interpreted in a realist mode, from what might be called a tragic and humanistic viewpoint. Tragedy always upholds the human spirit because it is an exploration of human nature in terms of its strengths. One simply cannot know strengths unless suffering, misfortune, and violence are explored quite frankly by the writer.

LS: In the case of Balzac, who was so enormously productive, there was a plan, which, as you know, later became *La Comedie humaine*. Since your books all seem to deal with American social unrest, are you following a specific plan in your own writing?

JCO: I certainly do have a general plan for my writing. But I am not accustomed to making statements about my writing, since this seems like self-advertisement. I would prefer to allow the books to stand on their own—even at the risk of being misinterpreted from time to time. Though I am ambitious about my writing I am not ambitious about my career in terms of recognition. Some understanding and sympathetic readers are the most I dare hope for.

LS: You can't leave the question half answered like that . . .

JCO: Since approximately 1965 I have set myself the task, in both novels and short stories, of exploring contemporary society on many levels. My focus has been a close examination of the sources of power. The political and social milieu; professions like medicine, the law, and most recently education and religion; and, to some extent, the predicament of the young and of women—all these have fascinated me.

LS: What is your position on women's liberation?

JCO: I am very sympathetic with most of the aims of feminism, but cannot write feminist literature because it is too narrow, too limited. I am equally sympathetic with male characters as with female, which has been a source of irritation to some feminist critics. . . . An unfortunate situation, but one which I cannot help.

LS: In his book *The Progress of the Human Mind* Condorcet gives an outline of history that ends on a hopeful note: that equality of men, equality of nations, and also "the real improvement of men" would some day come about. Since 1794 when his essay appeared, we have seen small wars, large wars, world wars, despotism, totalitarianism, natural disasters, the Holocaust, failures of all kinds. How do you assess the chances for "improvement" of the human condition?

JCO: First I must state my position about all forms of creativity, including my own: these acts are gratuitous offerings and bring something—a vision, an argument, an illumination of a certain corner of the world, a style, a music, an aspect of personality— into the world which did not previously exist. The creative act is an acte gratuite. It withdraws nothing from the world—not the intellectual world, not the material world. At its base it is a spontaneous birth, usually presented to the world as an offering or a gift. Consequently the creative act and its product are an end in themselves, complete. Like a bird's song—on a much higher structural level. The artist is forever being called upon in the

United States to justify himself or herself: and in a way that for instance the manufacturer of toothpaste, automobiles, cigarettes, every sort of material goods is not.

My feeling about art in every form is that, first, it is primarily a natural, spontaneous, inevitable motion of the soul, unique in our species; and, second, that it becomes transformed as it is directed toward a certain social, moral or religious context—at which point it generally acquires its "moral" dimension.

I am responding, of course, to your questions *only* in the spirit of the second category. My persistent and fundamental belief is that art is an expression of the human soul and need not ever, in any circumstances, justify its existence.

LS: And the "human condition" . . .

JCO: It has been greatly—enormously—in fact miraculously improved. One simply cannot look at the civilized world as it exists today, in 1980, and compare it to an abstract Platonic condition of perfection. Improvement exists in nearly every sphere of life, particularly domestic and social life, in civilized nations of the West, and elsewhere. One must go slowly, of course, and prudently, always with an awareness that Utopia is a myth, but if one considers the conditions of workers, for instance, in both the United States and Europe—not simply wages and work-hours, but working conditions, benefits, pensions—the progress within a few decades has been astonishing. I speak as the child of a working class family.

LS: Where did your family come from?

JCO: My maternal grandparents emigrated from Budapest in the early years of the twentieth century. Working and living conditions were extremely difficult at that time, as one might imagine.

In another sphere, that of women's rights, immense progress has been made. It is simply too easy to cast one's eye about to find faults, setbacks, "imperfections." They will always exist, our world is not Utopia. I could speak at great length on this subject, because I feel strongly about it.

LS: How do you relate to the "past?"

JCO: There is nothing more absurd than to hear someone, often an intellectual, speak romantically of the past: the nineteenth century, in which children of eight or nine toiled in sweatshops; the medieval period, in which mad religious struggles killed so many people; even antiquity, when the Greeks, a refined people, held onto their slaves and denied citizenship to women! Only someone without a realistic historical perspective can believe sincerely that "the past" is superior to the present.

LS: What do you think the arts can do to improve or develop people?

JCO: It was said by W. B. Yeats that "tragedy breaks down the dykes between people." This is true, and it is true for comedy as well. As soon as one opens a book, by an American, a Japanese, a South African, a Hungarian, one is in the consciousness of another. The psychological and emotional act of reading has yet to be fully explored or understood. In no other art is this really possible. For instance, I have taught classes of as many as 130 students, working with them on novels like Mishima's *Confession of a Mask*, which in many ways is a difficult novel for North American students to understand. Within a few days the students' sympathy and interest are remarkable. Or consider the work of Anzia Yezierska, a Jewish writer of the 1920s and 30s, now little known, whose novels about immigrant life on the Lower East Side did so much to bridge the gap between her people and Americans. Abraham Lincoln, meeting Harriet Beecher Stowe, commented that *here* was the person who had brought about the Civil War, hence the freeing of the slaves.

LS: Auden used to say that none of his poems had saved the life of a single Jew during the Hitler era . . .

JCO: That may be, but in recent times one might think of Solzhenitsyn. One can hardly measure the effect his books have had upon the world, politically as well as emotionally. It would be possible for me to name many writers who have had a considerable impact upon their culture, in both private and public ways. Dickens, for instance, Dostoyevsky. And Yeats, whose effect upon Irish nationalists was great.

LS: What can your own books do in that direction. Or, what would you want them to do?

JCO: Evidently my books are taught in university classes in various parts of the world. I can't be certain, however, how they are taught . . . or even how accurately they are translated. At a recent conference of Soviet and U. S. writers it was explained to me that my books were read in the Soviet Union, apparently with sympathy. I am surprised to learn that a group of short stories sold quite well in Hungary.

But, of course, I would be very modest about claiming that my books might "improve" humanity. The writer hopes to reach out to a reader . . . to a single reader at a time. The proper object of the writer's hope is not a crowd but an individual. Beyond that it is vainglorious to speculate. Writers who might be accused of being extremely self-absorbed, like Flaubert, for example, often create works of art that are devastating in their power to arouse sympathy in others.

LS: Take someone like Joyce . . .

JCO: Yes, it is rarely commented upon that his *Ulysses* is a masterpiece of empathy, for Leopold Bloom, the lonely Jew, who is at once a Dubliner and a member of the human species: an extraordinary creation for a writer whose reputation is generally considered elitist.

LS: Are your books used in courses in departments other than the English department?

JCO: At least in the United States; in sociology, for instance, or psychology, and then I am a bit apprehensive. For though the writer naturally hopes that various kinds of insights and information might be gleaned from his/her work, she/he does create a work of art primarily, which must obey its own internal laws of structure and aesthetic resonance. But I never write to lure the reader, or to "entertain," in the light sense of the word.

LS: Why not?

JCO: There are quite enough entertainments, especially in America, at the present time.

LS: But to diminish, mitigate or lessen problems?

JCO: Never! And never to solve problems by authorial fiat. My personal experience—both as a reader and a teacher of literature—is that difficult and troubling works of art, *King Lear*, for instance, are far more beneficial than happy works. One learns so much from Thomas Mann, Dostoyevsky, Kafka, Melville, and other great writers precisely because they refused to soften their vision of humanity. Yet, even including Kafka, they are by no means negative. I have written an essay on Kafka's mysticism, in particular his relationship to Taoism. He is a much misunderstood writer!

LS: Like many of his contemporaries, Condorcet hoped that science would explain human behavior. What hopes do you have for science in this respect?

JCO: Once again, outlawing the very concept of Utopia or perfection, I must say that science and its subsequent technology has done immeasurable good for mankind. Science is, of course, of two kinds, theoretic and practical. In the first category we might very well place great philosophical thinkers, for instance, who have helped mankind think its way through superstitions and other forms of ignorance. Great scientists, like Einstein, are usually mystics, guided by impulses (perhaps laws?) of creativity they cannot understand. I am convinced that the great scientists, like the great artists, are expressions of the evolutionary motion of a species.

LS: What would you say the novel has done which science has failed to do?

JCO: The novel, like all forms of art, is an expression of a subjectivity which might then be translated into the universal, while science deals only with the universal or the representative. One of the little-understood responsibilities of the artist is to bear witness—in almost a religious sense—to certain things. The experience of the concentration camps . . . the experience of suffering, the humiliation of any form of persecution. Ralph Ellison's novel *Invisible Man* is a brilliant portrayal of the experience of one black man in America—one cannot read it without being deeply moved. . . . The experience of being a woman in a patriarchal culture. . . . Any form of subjectivity that resonates with the universal power complements the function of science, the objective discipline.

LS: The gap seems to be widening between serious literature and light literature. Serious, intellectual literature requires more and more commentaries, it appears, for fewer and fewer readers. Is there, in your opinion, a risk that literature is becoming too intellectual?

JCO: No. I cannot agree that the gap is widening between serious literature and light literature! Our great age of modernism, in English, at least, is past. Though we read Joyce and, to a lesser extent, Pound, though we admire Henry James immensely, most of us who are serious about our writing have no interest in the high modernist position. One can point confidently to a writer of genius who has never been a self-consciously coy artist, and who has written books—at least one of them a masterpiece—that can be read by nearly anyone: Saul Bellow.

LS: What other writers are readily accessible?

JCO: Bernard Malamud. John Updike. Iris Murdoch. John Fowles, and many others.

LS: What about poetry?

JCO: We are, perhaps temporarily, in a period in American poetry in which difficulty, obscurantism, and private allusions are applauded by the critics, sometimes with justification—for a highly self-conscious writer, like Yeats himself, can also be an extraordinarily good writer. Certainly there are extremely obscure experimental writers—but their influence on the culture is quite minimal. Some of them are friends of mine—and so I can appreciate the sincerity of their art. It is their art; they haven't much choice about its degree of difficulty. Since I prefer Saul Bellow's writing to that of his experimental contemporaries, and since his books have been translated widely, and have made an impact, I can't feel pessimistic about this problem. Garcia Marquez's *One Hundred Years of Solitude* is another recent phenomenon: a lengthy, difficult, rather quirky novel in Spanish that has sold more than *Don Quixote*! Offhand I would say that in the U. S. the gap was far more serious in the nineteenth century. One can scarcely believe how our American masterpieces were ignored in favor of utterly insipid, improbable "novels" which became fantastic best sellers and are now completely forgotten. For a serious American writer—especially for a woman writer—this is by far the best era in which to live.

LS: How would you define your concept of beauty? And why is there so much sordidness in your books?

JCO: Beauty is a cultural ideal, often a cultural prejudice. In the abstract it really cannot exist, for even Einsteinian standards of

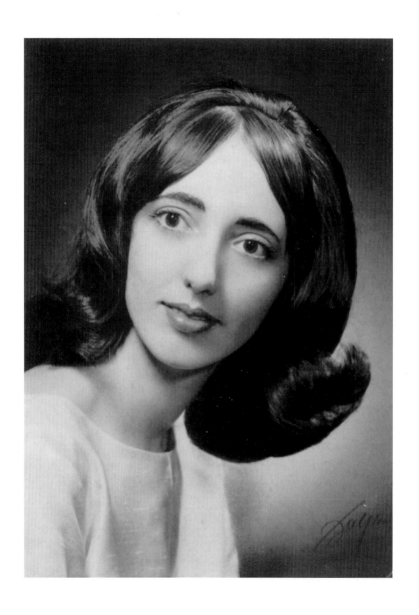

By the North Gate, 1963

With Shuddering Fall, 1964
Photo by Robert Benyas

National Book Award, *them*, 1970
Photo by Jack Robinson

Marriages and Infidelities, 1973
Photo by Fay Godwin

What I Lived For, 1994
Photo by Mary Cross

Blonde, 2000
Photo by Marion Ettlinger

Joyce with Greg Johnson, 1991

Heat and Other Stories, 1991
Photo by Norman Seefe

(Woman) Writer, 1988
Photo by Jerry Bauer

Rea Award for the Shorrt Stroy, 1990
Photo by Brian J. Berman

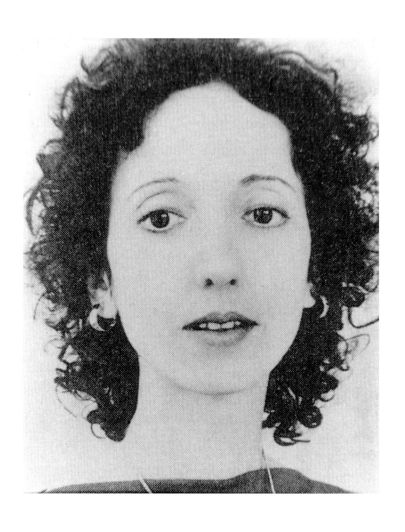

Angel of Light, 1981
Photo by Jerry Bauer

Joyce with Mike Tyson, Catskill, New York, 1986
preparing for an article for *Life Magazine* and for the book *On Boxing*

"Spinozan calm" have meaning only within the human imagination.

In my more recent stories there is probably less that is disturbing or violent since I have become far more concerned with the tragic within the human spirit. In *Son of the Morning*, the most extreme violence is that which occurs when the divine and the human intersect—and this is a subjective, interior experience, difficult to explain in ordinary language.

It should perhaps be re-emphasized that literature—particularly dramatic literature—focuses upon the moment in lives at which conflicts erupt. Think of Ibsen, Strindberg, Chekhov, and of course Shakespeare! Consequently it seems to concern itself with conflict; but this is not, strictly speaking, true. It concerns itself with the momentum of lives, the accumulating fears, tensions, lies, and illusions that then erupt on stage within a two- or three-hour duration. So very economic and condensed an art always appears to be more violent, or sordid, than in fact it is.

LS: Obviously it would be boring if there were too much sameness, if we were all alike, like polished grains of rice. The unusual, the unpredictable, that which is different, should command our interest. But why are so many of your most important characters on the boundaries of sanity?

JCO: Sanity, too, is a cultural prejudice, especially in nations that insist upon conformity in public affairs, like the United States. Many of the most imaginative and original thinkers—from Mozart to Newton to Einstein to Emily Dickinson—can be too casually dismissed by "normal" people as eccentrics. I agree with recent criticism of the psychiatric profession that focuses upon narrow and outmoded standards of normality and sanity against which people are presumably measured. Can Oedipus, King Lear, Ivan Karamazov, and Faulkner's doomed heroes be casually categorized as mad? On the contrary, it has always seemed to me, even as a much younger woman—as a high school student, in fact—that insane behavior of many kinds was the norm in our society.

LS: Would you give an example of what you have in mind?

JCO: As children of eleven and twelve we were forced to

participate in "atomic bomb" drills and told "Better dead than red!"—the idea being that the United States and Soviet Russia might blow up the world within a few years, and that this probably would have to happen since neither could tolerate the other's existence. Other aspects of collective madness, many of them frankly absurd, impressed upon me the fact that the individual who thinks for himself or herself, critically and unsentimentally, would probably be branded as eccentric or even crazy in such a society. I do not exactly accept the statement that many of my most important characters are on the boundaries of sanity: it seems to that these people extend the boundaries— that they are not to be measured by the usual conformist standards.

LS: In the event critics would venture to state that you tend to repeat yourself, how would you reply?

JCO: I am not really aware of repetition within my work. Each novel is a stylistic and structural experiment, from my point of view. Of course, all writers repeat themes, one way or another . . . Proust, Joyce, Faulkner, Bellow, certainly Kafka, Beckett, and others—but it is to be hoped that a new angle of vision, or a newer depth, makes the work innovative. Since I have written more than 300 short stories, for instance, it is perhaps unavoidable that some themes might be repeated; but from my personal point of view each project is new, and addresses itself to new problems and explorations. I am currently much interested in the drama, for instance, which forces a new perspective, and is very stimulating indeed.

LS: Do you think you have learned more from books or people? I refer particularly to books by others, but perhaps also to your own books, or writing them.

JCO: But one cannot distinguish between books and people! An excellent study of Mozart, for instance, leads us deeply into Mozart; a novel by Faulkner leads us into an aspect of human nature we have perhaps not yet encountered; poetry by one's friends and close colleagues reveals an angle of vision, and often a depth, or soul, not available in ordinary social discourse. No novelist scorns or undervalues reality, of course, for this is the very life-blood of our art: close observation of people, places, customs, beliefs, practices.

The writer also learns immensely from his own writing—for each work of art, particularly the lengthy ones, demands an immersion in thinking and experience that would not ordinarily be one's own; and of course the discipline in creating such long works is very strict and very rewarding. D. H. Lawrence believed that the novel was, among other things, an arena for the testing of the author's ideas—those which were weak would be revealed as weak, and those which were strong would triumph. This is perhaps not always the case, for there are powerful works of art whose "ideas" sometimes seem questionable but which satisfy as aesthetic accomplishment none the less.

LS: Whom did you have in mind?

JCO: Beckett, whose extreme nihilism puzzles me . . .

LS: This may be a ticklish question, but how do you rate some of your contemporaries?

JCO: I would not rate them, since it is offensive to my principles to "rate" human beings, especially in such very subjective terms.

But Faulkner is clearly the most significant writer. Hemingway is second. Others should not be rated along the same scale at all; they cannot be spoken of in the same context as Faulkner and Hemingway. I can't evaluate Dreiser and Sinclair Lewis, for example, as "artists," only as writers who have contributed important commentaries on social life in America. Dreiser's curious elephantine "mysticism"—in *Sister Carrie*, for example, when he speaks of an inevitable evolution, a "progress" in history—is intellectually indefensible. Lewis, though a good satirist, lacks subtlety and a sense of the depth of human experience.

LS: Among the older American authors Eudora Welty and Katherine Anne Porter are supposed to belong to your favorites?

JCO: Eudora Welty is a favorite of nearly everyone! A very fine, wise writer, less ambitious than the other authors we just mentioned, of course; but within the range of her intention she is completely successful. Of non-American women writers Isak Dinesen is much admired.

LS: What are your standards in determining what is important in literature?

JCO: Standards of greatness must encompass depth of vision; a breadth of actual work; a concern for various levels of human society; a sympathy with many different kinds of people; an awareness of and concern with history, or at least contemporary history; a sense of the interlocking forces of politics, religion, economics, and the mores of the society; concern with aesthetics; perhaps even experimentation in forms and language; and above all a "visionary" sense—the writer is not simply writing for his own sake, but to speak to others as forcefully as possible.

LS: It seems obvious especially in your later works that Jung is of importance to you. What books of his have you read and what have you got out of them?

JCO: I am a voracious reader and Jung is one of innumerable writers and thinkers I have read. Since I cannot accept his theories on the "male" and "female" archetypes I am not a "Jungian"—but I find his exploration of the Unconscious extremely intriguing. He is quite different from Freud, who imagines the unconscious as an adversary to consciousness. Jung understands that the wellsprings of life—creativity above all—reside in the Unconscious and its functions.

In Jung one confronts a bold, original, and "poetic" imagination, valuable for the questions it raises as much as for the answers it hopes to provide. I would set Jung beside Nietzsche; both men are brilliant and brilliantly provocative. One need not *believe* in their theories in order to learn from them.

LS: To what extent do you study influences with your writing students?

JCO: It is dangerous to place too much emphasis upon influences; this is a critical method of the past decade, as you know, exemplified by the Yale critic Harold Bloom, which has recently been subjected to wide and quite convincing rejection. Most novelists and poets are probably most powerfully influenced by their early surroundings: they wish to capture universal truths in the form of particular, even local types, and give life to the larger element of the human psyche by way of familiar images.

LS: You have indicated that it is the restless who interest you as a novelist, "for only out of restlessness can higher personalities emerge, just as, in a social context, it is only out of occasional surprises and upheavals that new ways of life can emerge." In what way can we expect that this point of view will be employed in your future novels?

JCO: My next novel, which is my most ambitious and also longest to date, is a complex parable of American aspirations and tragic shortcomings.

LS: Have you already decided on a title?

JCO: It is called *Bellefleur* and is imagined in the symbolist mode, though its concerns are very historical. It covers a period of time from approximately the American War of Independence until the present day, though time is treated symbolically. The elder members of the powerful Bellefleur family are destroyed but, one by one, their children—who may represent a younger or at any rate more selfless and idealistic America—escape their influence, and achieve their independence apart from the family's authority.

LS: That sounds like both tragedy and comedy.

JCO: It is. It is a tragedy in that many people are destroyed, in both a spiritual and literal sense, and a comedy in the higher sense that the instinct for survival and self-determination is celebrated. It was a considerable challenge for me, as the author, to imagine a conclusion that was both tragic and comic simultaneously . . . *Bellefleur* is, as I said, quite long, and filled with many characters and stories, all of them centering upon the American dream in both its daylight and nightmare aspects.

LS: Isn't there a certain risk that a work that mixes tragedy and comedy will be misinterpreted?

JCO: Sure. It has happened before. One of my longest books, *The Assassins*, was misunderstood by more than one critic. But if the new book is viewed as a poetic analysis of America, its meanings should not be elusive.

LS: Some of your short stories, such as "The Lady with the Pet Dog" and "Metamorphosis," are related to the work of familiar writers. Is this technique a lower form of creativity, not entirely original?

JCO: Postmodern writing often gains a secondary meaning by its juxtaposition to other works of literature or art. The stories stand on their own and were, of course, published on their own, but they are meant to have an allusive quality. Contrast is, of course, gained—but also a curious and ironic sympathy. The great writers were once young and unknown and struggling merely to be published; their works were not pronounced "great" for many years. I think the similarities between us all are far stronger than one might commonly realize.

LS: What are your feelings about experimentation? I would assume that a master stops experimenting at a certain point.

JCO: All serious writers are interested in experimentation. It is a means by which they honor their craft.

LS: Are there critical assumptions from which your stories operate?

JCO: The short story is the form in which I have worked most with experimentation. Virtually each story is an attempt to do something different—consequently it is extremely difficult for me to speak of my short stories in general terms. They proceed from a basis of psychological realism; however, often they take place in an individual's mind. I have become more and more interested in recent years in developing stories that are really miniature novellas: stories that deal with a person's entire life, greatly condensed and focused. An example would be "Daisy" in the 1978 volume *Night-Side*, which deals in a surrealist manner with some of the issues involved in the relationship between sanity and insanity—the story is based very informally on James Joyce's relationship with his schizophrenic daughter Lucia. Another story from the same volume, "A Theory of Knowledge," is a poetic attempt to dramatize the contradictions inherent in philosophizing—in abstracting from the world of sense experience and personal history: this story is very informally based on the later life of the famous American philosopher Charles Sanders Peirce. Of course it is entirely fiction.

LS: Are there any of your stories in which escape or humor, rather than interpretation or revelation, dominates?

JCO: I have written a number of satiric stories set in a fictitious university, gathered in the collection *The Hungry Ghosts*. These are serious stories, too, but their structure, pace, and characterizations mark them as deliberately light or humorous reading.

LS: Which is your favorite of your stories?

JCO: A very difficult question to answer. "Queen of the Night," which appeared in a special limited edition (Lord John Press, 1979), is one of my favorites. I am extremely fond of "Daisy," too, and "Stalking" and "The Dead" from *Marriages and Infidelities*; and "In the Region of Ice," "Where Are You Going, Where Have You Been?" and "How I Contemplated the World from the Detroit House of Correction . . ." from *The Wheel of Love*. "Famine Country" and "The Widows" (which I recently expanded into a play) from *Night-Side* are additional favorites.

A final comment on discursive conversations: as Nietzsche warns, "Talking much about oneself may be a way of hiding oneself." The most reliable introduction to any writer is simply the books.

A Taste of Oates

Jay Parini

Originally published in *Horizon* magazine, 1983, this essay is reprinted by permission of the author.

"I hardly see myself as being unusual," says Joyce Carol Oates, who at forty-five is one of America's most eminent writers of fiction. "I take my writing seriously, but I don't take myself seriously . . . that is, I don't feel pontifical or dogmatic. Writing is an absolutely fascinating activity, an immersion in drama, language, and vision."

Such modesty provides a dazzling contrast to her achievements, which include thirteen well-known novels, a dozen books of short stories (which many critics think are her best work), several plays, four remarkable collections of essays on a wide range of literary and cultural topics, and five poetry books. Her novel *them* (1969) received a National Book Award, and two others were nominated for that award. Her stories have often won the prestigious O. Henry Award, and she has been elected to the American Academy and Institute of Arts and Letters. Critic Robert H. Fossum said: "Oates may be the finest American novelist, man or woman, since Faulkner . . ."—an extreme statement, perhaps, but a sentiment shared to some extent by dozens of other critics since her first book of stories, *By the North Gate*, was published in 1963.

This month Oates will publish her fourteenth novel, *Mysteries of Winterthurn*, a complex tale of murder and the pursuit of love. The novel's hero is Xavier Kilgarven, an idealistic and glamorous detective who, in the course of this five-hundred-plus-page story, solves three exotic cases at decade intervals. Each case, in typical Oates fashion, involves bizarre twists, some violence, and unnerving consequences. In the midst of this, Kilgarven also manages to fall in love with his beautiful and intriguing half-cousin, Perdita. Their love affair forms a counterplot to the detective story, which all takes place in the mythical town of

Winterthurn during the latter part of the last century. Oates herself elaborates: "This is the third in a quartet of novels that have to do with American themes and settings and are meant to be slightly parodistic, but at the same time altogether serious as novels. The fourth novel, *The Crosswicks Horror* [set in Princeton in 1905 and 1906, when Woodrow Wilson was president of the university] will be published in 1985." [As of 2006, this novel still had not been published.] As usual, Oates writes on a grand scale; ambitious and productive.

As one might expect, any writer so prolific and so highly touted in general is likely to catch a good deal of harsh criticism, too; this seems especially true of Oates, whose hallucinatory and emotionally charged fiction disturbs many readers. Even her award-winning *them* elicited this remark from *Newsweek*: "This novel is a charnel house of Gothic paraphernalia: blood, fire, insanity, anarchy, lust, corruption, death by bullets, death by cancer, death by plane crash, death by stabbings, beatings, crime, riot, and even unhappiness." The London *Times Literary Supplement* snidely suggested that her novel *Wonderland* (1971) was aimed for "the sensation-mongering American market." A *Time* review of *The Assassins* (1975) referred to "the somewhat too prodigious Joyce Carol Oates." A percentage of reviewers has consistently been offended by Oates's industry and her use of violent subject matter, which includes her tendency to portray characters in states of mental extremity bordering on madness.

To these charges, Oates maintains a cool response. "Productivity is a relative matter," she says. "It's really insignificant. What is ultimately important is a writer's strongest books." As to the violence in her writing, she says, "Given the number of pages I've written, and then the 'violent' incidents dispersed throughout them, I rather doubt that I am a violent writer in any meaningful sense of that word." One does encounter numerous horrifying scenes in Oates's fiction, but her art is, as the saying goes, a mirror held up to life.

In person, Oates is warm, open, and generous. Tall and sylph-like, she has been described as "haunting" by many interviewers. Her striking black hair accents a face with large eyes and unusual features. According to her friend, Robert Phillips, "she is not photogenic; no photo has ever done justice to her appearance, which conveys grace and high intelligence." Her soft voice and courteous manners have sometimes been mistaken for aloofness. She avoids publicity and dislikes the personality cults that grow up around writers. Her immense output of books has attracted thousands of reviews and plenty of media attention, but Oates has been remarkably successful in keeping her personal life private.

She lives several miles outside of Princeton, New Jersey, with her husband Raymond Smith, who edits *The Ontario Review* and a special line of books from their home. They work from nearly adjacent offices in their home, which is a beautiful, glass-walled contemporary in a secluded area. Woods surround their house, which looks out onto a private pond; inside, the house is built around an atrium, conveying an atmosphere of greenery.

A professor at Princeton, Oates teaches literature with great gusto, according to her colleagues and former students. "I love teaching," she says. "I don't think I could do without it." It's not money that draws her to teaching; her recent novel *Bellefleur* (1980) has sold a million copies to date. "Teaching organizes my day," Oates explains. "I like to write in the morning and teach in the afternoons—the balance is right. It creates a rhythm for working."

Oates grew up in rural New York, near Lockport, in the region of Erie County depicted in her early fiction as Eden County. Her grandfather was a steelworker, her father a tool-and-die designer. She attended a one-room schoolhouse as a child, had few luxuries in growing up, and was the first person in her family to go to college. "We never thought she'd be *this* successful," says her father, Frederic Oates. "The turning point came when she won that short-story contest at *Mademoiselle*. She was still in college. Everything just took off from there." Her mother, Carolina Oates, traces her daughter's rise to fame back to childhood. "She was always so hardworking . . . a perfectionist at everything."

During her graduate-school studies at the University of Wisconsin, Oates met Raymond Smith, a student in the same department, and they married in 1961. Oates received her M. A. in English from Wisconsin and expected to continue for a Ph.D. She was just beginning her doctoral work at Rice, in Texas, when one of her short stories appeared on the honor roll of *Best*

American Short Stories. She decided to abandon the Ph.D. for fiction—a decision she has never regretted. In 1962, the young couple moved to Detroit, where they both taught English. Living through tempestuous years in that city inspired *them*, Oates's biggest early success.

In 1967, the University of Windsor offered Smith and Oates jobs on their faculty, so they moved to Ontario, Canada, where they lived for more than a decade. During this enormously productive time, Oates published twenty-seven books, including six full-length novels. She and her husband moved to Princeton in 1978, completing a migratory pattern that is not uncommon in academic circles. Having come back to the northeastern section of the United States, Oates was, in effect, "home." Her novel *Son of the Morning* appeared just as she arrived at her new job, and five other novels followed quickly.

Bellefleur is the most prominent of these. Consider one brief paragraph in this novel—a taste of Oates.

High in the mountains the seasons sped swiftly. Now the planet tipped north, now south. Now aurora borealis flooded the night sky and pitched into drunkenness all who gazed upon it; now all light was black—utterly and wordlessly black, as if eclipsed by the deep mire of man's sin.

Oates's well of creativity remains a mystery to her. "Whenever I finish a novel," she says, "I am certain that I have put literally everything I know into it—all of my feeling, my energy, my life— and that I can't possibly write another. Yet I continue to assemble notes, filling folders gradually, writing up sketches, little scenes, etcetera. If I'm thwarted in beginning a novel, as I often am—I was with *Bellefleur* for several years, also *Mysteries of Winterthurn*, which was devilishly difficult to think through—I write other, shorter things like poetry, short stories, essays. I've written entire novels—*Unholy Loves* was one—because I seemed to be blocked in writing a larger, more ambitious novel."

In her art as in her life, Oates has created a special preserve all her own, though not disconnected from America as we move to the close of this century. Her glass house near Princeton—with its mallard ducks floating in the pond, its deer and raccoons creeping up to the house—is as fragile as it looks. Oates knows this, and she knows, too, that nothing survives of us on this planet but our imaginings. "Life is energy, and energy is creativity," she says. "And even when we as individuals pass on, the energy is retained in the work of art, locked in it and awaiting release if only someone will take the time and the care to unlock it."

Joyce Carol Oates and the Hardest Part of Writing

Michael Schumacher

Originally appeared in *Writer's Digest*, April 1986. Reprinted by permission.

Joyce Carol Oates has come to typify the writer-as-artist. Shying away from interviews and public appearances, she prefers instead to work privately at her craft and teach her skills to others. Though the sheer bulk of her creative output seems to deny it, she revises her work tirelessly, rearranging words and passages—even titles of stories—to achieve their designed effects; on one occasion, she changed the entire ending of a novel between the time it was published in America and in England. Her idea of taking a break from the tension of writing novels is to write poetry or short stories.

When her first collection of short stories, *By the North Gate*, was published in 1963, few observers would have predicted that the quietly intense young woman from rural New York would develop into one of America's most prolific serious writers. Between then and now, Oates has published 16 novels, 12 story collections, five volumes of poetry and four books of literary essays, as well as plays and countless uncollected book reviews and short stories. *Prodigious* is an adjective often associated with her creative output, and her publishing history indicates the term is appropriate: at one point, she had three publishers—one handling her mainstream writings, another her poetry, and the third her experimental work. At age 46, Oates shows no sign of slowing down.

Reaction to her work has always been mixed, though generally favorable. As a college student, she submitted a short story to a *Mademoiselle* competition and won; in 1970, she won the National Book Award for *them*, a novel set in Detroit, her home for six years in the mid '60s. Her short stories are staples in the O. Henry and similar anthologies of award-winning pieces. Her work is studied on college campuses throughout the United States, in both literature and creative writing classes. One of her most recent novels, *Bellefleur*, sold more than a million copies and reached hardcover and paperback bestseller lists. She is a member of the American Academy of Arts and Letters.

Criticism of her work has mounted over the years, however; hostile reviewers dismiss her recent string of Gothic and romance genre novels as inappropriate or disappointing from a novelist who has proven herself so adept at contemporary themes. Her books have been assailed as too violent. Some critics have gone as far as to disapprove of the *number* of books she has written. It has been pointed out, to her displeasure, that she fails to "write like a woman"—whatever that means.

Though far from insensitive to critical reaction, positive or negative, she dismisses it with good humor. "I've never taken it very seriously, since for me the hardest part of writing is the writing, not the critical response afterward. Conversely, the writer wishes that good, strong, positive reviews had the power to convince him or her that the writing is successful. As John Updike has wryly said, we tend to believe the worst, and to think that the good reviews have simply been kind."

By all indications, Joyce Carol Oates is living a life rich enough for several people. In addition to her writing, she teaches at Princeton University, co-edits (with her husband, Raymond Smith) a literary quarterly, and publishes small-press books; for recreation, she enjoys cooking, jogging, bicycling, playing classical music on the piano, reading and taking brief excursions to nearby New York City. She admits, though, that little of what she does takes her very far from her writing and, conversely, that almost everything she does is somewhat connected to her work.

"My life is a sort of double narrative," she says—"*my* life running alongside an interior/fictional life. The external life is often absorbing in itself, particularly here at Princeton, but the internal life is ultimately the one that endures. I do subordinate nearly everything else in life to my writing—that is, the thinking about the story at hand. But this may well be simply analogous to the degree of saturation in thought—of self or others or of various projects—common to all human beings."

"Telling stories, I discovered at the age of three or four, is a way of being told stories," she wrote in a *New York Times* essay. "One picture yields another; one set of words, another set of words. Like our dreams, the stories we tell are also the stories we are told." Born in Millersport, New York, a crossroads in rural Erie County, the daughter of a tool-and-die designer, Oates recalls her childhood as a time of contrasts: a warmly protective family and household within a larger, more problematic rural community. Storytelling became an early fascination; Oates credits both her parents and grandparents as storytellers. Her paternal grandmother Blanche Woodside bought Oates her first typewriter for her 14th birthday.

Her short stories began to appear in literary quarterlies while she was an undergraduate at Syracuse University but it wasn't until she learned that one of her stories was chosen for an O. Henry award, in 1963 ("The Fine White Mist of Winter"), that she decided to pursue writing full time. "After my first publication," she told *Publishers Weekly*, "I immersed myself in writing for as many as 12 hours a day. Writing became the core of my 'professional' life."

When I ask if she could have done something other than write, she replies: "It seems to me in retrospect that I could not have done anything else, but the impulse to romanticize oneself is obviously dominant."

Writer's Digest: In a recent interview, you mentioned that you don't write for everybody, and that you don't expect everyone to read you. Who do you write for?

Joyce Carol Oates: This is a difficult question to answer. I doubt that any serious writer thinks of an audience while he or she is writing. My primary area of challenge—or tension, or at times anxiety—is simply the work at hand, the next morning's provisionary and often endlessly revised and retyped scene. In structuring a novel, I have a quite detailed outline—even an "architectural" sort of design affixed to my wall—but as each chapter or scene is written, the whole design is altered. So I am in a constant state of tension while writing a first draft, as I am at the present time. Even the first draft is the consequence of what seems to be endless revisions of chapters, pages, even paragraphs. The primary focus of concentration is therefore the work at hand. To think of an audience—of anyone!—reading the material is virtually impossible. It's analogous to worrying about what you'll wear on the morning of March 10, 1988.

When the work is completed, however, one can make some sort of judgment, as editors and publishers do, about whether it is likely to be popular or not. I can't see my writing as ever being *popular*; much of it, to make even literal—not to mention emotional, psychological or thematic—sense, has to be reread. When *Bellefleur* became a bestseller in both hardcover and paperback, no one was more surprised than I was, but I'm sure that many of the copies sold went unread or unfinished. For this, a writer does feel some slight guilt, I think, and hence my statement that I really *don't* see myself as writing for a very large audience.

WD: Over the years, you've addressed a number of critical attacks concerning the violence in your work, yet I can't help but wonder if there's a gender identification connected with the criticism: If Norman Mailer writes about a man finding the severed head of a woman, it's macho art form; if you write a novel about a boy who murders his mother, or a novel about the assassination of a politician, critics question your motives. It's as if women are expected to be "civil" (in the Austen sense of the word) and controlled.

JCO: Yes, it's purely a sexist response but I think it's beginning to diminish. In the past, it may well have seemed even to responsible critics that a woman's natural art form was needlework; hence, any deviation from this genteel activity was alarming. I did draw a good deal of angry abuse—"sickening," "loathsome," "disgusting," "mere trash"—and perhaps I still do. I've never taken it seriously.

WD: Did you read Mailer's *Tough Guys Don't Dance?* Though the book is contemporary, it seems familiar with much of what you were doing in *Mysteries of Winterthurn*. Both books seemed to be working to establish correlations and contrasts related to physical and psychological violence.

JCO: I haven't read Mailer's novel yet, but I would suspect that Mailer and I have many concerns or obsessions in common. However, the relationship between physical and psychological violence is one fairly generally explored, isn't it? I know I have been exploring it since my first published stories.

WD: About *Mysteries of Winterthurn*: You've said that book taught you a new way of writing. What did you mean by that?

JCO: The detective-mystery novel must be imagined both forward and backward. Unlike most novels--most serious novels, in any case—this peculiar and highly challenging genre demands absolute accuracy in terms of time, place, details, clues, etc. I realize, of course, that in conventional detective-mysteries the plot is all, or nearly all, but my concern was with writing a "double" novel in a sense, a novel of character and theme that nonetheless required the classic structure of the mystery. The novel I have written, however, is in fact an anti-detective-mystery, a critique of the genre from the inside. As I grew to love the form, I grew to realize the strange nature of its restrictions and its many necessary exclusions—as in, for instance, a game of chess one must abide by the rules and take for granted that the world "beyond" the game board scarcely exists, in fact does *not* exist. Otherwise the game is jeopardized.

WD: That book, as well as the other period pieces you've written recently, not only recreated the times but was also authentic in duplicating the writing style of the day. How did you research this? Did you read a lot of 19th-century Gothic novels?

JCO: I've done a good deal of reading over the years, of course. But the 19th-century novel is immensely varied; what is meant by *Gothic*, in fact, is debatable. I read a number of novels by women writers of the mid and late 19th century. Susan Warner is the outstanding example. And etiquette books, handbooks on how to live—with such titles as *The Young Christian Wife and Mother*, which I discuss in *The Profane Art* in a long essay on stereotypical female images in Yeats, Lawrence, and Faulkner.

WD: You've worked in widely diverse styles in your stories and novels. The obvious question: Is style something that you can control, or do your stories dictate the way in which they are told?

JCO: It's a mysterious process. The character on the page determines the prose—its music, its rhythms, the range and limit of its vocabulary—yet, at the outset at least, I determine the character. It usually happens that the fictitious character, once released, acquires a life and will of his or her own, so the prose, too, acquires its own inexplicable fluidity. This is one of the reasons I write: to "hear" a voice not quite my own, yet summoned forth by way of my own.

WD: Your story collection *The Poisoned Kiss and Other Stories from the Portuguese* went as far as to name a fictional character as your "collaborator," giving the book a sort of visionary glow. Could you explain how that book came into being? Is this an example of what you mean when you say that writing is a transcendental function?

JCO: The appeal of writing—of any kind of *artistic* activity—is primarily the investigation of mystery. Somehow, by employing a deliberate speech-rhythm, or by unlocking it, one is able to follow a course into the psyche that reveals different facets of the self. *The Poisoned Kiss* is a "poetic" record of an extreme experience of my own along these lines: Actually, I gave to the *voice* of the stories the adjective "Portuguese" because I knew only that it was foreign, yet not familiarly foreign. Beyond this, it is difficult to speak.

I should stress, though, that the *voice* of these tales was firmly joined to a fairly naturalistic setting by way of subsequent research and conversations with friends who knew Portugal well. And the tales were rigorously written and rewritten.

WD: Could you talk a little about revision? I understand that you spend a great deal of time reworking your novels and stories.

JCO: I revise endlessly, tirelessly—chapters, scenes, paragraphs . . . I don't like to push forward with a story or novel unless it seems to me that the prose is strong enough to be permanent, even though I know very well that once the work is finished I will want to rewrite it. The pleasure *is* the rewriting: The first sentence can't be written until the final sentence is written. This is a koan-like statement, and I don't mean to sound needlessly obscure or mysterious, but it's simply true. The completion of any work automatically necessitates its revisioning. The same is true with reading, of course—at least of a solid, serious, meticulously written work.

WD: How does a novice writer perfect revision skills?

JCO: Since we are all quite different, I can't presume to say. Rereading, with an objective eye, is a necessity—trying to *see* one's work as if it were the work of another, setting aside involvements of the ego. . . . Revision is in itself a kind of artwork, a process of discipline and refinement that has to be experienced. It cannot really be taught. But my students are amazed and excited by what they learn by revising; they're usually very grateful that they are "strongly encouraged" to do so.

WD: Is it possible to revise too much? Can one be too much of a perfectionist—such as the painter who keeps adding brush strokes to a canvas until the original picture and its inspiration are painted over or altered beyond recognition?

JCO: Certainly. Some people think that, on some pages at least, *Ulysses* is over-polished, its slender narrative heavily burdened with various layers of significance, symbol-motifs, allusions. I am temperamentally hostile to the weighting down of a natural and spontaneous story with self-conscious Significance: to me, the hard part of writing *is* the story. The gifts of a Thomas Hardy, for instance, are far more remarkable than the gifts of a writer like Malcolm Lowry, who so painfully and doggedly and willfully created a novel of symbols/ideas/Significance.

I admire Joyce immensely, of course; I've written a good deal about him. But he had the true Jesuitical mind—as he himself noted—plotting, calculating, outlining, dissecting: In *Portrait of the Artist as a Young Man*, Stephen experiences the "seven deadly sins" in a programmatic way, for instance; once one knows the key, the story seems willed, artificial, slightly tainted by the author's intention. It's ideal fiction for teaching, however.

WD: Where does your writing fit in?

JCO: Temperamentally, I may be more akin to Virginia Woolf, who worked very hard, as she noted in her diary, to achieve a surface of "fluidity, breathlessness, spontaneity." One wants the reader to read swiftly and with pleasure, perhaps even with some sense of suspense; one hardly wants the reader to pause and admire a symbol. In my genre novels, I had to use conspicuously big words since, to me, that is part of the quaint humor of 19th-century fiction—its humor and its power—but these are not my words, they are those of my narrators.

At the present time, I am writing a novel, set in the years 1947-1956, called *The Green Island.* My hope is to create a colloquial, fluid, swiftly moving prose that sounds, in places—when certain characters are on stage, for instance—rather rough, sheerly spontaneous. Yet I write and rewrite to achieve this "roughness." My prose tends to be more polished, to a degree, in its first state— at least more systematic and grammatical. To find the right voice for this novel, I have had to break down my own voice.

WD: You've drawn a distinction between ideal fiction for reading and ideal fiction for teaching. Have you, through your mainstream and experimental fiction, been seeking a compromise between the two?

JCO: Yes, I believe every writer wants to be read by as many people as possible—with the stress on *possible*. That is, one doesn't want at all to modify his or her standards; there is the hope that readers will make an effort, sympathize, try just a little harder, reread, reconsider—the effort that is routinely made with Modernists like Joyce and Yeats. Since I work so particularly hard on rewriting, and can do a dozen versions of an opening section after I've completed a novel to get it right or in harmony and proportion with the rest of the book, it would seem that my opening sections should be reread, too. Yet I doubt that many— any?—reviewers trouble to make the effort. However, I do keep trying. I must be incurably optimistic.

WD: Did you ever find yourself beginning a story or novel which was difficult or impossible to execute?

JCO: I have never begun a novel that hasn't been *impossible* for the first six or more weeks. Seriously! The outset of a novel is sheer hell and I dread beginning. But it must be done. . . . I've written 100 pages or more to be thrown away in despair, but with the understanding that the pages had to be written in order that the first halfway-good page might come forth. When I tell my students this, they stare at me in pity and terror. When I tell them that my published work is perhaps one half of the total work I've done—counting apprentice work, for instance—they turn rather pale. They can't seem to imagine such effort and, in retrospect, I must confess that I can't, either. If I had to do it all over again, I'm not sure that I could.

WD: Much of your prose has a rhythmic and lyrical quality about it that approaches poetry. Do you consciously write for the mind's ear? Do you ever read passages aloud to hear what they sound like?

JCO: Absolutely, all the time. It's a practice I am totally dependent on, and have grown to love, though I don't usually read the passages out loud. *Silently out loud*, if that makes sense.

WD: Your use of ellipses, as well as your intermixing of short and long paragraphs on the same page, makes me wonder if you work to achieve a certain physical effect in your writing for the printed page. Are you looking for something physical?

JCO: Sometimes—certainly in my poetry and in some short stories. In *Childwold*, I had wanted varying spaces between the chapters to suggest varying "spaces" in the narrative and between characters, but my publisher didn't want to print the book that way.

WD: As it is, that was one of your most experimental major works. Your use of the second-person singular was one of your most interesting experiments in language. How did you come to choose that particular way of telling that story? Was it a difficult book to write?

JCO: *Childwold* was written first, almost in its entirety, in longhand. When I finally began typing it, I think it went rather smoothly. The *you* seemed necessary for Laney because, though Laney was not *me/I*, she lived through and saw numerous things that I experienced at one time or another. Her focus of consciousness seemed to demand the second-person singular, which I don't believe I have ever used since.

WD: I felt a Faulkner or Flannery O'Connor influence in that novel. Do you find yourself influenced by certain writers when you're working? Do you ever go back and reread one of the classics in an effort to capture a particular flavor or style?

JCO: My reading is so wide, varied and idiosyncratic that it is impossible for me to say anything specific or helpful. I was reading Faulkner, Dostoyevsky, Thoreau, Hemingway, the Brontës, and many other classic writers, in my early teens. These influences remain very deep, I'm sure. Only in my late teens and 20s did I read Lawrence, O'Connor, Thomas Mann, Kafka—yet these influences are still quite strong, pervasive. The curious thing, which I try to explain to my students, is that one can try very hard to be influenced but not succeed. Much of what we read is in a voice so alien to our own that there is no possibility of influence, though we might admire it a good deal. For instance, I *admire* Huxley, yet I could never have been influenced by him.

WD: Your books are filled with richly descriptive narrative passages. Do you keep notebooks or jot down ideas as they come to you?

JCO: I do both, I suppose. For me, writing—and reading—are ways of seeing: I have a sharply visual imagination and love to see by way of words, and there are many writers (one might name Emily Brontë, Thomas Hardy and D. H. Lawrence) whose visual imaginations are so powerful that one is immediately transported to an alien but totally convincing world by way of their prose. Oddly, merely viewing without the filter of words, as in a film, seems to me less satisfying. I get a good deal of happiness out of transcribing scenes in retrospect, by way of memory—evoking the formidable city of Detroit, for instance, in *Do with Me What You Will*, while at the time I was living in London, England, for a year; writing *Bellefleur*, set in the mountains of a region very much like upstate New York, while living in Princeton; and writing my current novel, *The Green Island*, with a Buffalo/Lockport, New York, location, again while living in Princeton. Conversely, I get no satisfaction out of writing about things immediately at hand; they don't interest me at all. Part of the motive for writing seems to me the act of conscious memory.

WD: A few questions about your writing habits. What is your daily schedule like?

JCO: I try to begin work around 8 a.m., stop at 1 p.m., begin again at 4 p.m., and work to perhaps 7 p.m. Sometimes, I will work in the evening—in longhand, not at my desk— but throughout the day I am *working* in my head so far as possible. This makes it sound rather constant and perhaps it is, but the activity is rather more exciting than tiring, at least when the story is moving along well. This schedule is an ideal day when I am not in the university or involved in other activities. Obviously, my two teaching days are radically different; I'm gone through the afternoon.

WD: Do you still work in longhand?

JCO: Yes, I'm very dependent on working in longhand. All my poetry and most of my novels are taken down in longhand first. It seems close to the voice, more intimate, less artificial.

WD: In what way? Could you explain that further?

JCO: I don't think I can, really. Most poets write in longhand; even many of my students, who then turn to their word processors. I am not averse to using the typewriter, of course, at certain more pragmatic times.

WD: How do you feel about word processors? It would seem ideal for someone like you, who is usually involved in several projects at once.

JCO: I am not usually involved in several projects at once; in fact, when deep at work on a novel, I try to do very little else. My short story writing has sharply abated in recent years since I've been working on exceptionally long, complex novels.

The word processor isn't for me, since I am dependent on so many systematic, slow, deliberate rewritings. Often I retype a page that seems to me finally finished, only to discover in retyping that I've tightened it, or added something that, in retrospect, seems obvious and necessary.

WD: Can you talk about the different sorts of writing projects you undertake? Let's start with the short story. What role does the short story play in your activity as a writer?

JCO: I seem to have published more than 300 short stories since 1963, so their *role* is virtually indistinguishable from my life! Most obviously, the short story is a short run—a single idea and mood, usually no more than two or three characters, an abbreviated space of time. The short story lends itself most gracefully to experimentation, too. If you think about it, the story can't be defined, and hence is open, still in the making. Radical experimentation, which might be ill-advised in the novel, is well suited for the short story. I like the freedom and promise of the form.

WD: Do you find that, like a painter, you consciously work your stories into a series of common themes or colors—such as in *Crossing the Border* and *Night-Side*—or do they sort of gather that way after a period of time?

JCO: Yes, I think the process is rather like that of a painter's: There are common concerns, common themes and obsessions, in a certain period of time. I collect only a few stories in proportion to the number I publish. To me, hardcover publication is the final imprimatur. When I assemble stories, as in *Last Days* and *A Sentimental Education*, my most recent collections, I rewrite them, at least in part, and arrange them in a specific order. My story collections are not at all mere collections; they are meant to be books, consciously organized. Unfortunately, a number of stories I am fond of have never found their way into hardcover print, because their themes or voices were unsuited for a volume.

WD: You've written a substantial amount of poetry—enough to merit a volume of collected poems. How does poetry fit into your life as a writer?

JCO: Poetry is my *other* world, my solace of a kind. I love both to read and to write—or to attempt to write—poetry as a means of escape from the strain of prose fiction. It is also an extremely personal mode for me, as fiction is not. I can employ autobiographical landscapes and even experiences in my fiction, but *I* never exist—there is no place for *I*.

In any phase of poetry writing, I feel that I am most at home in poetry. There is something truly enthralling about the process—the very finitude of the form, the opportunity for constant revision—an incantatory solace generally missing in fiction. Poetry requires no time in the reading as prose fiction always does, particularly the novel; the demands of the novel on both reader and writer are considerable, after all. After finishing a long, difficult novel, I always enter a phase of poetry. It can last for perhaps six or eight weeks. Of course, this phase is by no means without its own difficulties, but its pleasures are more immediate and forthcoming. One can even *see* a poem in its entirety—a source of amazement to the novelist.

WD: What about book reviews and literary essays? What function do they serve in your career?

JCO: I don't know that they serve any *function*; they are vehicles for my more discursive voice, I suppose. Like most critics, I write about what I like and hope to know more thoroughly by way of writing and analysis.

WD: One final question: If and when you write your memoirs, what period of your career would you consider to be your happiest?

JCO: I can't answer that—perhaps I don't yet have the perspective to make such a judgment. My husband and I are quite happy here in Princeton, and I've been extremely productive here, but I well remember feeling idyllic in Windsor, if not always in Detroit, where we lived from 1962 to 1968. Also, the concept of a *career* is rather foreign to me, since a *career* is so outward, while *life* is so inward, a matter of daily experience. Many a writer has enjoyed an outwardly successful career while being personally unhappy, and the reverse might well be true. The most sustained and experimental—if not audacious—work of my career is the five-volume sequence of novels written here in Princeton. So I suppose this period, from 1978 onward, might be later seen as my "happiest" time.

An Interview with Joyce Carol Oates

Lawrence Grobel

Originally appeared in *Playboy*, November 1993. Reprinted by permission.

Joyce Carol Oates is one of the most prominent writers in America. Her critics even complain that she writes too much. She has written more novels than Nobel laureate Saul Bellow, more short story collections than John Updike, more books of essays than Norman Mailer, more words of poetry than Emily Dickinson and more plays than Chekhov. Critic Harold Bloom considers her "our true proletarian novelist." Author and critic John Gardner called her "an alarming phenomenon— one of the great writers of our time."

She has been described as shy, mouselike, intense, perceptive, brilliant. She can cook, play the piano and quote James Joyce, and she writes about boxing with style and authority (in her "Life" magazine piece on Mike Tyson she couldn't resist quoting Thorstein Veblen, Shakespeare, Virginia Woolf and Wallace Stevens). She writes about troubled lower-class people and the way they sometimes brutalize one another. She's been criticized for being too fascinated with violence and praised for writing about life as it is. She doesn't shy away from rough language, and in her imagination she can commit the most horrendous crimes: murder, incest, self-abortion.

More than 20 years ago "Newsweek" called her "the most significant novelist to have emerged in the United States in the last decade." Oates has a loyal cadre of readers who line up outside bookstores, usually carrying an armful of their favorite titles, whenever she's signing. "Nobody else writes nearly as much as she does," said critic Bruce Allen in "The Hudson Review." "The really alarming thing is that so much of what she writes is good."

Adds book reviewer Marian Engel in "The New York Times," "It has been left to Joyce Carol Oates, a writer who seems to know a great deal about the underside of America, to guide us—splendidly—down dark passages."

Allen agrees: "We are a country of intensely destructive (and self-destructive) people, she seems to keep saying. What is there in us—and outside us—that makes us act as we do?"

Despite her acclaim, Oates is not a hugely popular novelist along the lines of Stephen King or Larry McMurtry. Her themes are dark and complex. Her writing style changes from book to book. One doesn't pick up an Oates novel, as one does a book by Raymond Carver or Elmore Leonard, with predetermined familiarity. Her writing, like her subject matter, is neither predictable nor comforting.

Hers is an intellectual life. When she isn't writing she's teaching students at Princeton about writers and writing. A friend, critic Elaine Showalter, once noted, "In the midst of a quite ordinary conversation about the news or television or the family, Oates often inserts remarks whose philosophical penetration makes the rest of us feel like amoebas in the company of a more highly evolved life-form." Oates is married to a teacher and editor, Raymond Smith. Together they founded the "Ontario Review" and the Ontario Review Press, which publishes work by up-and-coming writers.

There is no other writer in America, male or female, who quite compares with Oates. In 1970 she won a National Book Award for an early novel, "them," and she has been inducted into the American Academy and Institute of Arts and Letters. In 1990 she received the Rea Award for Achievement in the Short Story, the Bobst Lifetime Achievement Award and the Heideman Award for One-Act Plays.

Born in the small town of Millersport, near Lockport, in western New York on June 16, 1938, Joyce Carol Oates came from a working-class family. Her father was a tool-and-die maker and neither of her parents graduated from high school. Her grandfather was murdered when her mother was a baby, an act of violence that indelibly altered Oates's development.

She began writing as a young girl, throwing away novel after novel as quickly as she completed them. When she was 14 a relative bought her a typewriter to help her churn out her stories. One of them, "In the Old World," written when she was 19, was a co-winner of the "Mademoiselle" magazine's college fiction award. After graduating as valedictorian and Phi Beta Kappa from Syracuse University in 1960, she went to graduate school at the University of Wisconsin, where she received her master's degree in English and met and married her husband. While she was enrolled in a doctoral program at Rice, one of her stories was given an honorable mention in Martha Foley's "Best American Short Stories." That was the acknowledgment she needed to convince herself that she was, truly, a writer. She dropped out of Rice and never looked back.

Her first book of stories, "By the North Gate," was published in 1963, when she was 25. A year later came her first novel, "With Shuddering Fall." Then another book of stories, "Upon the Sweeping Flood," followed by her second, third and fourth novels, "A Garden of Earthly Delights" (1967), "Expensive People" (1968) and "them" (1969). While living in Windsor, Ontario, she also managed to squeeze in two books of poetry during 1969 and 1970. In the Seventies she published seven novels, nine books of short stories, four volumes of poetry and two collections of essays. Nine more novels were written in the Eighties, including her trilogy of gothic, romance and mystery novels: "Bellefleur," "A Bloodsmoor Romance" and "Mysteries of Winterthurn."

You need a calculator to keep track of her work. In the 30 years that she has been a professional writer, Oates has written and published 27 novels, 17 collections of short stories (she has contributed nine short stories to PLAYBOY over the years), seven books of poetry, five volumes of essays, 15 plays and more than two dozen works published by small, independent presses. She has, by her own estimate, written more than 300 short stories, most of which have not been collected in book form, and other novels that she has not seen fit to publish. She has edited numerous volumes of essays, story collections and interviews with other writers on their craft. She has also written four psychological suspense novels ("Lives of the Twins," "Soul/Mate," "Nemesis," "Snake Eyes") under the pseudonym Rosamond Smith.

What is astounding about her output is the breadth and depth of her subjects as well as the quality of her prose. "With Shuddering Fall" deals with cars and leaving home; "them" with corruption, race riots and death. "Wonderland" deals with family murder and the psychology of medicine; "The Assassins" with politics; "Son of the Morning" with religious fanaticism; "Do with Me What You Will" with irrational, possessive, adulterous love and the legal profession; "Angel of Light" with revenge; "Unholy Loves" with faculty life at an American college; "Solstice" with female love; "American Appetites" with turning 50;

"You Must Remember This" with coming-of-age and loss of innocence; "Because It Is Bitter, and Because It Is My Heart" with racism and alcoholism. Her book "On Boxing" was an insightful look at an often brutal sport.

A recent novel, "Black Water," which was just released in paperback, is a fictionalized account of Senator Ted Kennedy's incident at Chappaquiddick, where Mary Jo Kopechne drowned in a car accident that spoiled any chance Kennedy had of becoming president. The reviews were mostly raves. "The New York Times" said it was as audacious as anything in recent fiction, "a brilliant vision of how a culture has learned to associate political power with sex. Taut, powerfully imagined and beautifully written, [it] ranks with the best of Joyce Carol Oates's already long list of distinguished achievements."

Reviews have also been good for her latest book, "Foxfire," which is written from the point of view of a female high school gang member from upstate New York.

To find out what keeps Oates writing as much as she does, PLAYBOY sent Contributing Editor Lawrence Grobel (whose previous interviews include Robert De Niro and Robin Williams) to Princeton, where she lives with her husband and their four cats. Grobel reports:

"The street Oates lives on is quiet and idyllic, the area exclusive and privileged, the nearby university elite and prestigious. Her study and living spaces are crowded with books—on shelves, tables, even floors. There is a healthy garden outside where vegetables are tenderly cared for by her husband.

"She appears fragile, with short curly hair and enormous eyes. During the week we spent talking, she tired each day after a few hours. But that's because she's not used to talking about herself. Her time and energy are almost always focused on her work.

"What she seemed to look forward to were the times when we stopped and went out for dinner, or to a party hosted by one of her Princeton friends—times when she could relax and enjoy the food and conversation. But during the days we taped—at her home, in a limousine taking her to and from a book signing, at a restaurant—Oates was all business: concentrated, thoughtful and very, very smart."

PLAYBOY: Since you seem to be a compulsive writer, what is it that excites you most about putting words on paper?

OATES: Getting the inner vision out. I love to write. I feel I have something to say. It's exhilarating once in a while, but most of my experiences are fraught with frustration because I always feel dissatisfied. An entire day can go by and I'll feel I haven't accomplished anything. My husband was asking me about this. He said, "You get a lot done in a day." I guess I do, but I don't feel I have. I always have a feeling, which is subterranean, of being profoundly dissatisfied with what I'm working at.

PLAYBOY: Does dissatisfaction lead to compulsion?

OATES: Compulsion probably accounts for virtually any achievement. There are people who say they are envious of me, who write "I wish I were you." These people don't know how hard I work. You have to have a driving, almost feverish energy. It's like the tremendous hunger you saw in the young Mike Tyson. How many other men who fantasize about being a boxer would really want the kind of burning passion, hunger and desire to hurt other people that a great boxer must have? To be a writer you have to be compulsive, eccentric. You have to want to stay up all night writing because you have some brainstorm. The energies are demonic. You can't be a normal, contented person and be a great novelist or a great filmmaker or actor. You have to be a little crazy.

PLAYBOY: How crazy do you get?

OATES: Well, I write all over, and sometimes I can't stop taking notes. Maybe I shouldn't say this, but I've actually written while I was being introduced to give a talk. It's a good way to use time. I really begrudge the hours that I have to sleep, because sleep is a waste of human energy. Think of all the hours you spend asleep. Sometimes when I travel I don't sleep at all. It's like a chaotic rush of images, a kaleidoscope, that keeps me awake all night.

PLAYBOY: Does this drive you to be so prolific?

OATES: I don't know how it adds up. I must have a different time zone. People ask me how I find the time. I have the same amount of time as anybody else. I just try to use it. It might have to do with the tachycardia I have, where with every tick and every heartbeat, if I'm not getting something done, I feel I've just wasted that moment. Whereas a more normal person would feel, well, why not relax for the whole afternoon and go sailing?

PLAYBOY: What is tachycardia?

OATES: A little malformation of the heart valve. It's often associated with people who are tall and lank. A tachycardia attack sends a person into hyperventilation, the heart speeds up and pounds hard. A person may faint or feel he or she can't breathe. Then the extremities start turning icy cold because the blood's not circulating. It's like a mimicry of death. It's terrifying because you feel that you are dying.

PLAYBOY: Do these attacks happen often?

OATES: I've probably had over 50 in my life. I've been admitted to the emergency room at Princeton a couple of times, but not recently. I take digitalis every day. It started when I was 18. I was playing basketball at Syracuse and I was knocked down. I started having this attack and it scared the life out of me and everybody else, including my gym teacher. She thought I was going to die in front of her eyes. It was terrifying. It's because of these attacks that I have a heightened sense of mortality and time. That's why I'm always working and why I'm concerned with wasting time. Almost every minute of my life is plotted very carefully. Thoreau said, "You can't kill time without injuring eternity." That's probably part of the reason I seem prolific.

PLAYBOY: So you're unlikely to hang out at the beach?

OATES: I would go crazy. I could sit on the beach for maybe three minutes. I was even wondering before you came if we could do this interview while jogging, but I realized that was absurd.

PLAYBOY: No wonder your output is so staggering. So you see yourself as successful?

OATES: No, I don't think of myself as successful. I experience dissatisfaction or relative degrees of failure more than success because I'm always rewriting. I have to be careful not to put too low an evaluation on myself. Probably the only people who are successful are people who are dissatisfied. What else pushes them on? Some people are quite content, and they were content when they were eight years old, affable, happy people who are not going to be successful and don't care. And none of them is a writer or creative artist because they don't have that push. All art begins in conflict. Even situation comedy.

PLAYBOY: Has any of your success, such as winning a National Book Award in 1970, caused problems for you?

OATES: I was young when I won that, about 31 or 32. It got me much more exposure, but it turned many people against me. People don't like it when someone's successful. Norman Mailer is the classic example. He started big and then got terrible reviews of his next novel. Since then, Mailer has always been a kind of punching bag.

PLAYBOY: Did you lose friends as your career took off?

OATES: There was a male writer whose career I helped—I got him my agent, gave him a quote for his first novel—and he really turned against me. He just couldn't take my winning that award. He threatened my life and did all sorts of strange things. He wanted me to write a review of one of his books for *The New York Times Book Review* and I said I couldn't do it. He went crazy. For years he would write me letters. It had to do with the National Book Award. He felt that suddenly I had fame and power and I could get a review published. I tried to explain that even if I wanted to do it, I wouldn't do it. He wrote a story called "How I Killed Joyce Carol Oates" and sent me the manuscript. I don't know if it ever got printed. It was pretty extreme. I once talked at the Modern Language Association and he was in the audience and at the end he came toward me. He was going to throw something at me. Somebody found it on the floor and wouldn't let me see it. I think it was a razor.

PLAYBOY: Since your work often deals with violence, was that the only time you've been threatened?

OATES: I get a lot of letters from people in prisons—always men, never women. They obviously haven't read anything of mine, but they see stuff about me in *People* magazine. I can't be bothered.

PLAYBOY: In what other ways has fame affected you?

OATES: It's very complex. If one is famous, one has a certain amount of power, but maybe power is corruptive and corrosive. Look at the phenomenon of Marilyn Monroe. She had celebrity and extreme fame yet seemingly had no personal life nor any control. Fame exacerbates one's personal failing. Celebrity, if one doesn't have inner strength, can be corrosive. It's as if the flaws in your character, like cracks in a façade, become magnified in the public eye. And you can't hide them. I feel my heart sink a little when people recognize me, because then I have to put on this identity. At the supermarket I've sometimes had to sign autographs on people's grocery lists. It's embarrassing to me.

PLAYBOY: Yet yours is a modest kind of fame compared with a Monroe or a Madonna.

OATES: That's probably true. The outsider looking in would have thought Marilyn Monroe was a tremendous success. It must have been keen and sharp and terribly ironic for her to realize that her image was out in the world and she scarcely shared in that. It's a bizarre, almost schizophrenic experience. I recently saw *The Misfits* on video and I was really struck by Marilyn Monroe as a kind of female impersonator. There were real women in that movie and they walked around in regular shoes, and then she would come on the screen completely confectionary, her hair, her manner, her walk, her physical being. It was as if she were a female impersonator in a way that we don't experience women now—stuffed into a dress, teetering on high heels. It's kind of like being an anthropologist and going back in time: Was this really an ideal of female beauty or was it, even then, exaggerated and a little absurd? She said to one interviewer, "Please don't make me look like a joke." So she was aware of that.

PLAYBOY: When you were growing up, did you ever want to look like her or any other star?

OATES: No, then you'd have to deal with so many men being attracted to you, and that's hard. In Arthur Miller's *After the Fall*, the figure who represents Marilyn Monroe can barely walk down the street without three men following her, accosting her, talking to her. Who would really want that? The most attractive girls in school were the ones who ended up getting married and having babies right after graduation. In a sense their lives are finished. So being very beautiful and having a strong appeal for the opposite sex is a handicap, though it's not perceived that way when one is young.

PLAYBOY: Have you always been satisfied with who you are?

OATES: I don't really identify with my physical self that much. My spiritual self, my inner self, my imagination is probably my deepest self, and that expresses itself in language in my books. My physical and social self is just another person.

PLAYBOY: Do you feel being a woman allows you a certain invisibility?

OATES: A woman is often judged by her physical appearance or by the fact that she's a woman. But a man is judged by his work. It would never be said about a male novelist that he was very handsome. You also don't say, "Hemingway, a male novelist, has written some good books." But people describe women writers in such a way that we are lumped together in some strange category that's heterogeneous and kind of promiscuous. I have books of literary criticism that list "women's novels" and I'll find myself in that chapter along with women who write about romantic experiences or domestic life or children. And my real kinship would be with someone in the realistic-novel category who's a man. But I'm not put in that chapter because I'm a woman.

PLAYBOY: And yet you also believe that this is the best time in history to be a woman.

OATES: I think so. Women are being published in great numbers, women are being read, women support one another—and this was not always the case. Women are directing plays and having roles in the organization and administration of theaters, which has been very male-dominated. There are women's studies programs at universities. Young women are going into medical school, there are women lawyers. They still encounter sexism, of course, but it's not the way it used to be when women couldn't get in at all. To me, it's by far the best time for women professionals.

PLAYBOY: Do you think we'll see a woman president in our lifetime?

OATES: I seriously doubt that. Vice president, possibly.

PLAYBOY: Do you take the radical-feminist attitude that men are the enemy?

OATES: Even though I am a feminist, I've never felt that men are the enemy. I've also never had any real animosity toward men. Some radical feminists have attacked me in the past because I write about men with a certain amount of compassion or because I defend men. They feel that I've betrayed them. I was attacked in a women's journal because I had written a novel called *Solstice*.

The woman who attacked me was a lesbian and she said that this was a thinly disguised novel about an evil lesbian. In fact, the novel doesn't have a lesbian in it. She was projecting her own propagandistic vibes into the novel. I'm a counterpuncher, so I wrote back, "If I want to write a novel about a lesbian who is evil or a silly lesbian or a brilliant lesbian, I will do it. This is my prerogative as a writer and I don't subscribe to any ideology except writing." Feminist literature per se is propagandist literature. And feminism, like any ism or ideology, exacts too high a toll. You can be politically incorrect and people get angry with you. I will always place a much higher value on aesthetic integrity than on any kind of political correctness, including feminism.

PLAYBOY: How do you define feminism?

OATES: In a root way: Everyone should receive equal pay for equal work. To me, feminism is basically economic.

PLAYBOY: Are there differences between the sexes?

OATES: Your question is particularly appropriate for *Playboy* because I really have to go against some feminist thinking. No, I don't think the two sexes are that different. There's an intensification of aggression, especially sexual aggression, in the male: Sexual feelings, instincts and desires of the male are in many cases more intense than in the female. For instance, female rapists or sex offenders are virtually nonexistent. There are 17 times as many male criminals as female criminals, and the sexual component has a lot to do with that. But it's a continuum. If you got rid of all men and had only women left behind in some bizarre dimension, you would find them clustered toward one end of the continuum these adversarial and aggressive women. And they would be the "new men." So I don't feel the sexes are different in kind, only in degree.

PLAYBOY: Camille Paglia, the author of *Sexual Personae*, suggests that "male aggression and lust are the energizing forces of culture, and that if civilization had been left in female hands, we'd still be living in grass huts."

OATES: That's ridiculous. She obviously hates being a woman. And she's identifying with what most men consider the worst traits of maleness. The men I know in Princeton and elsewhere, and the men in my family, are not marauding males energized by lust and aggression. They're energized by desire for creativity. Norman Mailer once said that nobody says to a woman, "Come on, be a woman!" But to be a man, it's either explicit or implicit: "Come on, be a man!" And that admonition to be a man is fraught with a good deal of anxiety. What does it mean? Be a man like Mozart? Like Einstein? No, it really means be a tough man, a physical man in terms of other men.

PLAYBOY: Aren't there differences between men and women in the area of sports?

OATES: Sports may be an area in which women and men are different. And that's too bad. For the men I know who play squash or tennis or poker, it's a celebration of friendship. They love one another and they love what they're doing. And men experience sports that way. Women don't have the same thing. I don't know why not. When I watched a lot of boxing, virtually everyone I was with was male. It was a male experience, and when I was in it, it was as if I were a male. But other women experience it differently and they put their hands over their eyes: "Oooh, this is awful. How can you look at this?" As if by watching boxing I had abrogated my femininity.

PLAYBOY: What is it about boxing that fascinates you?

OATES: It's a paradigm of life where you don't know what's going to happen. It's a mimicry of a fight to the death, mortal combat. Whereas tennis or chess is a stylized mimicry of a fight— the chess players are the kings and their pawns are soldiers and they're fighting on a board, but it's only a game—boxing is not a game. It is the real thing. It inhabits a special dimension in the history of sports because it arises out of mortal combat in which one man would die. It's different from other sports not in degree but in kind. To me boxing is mainly about failure. It's about getting hurt but doing it with nobility and courage and not complaining. I tend to be sympathetic with boxers. I'm not sympathetic with the managers or with the business side of boxing, because they exploit boxers.

PLAYBOY: Are men fascinated by boxing because it suggests that masculinity is measured in terms of other men?

OATES: That's true. And boxers have a camaraderie with other boxers and with the history of boxing that excludes women.

Women have nothing to do with it. Women can admire boxing, as I do, but boxers are basically boxing for other men and for other boxers.

PLAYBOY: Was Mike Tyson surprised by your interest when you were interviewing him?

OATES: I was never really interviewing Mike Tyson in a formal way and I didn't have a tape recorder. I was doing it by hand. We were in [his then-manager Jim] Jacobs' apartment in New York sitting on a sofa, talking about fights, seeing boxing tapes. Mike was from a world in which everybody knew boxing, including women. To him it wouldn't have been surprising that a woman could talk about Jack Johnson or any other fighter.

PLAYBOY: Had Tyson read any of your writing?

OATES: He wouldn't have had time. He had his karate videos and splatter films. He didn't have time to turn the pages of a book and move his eyes.

PLAYBOY: Did Mike Tyson surprise you in any way?

OATES: Mike always surprises people when he walks into a room because he's so short. He's not a Sonny Liston or a Muhammad Ali. When I knew Mike he was only 20 years old. He was soft-spoken. He's not the same person anymore. Getting married and signing with Don King accelerated his aging process. He's a much older person physically. He's probably abused his body, his reflexes may be gone.

PLAYBOY: Are you saying that you think he's finished as a fighter when he gets out of prison?

OATES: I'm an optimist. When Mike gets out of prison he may come to his senses and realize that he's been behaving self-destructively. I think he could make a comeback. If he wants to do it he can do it. And if he were in condition he could beat the current crop of heavyweights handily: Bowe, Lewis, Holyfield, Morrison, Foreman—it hasn't been a distinguished time for boxing since Tyson lost his will to fight and his title.

PLAYBOY: Do you feel Tyson got the punishment he deserved?

OATES: It's hard to know what anyone deserves. Do we get what we deserve? Or do we deserve what we get? I'm not a person who judges happily. I guess that's why I'm a novelist; judgment is usually suspended in a novel.

PLAYBOY: What other boxers and fights do you admire?

OATES: One of the things I liked about Sugar Ray Leonard was that, like all great boxers, he was most dangerous after he'd been knocked down. Once the average boxer is knocked down, something goes out of him. But when Leonard was knocked down and then would get up he was much more dangerous than before. I liked Leonard near the end of his career a lot more than I liked him earlier. Like many people, I wanted Marvin Hagler to win their fight and couldn't believe it when Hagler lost. Looking back, we might say that Hagler's finest moment—when he fought Tommy Hearns—turned him into a lesser boxer because of the beating he took from the man he beat. If Hagler had fought a different fight he might have beat Hearns anyway, but he would not have been hurt as much. They both took terrible beatings. That was a fantastic fight.

PLAYBOY: What about the heavyweights?

OATES: I don't like heavyweights that much, except for the outstanding ones like Ali. But most heavyweights, like Gerry Cooney, what can you say? I don't even want to see them. I never watched George Foreman during his comeback. I refuse to look at a boxer whose physical being is an insult to a great sport. I don't want to see an overweight boxer in the ring. The sport is too important and has a history that the men who are in it should respect. That's why I was so shocked when Tyson came in out of condition with Buster Douglas. I couldn't believe he would demean the heavyweight title. I found it hard to watch Mike fight because I knew him, and when I saw him lose the title to Douglas I was stunned. I literally couldn't believe my eyes. When he came into the arena that night I could see he was dry, he hadn't been sweating, he didn't look good. He hadn't trained. To me that's much more profoundly disturbing and bizarre than the things he did in his private life, which I can understand. I don't condone raping a woman but I can understand that a lot more than I can a heavyweight champion coming in at a young age and not being trained. That was shocking to me.

PLAYBOY: Was it also shocking to you that your book *On Boxing* was praised by so many aficionados, including Norman Mailer?

OATES: Yes. Norman has said he feels a kinship with me. It was nice of him to say. He introduced me at Lincoln Center for a benefit evening and he said, "This person wrote an essay on boxing that was so good I thought I'd written it myself." And he didn't know why people were laughing. He meant it sincerely as the highest praise. I came out and said, "It's considered high praise to be told you write like a man, but to be told that you write like Norman Mailer is off the scale." And in my novel *You Must Remember This,* I'm really inside a person who's a boxer. I just love that part of the novel, that whole masculine ideology and the camaraderie of men in the gym. I don't suppose any other women novelists would even want to write about that.

PLAYBOY: You're working on screenplays based on your works. Are you ever asked to write original scripts—not based on your stories—for actors?

OATES: I was asked to write the Jeffrey Dahmer story for HBO. I thought it was a strange invitation. And I was invited to write something on Mike Tyson for HBO and I declined. I don't have much time. I'm usually working all the time, sometimes up to midnight. I'm now immersed in a novel I've been planning for a couple of years. It's called *Corky's Price* [later retitled *What I Lived For*] and it's my attempt to get inside the skin of a man, to deal with male sexuality in a candid and nonjudgmental, realistic way. It's a challenge because I certainly could fail. I can't fail writing about women—I've written about women's sexuality many times—but this is something I've never really done before. The entire novel is this man going through four days of his life. It took me about two years to get the voice for this man—a lot of profanity, obscenity, but funny. I want him to be an average man.

PLAYBOY: What male writers do you think have best captured the way a woman thinks and feels?

OATES: D. H. Lawrence is one of the pioneers in the male attempt to write about women. Lawrence had a sensibility that was androgynous. Although he was a heterosexual male, he was also possibly homoerotic. He was attracted to men, too. He was an ideal artist in that he had an erotic feeling for much of nature. This kind of intense identification with some other living presence is probably necessary for a writer. But I can't think of many of my male colleagues who've written compellingly or convincingly about women. Faulkner is an example of a truly great talent who could not create any women characters of any depth; they tend to be caricatures. Melville has no women characters. Saul Bellow is a great writer who has concentrated on male portraits. His female portraits in some cases are compelling, but it's the male portraits that are really brilliant and memorable. Shakespeare was a great writer whose masculinity is evident. He's created some great women, such as Cleopatra, but they tend to be somewhat mannish women.

PLAYBOY: Aren't you worried, then, that your male character might be considered a female-ish man?

OATES: Absolutely not. I feel that I know men from the inside. I've created a lot of male characters.

PLAYBOY: Why do you suppose that your contemporaries have such difficulty capturing women but you don't have any difficulty capturing a man?

OATES: It's just a measure of what one's trying to do. I don't value one achievement over the other. Faulkner and Melville are great writers. It doesn't matter that they couldn't capture women as well as F. Scott Fitzgerald or D. H. Lawrence. The measurement of genius is sui generis. Geniuses are not compared with one another. I mean, it's not held against Chopin that he never wrote an opera.

PLAYBOY: Do you measure yourself against other writers?

OATES: No, that would be discouraging. I don't like the idea of competition. We have great writers living today. It's difficult for contemporaries to accept one another. Virginia Woolf said it's impossible. I agree.

PLAYBOY: Since Melville is often considered America's greatest writer, isn't that comparison somewhat overwhelming?

OATES: Melville lived for years as a complete failure. That a man of such genius would think he'd been a failure is heartbreaking. That's one of the saddest stories in American literature. When he was writing *Moby Dick* there was no prototype for it. It was an adventure story, a Shakespearean tragedy, it was metaphysical and philosophic speculation. Nobody had ever done that before in America. And then it was published and got the most vicious, ignorant, jeering reviews. Obviously his heart was broken, he didn't make any money and after that his life took another turn. I kind of identify with him. Many writers do. It's like we've done the same thing but we're more lucky. When he died his obituary in *The New York Times* was about Henry Melville—it even got his name wrong.

PLAYBOY: Hemingway said American literature starts with *Huckleberry Finn*, and Mailer said that William Burroughs changed the course of American literature. Do you agree?

OATES: No. In terms of history, Walt Whitman changed the course of American literature. He was saying things that nobody ever said before. Not William Burroughs, because few people have even read him. But Whitman came along with *Leaves of Grass* in 1855, and he was saying things in his poetry and he had a musical, incantatory voice in which he talked about being both male and female, about homoeroticism, about having a baby. This was profoundly contemporary and was so deeply disturbing to his contemporaries that he was considered extreme. And yet he has affected so many people.

PLAYBOY: Can a major writer alter, as Mailer called it, "the nerves and marrow of a nation"?

OATES: Not the United States. But definitely individuals are affected. Whitman, Dickens, Dostoyevski, Tolstoy, Solzhenitsyn. Harriet Beecher Stowe and Upton Sinclair had effects upon legislation in America. Emily Dickinson had an effect upon individuals. People have told me that their lives have been changed by things I've written. A nun actually left the convent after she read a story of mine. Obviously she was inclined to feel that way and then the story gave her a push.

PLAYBOY: How much of a class society is America?

OATES: Oh, very much a class society. It's getting more and more evident. Segregation is more marked than it was in the Sixties. We have a new division between fundamentally illiterate people and the rest of our society, which is educated and has knowledge of computers and the electronic medium. Along with other problems of poverty, ghettos, drugs, I don't know what's going to happen. The Los Angeles riots demonstrated that.

PLAYBOY: You dealt with an earlier city riot, the one in Detroit in 1967, in your novel *them*. Did you actually experience the riot?

OATES: We were only one block away from some of the burning and looting, and I'd never been in any situation like that where your physical being is at risk. You never forget it and as a writer you want to deal with it. It was not an easy time. Living in Detroit changed my life completely. I would be writing a different kind of work right now had I not been there. I came from this rural background and suddenly I was thrust into the city in the Sixties. It was so alive and fraught with excitement.

PLAYBOY: Do you miss the rural background of your youth?

OATES: I don't want to make my childhood sound like something out of *Tobacco Road*. It wasn't. But I went to a one-room schoolhouse and the other students, particularly the boys, were very rough, really cruel kids. A lot of things frightened me, but I had to face it day after day. At one point there were eight grades and some of the boys were big, like six feet tall, farm boys, very crude. We heard tales of things that had been done to other girls, an act of incest—an older brother forcing himself on a younger sister, then boasting about it. And I certainly was the object of molestation of one kind or another.

PLAYBOY: Verbal or physical?

OATES: Verbal is nothing, who cares about verbal. No, really physical. Being chased, being mauled. I was molested when I was about nine or ten. I was not raped, but it would be considered sexual molestation today. And I couldn't go to my mother and say I was sexually harassed at school. I was threatened and ordered not to tell. However, I'll never forget it.

PLAYBOY: Did you have anyone you could talk with?

OATES: There was no consciousness then. Molested, battered children were in a category that was like limbo. There were no words, no language. If you tried to talk about it, you'd say, "I was picked on." Then there was a certain amount of hesitancy, if not actual shame, to say anything about your body, so you wouldn't want to say where you were harassed. So a lot of this was never spoken. It was extremely important for me, retrospectively, to have these early experiences of being a helpless victim, because it allows me to sympathize—or compels me to sympathize—with victims. I know what it's like to be a victim, but I also know what it's like to get away and not have been damaged or scarred. I was part of a world in which almost everybody who was weak was victimized. This seems to be the human condition: to be picked on, to be a victim.

PLAYBOY: Did this drive you inward, turn you to writing at an early age?

OATES: I was always writing little books when I was five or six. I would use a tablet and do drawings. I was never interested in dolls, I gave my dolls away. I was reading books like *Alice in Wonderland* and *Through the Looking Glass* when I was very young. I obviously was greatly influenced by Alice, who was a little girl but has some of the courage and resilience we associate with adults. And, of course, she's a female protagonist, and that made a strong impression on me.

PLAYBOY: Was your family religious?

OATES: My family became religious when my grandfather died of emphysema. He worked at a foundry and his lungs were filled with bits of metal. Our household was traumatized by that. My parents had been Catholic and they had lapsed. That's a joke to other people, but to Catholics you are never not a Catholic. You're born Catholic and you're baptized, then you become a lapsed Catholic for the next 90 years. It's like an alcoholic—you're never not an alcoholic. I'm not a person who feels very friendly toward organized religion. I think people have been brainwashed through the centuries. The churches, particularly the Catholic Church, are patriarchal organizations that have been invested with power for the sake of the people in power, who happen to be men. It breeds corruption.

I found going to church every Sunday and on holy days an exercise in extreme boredom. I never felt that the priest had any kind of connection with God. I've never felt that anyone who stands up and says "Look, I have the answers" has the answers. I would look around in church and see people praying and sometimes crying and genuflecting, saying the rosary, and I never felt any identification. I never felt that I was experiencing what they were experiencing. I couldn't figure out whether or not they were pretending.

PLAYBOY: Yet haven't you had some mystical experiences?

OATES: I actually had some experiences that were electrifying and changed my way of looking at life. But I haven't had them for a long time.

PLAYBOY: Can you describe what happened to you?

OATES: I can't talk about it. A mystical experience is ineffable and you can't put any language to it because as soon as you do you demean and reduce it. You wouldn't have a mystical experience in a Sunday Mass, you would have it out in the wilderness. You'd have to be alone. It might not have any god involved. It would be more like an activation of the deepest psyche. I've been interested in religious experience and the spiritual side of all of us, and mysticism. But organized religions such as the Catholic Church are the antithesis of religious experience.

PLAYBOY: Do you feel the same way about astrologers, numerologists, tarot cards and Ouija-board readers?

OATES: The persistence of crackpots, pseudoscientists like astrologers, suggests the failure of science and education. How can people still be superstitious, still believe in nonsense and astrology and grotesque demonic religions of every kind, every fundamentalist religion crowding us on all sides? How can we have these phenomena and say that science and education have not failed? That's embarrassing.

PLAYBOY: It sounds as if you're not the kind of person who would turn to therapy.

OATES: I can't begin to imagine going to a psychotherapist. You're going to another person who has some dogmatic ideas and his or her own agenda. Why go to somebody else, anyway? Theoretically they're listening, but in fact they're not, they're looking at the clock, thinking, How can I bend this person to my own theories? Go for a long walk or go jogging, take a retreat and meditate and think. Or read Walt Whitman.

PLAYBOY: Would it be fair to categorize your philosophy as: Shut up, don't complain and get on with it?

OATES: I have strong interior models from my parents and grandmother how a human being should behave with dignity. Not that I always live up to it, but I sure know how you die, how you deal with life without complaining, with as much strength as possible. I'm in a profession where people are so quick to complain about the smallest things. Their vanities and egos are really bruised. To me this is just absurd. The harshest facts of life have to do with the economy, with one's own economy. If you are poor, if you are living at or below the poverty line, then you're right up against life in a way that literary and academic or professional people are not. I come from a world where there was a fear that there wouldn't be enough money, not enough food to eat. I remember that. Now I'm in a world where somebody fears they'll get a bad review.

PLAYBOY: You also come from a world where one relative was murdered and another committed suicide.

OATES: My mother's father was murdered in a saloon fight when she was a baby, the youngest of eight or nine children. Their family was extremely poor, so she was given away to relatives. I only found out about it as an adult. Then I found out, many years later, that a relative put a gun in his mouth and shot himself while my father's mother was with him. This took place before I was born, but it's part of my parents' life. I'm pretty close to my parents and a lot of my writing draws on their experiences. They really had adventurous and arduous lives growing up in the earlier part of the century in a rough part of America, and they came of age during the Depression. They were brave, strong people.

PLAYBOY: Their lives weren't made any easier after you were grown and your sister was born autistic. Being as verbal and articulate as you are, that must have been quite a shock.

OATES: I've written about the phenomenon of one person living in language and the other not having any language. My sister has not really ever spoken. She was born at a time when virtually nothing was known about autism. An autistic person has a little bit wrong with the brain chemistry. It's a mystery. She's now in a special home.

PLAYBOY: Given your history, it's understandable why you would lean toward tragedy.

OATES: I'm always struck by that wonderful remark by Henry James, how what's bliss for one person is bane or evil or pain for another. That's so true in life—what's happy for one person can be painful for another. If you have a happy ending in a novel, it's probably not going to be happy for everyone.

PLAYBOY: Why are difficult and troubling works of art more beneficial to readers than happy ones?

OATES: Well, the classic theory of tragedy is that it allows people to be ennobled. We see people pushing the limits of their courage and their involvement. King Lear, for instance, rises to a stature by the end of the play that he didn't have in the beginning. If it were a situation comedy and Lear were just dealing with a funny daughter, he would always be on the same level. Serious works of art push people to the extreme. That's why creative artists try risking things that could fail, because they feel that's how they learn more about themselves.

PLAYBOY: Can fiction show a person how to survive?

OATES: Oh, definitely. We pick our models from art. In the past, prose fiction and drama provided models for people. I'm sure many young people now get their role models from the movies and television, which may not always be good.

PLAYBOY: Are there any TV programs that interest you?

OATES: I don't watch television. I don't have time.

PLAYBOY: What about news events such as political conventions or the Olympics?

OATES: No. If I wanted to know about the conventions I'd read *The New York Times*. And I'm sorry to say that I was no more interested in the Olympics than those athletes are interested in my writing. As many athletes as there are crowding one another at the bookstores to get hold of my books, that's as much as I watched the Olympics. I like to read. Television is a different kind of medium: It's for people who are skimming along on the surface of life.

PLAYBOY: With the way you work, would you have felt trapped if you had children?

OATES: I was never driven by a strong maternal instinct. Nor does my husband have a strong paternal instinct. We never really thought about it much.

PLAYBOY: Did you think about marriage before you met Ray?

OATES: I grew up in a time when young women wanted to be engaged as soon as possible. When I graduated from college in

1960, to get married was the ideal. But I was different. I was always bent on either teaching or being a writer.

PLAYBOY: How old were you when you met Ray?

OATES: I was 21 and he was 30, so he was an older man. This has a certain romance about it. He was getting his Ph.D. and I was beginning my M.A. I guess it was love at first sight. Or love at first conversation. We met at a social gathering and we started talking. I think of marriage and/or love as a long conversation that has many modulations to it. Ray's a stabilizing force in my life. When I have trouble writing, he is a voice of calm.

PLAYBOY: Is that the secret to a successful marriage: Stay calm and have long talks?

OATES: The secret is that one is closest friends with one's spouse and it's a relationship that deepens with time.

PLAYBOY: Does Ray ever appear as a character in your books?

OATES: No, I'm so close to him that in a way I don't see him. I have assimilated him, which is typical for people who have been married quite a while. There's a kind of pronoun "we" consciousness.

PLAYBOY: Do "we" share the housework?

OATES: I do all the housework and Ray does all the outside work—the lawn, the garden. I start making dinner at eight, which is pretty late. My take on cooking and housework is that it's part of my writing. Sometimes my brain is like a computer screen and I can do my revisions and copyediting of the day's work while I'm preparing a meal. When I'm done I'll go to my desk and make those corrections, then the whole thing's erased in my head.

PLAYBOY: Is it true that your husband never reads your work?

OATES: I have always felt that I didn't particularly want people closest to me—my parents, my husband—to read my work. I wanted freedom and I didn't want people peering over my shoulder. I didn't want them to feel they had to like it. I'm not a person who gives her writing to her friends to read. I would feel very embarrassed to do that. Joan Didion and John Gregory Dunne read each other's work all the time. This is a healthy, symbiotic relationship they have worked out. But Ray has so much of his own work to do, he just wouldn't have time to read any of my work.

PLAYBOY: Who takes care of the finances in your house?

OATES: Ray is the one in charge of the finances. When he married me many years ago, he could not have anticipated that he'd spend a lot of time dealing with accountants and investors and money men. It's nothing that he's interested in. We're both literary people and interested in culture.

PLAYBOY: Are you also very rich?

OATES: How can you ask a question like that? If I said yes I'd have a burglar visiting immediately. I don't have much idea of how much money we have, but we're not really wealthy. We don't spend money, put it that way. We live quite modestly. I'm not concerned with money.

PLAYBOY: Still, with all those books in print, you must constantly receive royalty checks from around the world.

OATES: Over the years I'm surprised by checks that come in because I don't expect them. I could probably live comfortably on my income just from Germany and Sweden.

PLAYBOY: What does the money mean to you?

OATES: Money is a kind of burden because one feels one should spend it intelligently. You can spend money in a consumptive way and waste it, but to spend money intelligently, to direct it toward meaningful goals, to give to charities that are not exploitive, that's difficult. We subsidize our friends in terms of publishing ventures. James Michener has given away millions of dollars. Giving away that amount of money has probably caused him creative angst.

PLAYBOY: Are you uncomfortable talking about the subject of money?

OATES: When I grew up, sex was not talked about—it was a classic taboo subject. These days, I think money may not be talked about. If a child were to ask his parents, "How much money do you make? How much do you have in the bank?" that might be the taboo subject today.

PLAYBOY: So let's talk about sex. Norman Mailer says sex that makes you more religious is great sex.

OATES: How does Mailer know what's great? Maybe what he's experienced is puny, but he has only his own experiences. Norman has a sense of being an entertainer. He's like a boxer—he feels you get into the ring and you put on a show and it's adversarial. I'm not like that. Maybe I would be more like that if I were a man.

PLAYBOY: Was sex a scary subject for you growing up?

OATES: Girls were, and probably still are, afraid of sex—for good reason. Getting pregnant was always the fear. It was a sense of public humiliation.

PLAYBOY: For many boys of your generation the novels to read were usually written by Henry Miller. Did you read him as well?

OATES: I read some of Henry Miller, but it's on the level of a comic book. People seem shallow, nothing that has any appeal to me. I do remember going to the adult section of a library when I was about 12 and I pulled *Ulysses* off the shelf and the whole book seemed to glimmer with a forbidden glow. It was erotic and forbidden and exciting and sacred. Now when I look at it I feel this identification with James Joyce, who was 38 when he finished *Ulysses*. But he was a struggling writer and that's the effort of his great struggle.

PLAYBOY: Which of your own novels are watershed in terms of your career?

OATES: Evidently *them*—it's the one people talk about. Maybe *Because It Is Bitter, and Because It Is My Heart* and *You Must Remember This*—so much of my own life and heart went into them. I can't tell, it's hard to get a bead on one's own self.

PLAYBOY: You omitted *Wonderland*, which caused you quite a bit of anxiety when you wrote it.

OATES: Probably the closest I ever came to cracking up was in the writing of *Wonderland*. Appropriately enough it's about the human brain, examining a crisis in American society by way of one representative man. It's hard to talk about. I thought I had this neurological problem and had to see a specialist, but it was more a biochemical problem caused by stress. I put so much energy into that. It was such a monumental novel, very daunting to write. It left me kind of breathless. I felt when I was done that I didn't want to write any more long novels.

PLAYBOY: Are the novels of Rosamond Smith the kind of novels that Joyce Carol Oates would write? Or did you simply choose that pseudonym to escape from your identity?

OATES: I wanted to write psychological suspense novels that would be more cinematic than my other novels. However, as time has gone by they have gotten more intellectual and analytical, more Jamesian, more interior. All the Smith novels are about twins of one kind or another.

PLAYBOY: How strongly did you want to keep your identity a secret?

OATES: I wanted badly to keep it a secret. It was like being 11 years old again, like a little girl. I would have had reviews that were for a first novel, and everything would have been new and fresh and untried. But then the secret got out. My editor was upset and had reason to be. I didn't think it was that important if I wrote a novel under a pseudonym. Why would anyone care? But it's hard to have a secret identity because one has to have a Social Security number, income tax forms.

PLAYBOY: Why did you feel the need to go undercover?

OATES: Because people don't judge the new work as new work. In my case they say, "This is Oates's 25th novel, or 50th book." Whereas with my new identity it would have been, "Here is a new novel by a writer we haven't heard of." And the attentiveness would have been for the text itself.

PLAYBOY: Were you disheartened when you were discovered?

OATES: It was sad. Disappointing.

PLAYBOY: Critic Alfred Kazin said that you write to relieve your mind of things that haunt us rather than to create literature that will live.

OATES: Well, Kazin doesn't know. It's sort of a statement like, "Does she dye her hair?" It's a haphazard pomposity that one gets from people who have no idea what they're talking about.

PLAYBOY: Do critics ever know what they're talking about?

OATES: It's unpredictable. I get extremely good reviews or angry reviews. People have said they admire that I keep going. They have a different reading of the enterprise of being a writer. My worst problems are inner-generated. They come from my own self.

PLAYBOY: You've said that a writer who has published as much as you have develops a skin like a rhino's. How necessary is it to be thick-skinned?

OATES: It's scar tissue over the years. I started writing before women's liberation, publishing since 1963. I came under a lot of attack because I was a woman writing about subjects that men usually write about. John Updike once said that I really took a lot of hostile criticism. Some writers stay down in the mud. D. H. Lawrence called it the scrimmage of life. I consider myself still down there. I'm fair game for the attack.

PLAYBOY: Let's talk about some of those people. We'll name a writer, you say what you think. We'll start with Norman Mailer.

OATES: If anyone has literary presence and power in New York it is Mailer. He has been courageous and adventurous, and he obviously loves the craft of fiction. He also gets negative reviews. People are either jealous of him or they have an ax to grind. Norman and I try different things all the time, different voices. We are much more vulnerable than many writers who repeat the same formulas for success. But Norman has taken a good deal of abuse. And it's good for him. He's a fighter, a counterpuncher. One should defend oneself.

PLAYBOY: Doris Lessing.

OATES: She's in the tradition of George Eliot—she tries to write about society in an ambitious way. Lessing's more like Norman Mailer and like me, for better or worse. She's tried different things.

PLAYBOY: John Updike.

OATES: A great writer, a major, important writer. I write to John Updike and he writes to me quite often. He's a wonderful letter writer.

PLAYBOY: Iris Murdoch.

OATES: I have read a lot of Iris Murdoch and I have written about her. There was a time when I would be asked to review every new Murdoch novel that came out. Her novels are somewhat repetitive.

PLAYBOY: Tom Wolfe.

OATES: He's obviously a satirist and a social critic. I don't think of Tom Wolfe as a literary figure, but he's amusing.

PLAYBOY: Flannery O'Connor.

OATES: She's an American classic. A very special, very indi-
vidualistic, very idiosysncratic and, in an odd way, very Catholic
writer. She had a gift for satire and treating character quickly.

PLAYBOY: Eudora Welty.

OATES: She has a broader humanity than O'Connor. O'Connor
was very narrow and good at what she did—she never wrote
about romantic love, perhaps knew nothing about it. Welty tried
many more things. She's more ambitious.

PLAYBOY: Saul Bellow.

OATES: Bellow's brilliant. Bellow is a genius. A great writer.
Brilliant themes. Saul Bellow is off the scale of even Truman
Capote, Thomas Pynchon or Thomas Wolfe. You can't compare
him with those others.

PLAYBOY: How about Philip Roth?

OATES: Roth is not as ambitious as Bellow. He hasn't tried as
many things. But what he does he does brilliantly.

PLAYBOY: T. Coraghessan Boyle.

OATES: Tom Boyle is a wild writer, very inventive, surreal,
funny. He's a serious person.

PLAYBOY: Gabriel Garcia Marquez.

OATES: I've enjoyed him very much. My favorite Marquez is
the Faulknerian *Autumn of the Patriarch*. It's his best novel.

PLAYBOY: You're a big Faulkner fan, aren't you?

OATES: Faulkner was ambitious and courageous in what he
did. And that accounts for a lot. The South American writers
were immensely influenced by Faulkner. Without Faulkner,
Marquez wouldn't have been Marquez. To speak of greatness,
we're speaking of Faulkner.

PLAYBOY: How about J. D. Salinger?

OATES: He was, or is, a winning and appealing writer who had
a strong appeal at a certain time. But there's no comparison with
Faulkner. I wouldn't even put them in the same room together.

PLAYBOY: F. Scott Fitzgerald.

OATES: He was a brilliant, gifted, somewhat limited writer
who needed to live longer. He simply didn't develop.

PLAYBOY: Ernest Hemingway.

OATES: I've always read Hemingway for his prose. I've
never thought his characters were interesting, they seem to be

flat and childlike. His dialogue seems infantile, but his eye for nature and his ear for language were breathtaking. You don't find subtleties of character in Hemingway, you find them in Henry James.

PLAYBOY: Henry James.

OATES: A great master, he's up there, he's like Shakespeare.

PLAYBOY: What would you say has been your most influential work?

OATES: One short story, "Where Are You Going, Where Have You Been?" has been anthologized a good deal and made into a movie called *Smooth Talk*, and everywhere I go people ask me about that.

PLAYBOY: Martin Scorsese plans to produce *You Must Remember This*, which Martha Coolidge will direct from your script. Are you excited about this?

OATES: Excited is a word that's not in my vocabulary, but I'm very hopeful.

PLAYBOY: When the movie is made of your life, who should play you?

OATES: Oh, that's really science fiction.

PLAYBOY: Capote thought the ghost of Eisenhower would be right for him.

OATES: Oh, well . . . the ghost of Henry James.

PLAYBOY: We haven't talked about how you write. Do you use a computer?

OATES: I don't have a word processor anymore. I write in longhand first—that's the only way I can be in touch with the emotions that the characters go through. Then I go to the typewriter and it starts to be something different. Much more in control and meticulous. That's a different process. Ninety percent of what I do now is revision.

PLAYBOY: How important are names for your characters?

OATES: Absolutely important. I spend a long time naming names. If I can't get a name right I can't write, I can't begin. I have a lot of names that begin with J, especially men. It's like my alter ego. I always go for the J if I can get away with it.

PLAYBOY: Have you ever used drugs to stimulate your thinking?

OATES: No, I'd no more do that than I'd take a bottle of ink and pour it on my rug. What if you stained your consciousness permanently? It's not a gamble that I would consider.

PLAYBOY: You teach two writing classes at Princeton. Can writing be taught?

OATES: We're not teaching writing, we're teaching writers. I believe in helping gifted students get published. I really want to be like a trainer, where you keep pushing and pushing the gifted writer. I'm looking for my Mike Tyson.

PLAYBOY: *Newsweek* declared your subject to be "passion and its irrational power over human destinies." Is that accurate?

OATES: That may be part of it. I certainly do feel that we're guided by subterranean impulses. I don't just mean individuals, I mean the collective. I mean entire nations. You see it in countries such as Iraq and Iran. It seems like a wave of irrationality rushes through an entire people and could carry them almost to suicidal behavior. And then you see it in individuals. Nietzsche said that madness in individuals is a rarity but in nations it's the norm. It's a good point.

PLAYBOY: In *Black Water* you attack former president Bush as evil, exploitative, hypocritical and shallow. Would he qualify as a mad Nietzschean individual?

OATES: You're being too meticulous. I'm amazed that Bush got away with such blatant falsehoods. He said things that were screamingly untrue, like Clarence Thomas is the best person—male or female, black or white—to sit on the Supreme Court. Nobody would believe that, including Clarence Thomas.

PLAYBOY: We take it that you voted for Clinton?

OATES: Yes. As long as I don't have to listen to him speak. Or listen to Al Gore go on and on shamelessly about his son.

PLAYBOY: You obviously lean more toward the downtrodden and invisible people of our society than those in positions of power. Do you feel a responsibility to be a voice for the powerless?

OATES: Yes, I do. There are a lot of people whom nobody cares about. They work at the minimum wage, they're exploited, they exist all around us, but they're invisible. They can't write about themselves, they don't have any language, sometimes they're illiterate. So if anybody's going to write about them, it has to be someone who can feel sympathy for them. And I've always felt the sense of "there but for the grace of God go I."

PLAYBOY: With such a body of work already behind you, what are your thoughts about immortality?

OATES: It's just a word, a wishful word. People are not immortal.

PLAYBOY: Why do we feel haunted by the dead or by thoughts of death?

OATES: It's sad how we love people and they are so fiercely individual and so priceless and they pass away. Then as we in turn pass away, their memories are gone. It's the eternal drama of a species, of time burying the dead. The wheels keep turning.

PLAYBOY: If your life ended suddenly, would you feel you had accomplished much of what you wanted to?

OATES: I will never live long enough to execute all the ideas I have. Probably everybody has serious work to do and wild stories to tell, but life gets in the way. Everybody has a novel to write.

PLAYBOY: But not everybody who writes one has a chance for a Nobel Prize. How would you feel if you were so honored?

OATES: It would be a great honor, and it would bring honor to a body of work and to a group of people—American women writers. And it could probably change my life irrevocably. If it comes too soon it can have an adverse effect, like with Albert Camus, who was one of the youngest Nobel Prize winners. I think he was only 44 when he won it. He seemed them to have felt that he could not live up to it. But if it comes at the end of a career, obviously that's different.

PLAYBOY: So it's still something a long way off in your dreams?

OATES: I'm sure I have a long way to go. I won't hold my breath.

The Sunny Side of Joyce Carol Oates

Laurence Shyer

Originally appeared in *American Theatre* magazine, 1994. Reprinted by permission.

Joyce Carol Oates has always been drawn to the underside of the American imagination. Serial killers, rapists and youth gangs stalk the pages of her novels, and scenes of domestic violence, economic deprivation, loneliness and rage are commonplace. The emotional climate is intense; the language often unflinching; the vision corrosive, even apocalyptic.

Now the writer once called "the Dark Lady of American Letters" has stepped into sunlight. *The Perfectionist*, which premiered at the McCarter Theatre in Princeton, N.J. last October, was Joyce Carol Oates's first "romantic comedy," and it came complete with a cast of good-hearted characters, a cheerful suburban setting and all the happy contrivances that go with the genre. The whole enterprise was rather unlikely and disconcerting, as if Jane Austen or Madame de Stael had suddenly turned herself into Jean Kerr—and no less surprising is how Oates mastered the rudiments of Broadway light comedy without ever having seen one. There are, to be sure, a few discordant rumblings along the way as well as some of the disruptive impulses that underline the rest of the novelist's work—intimations of illness, death and drug dependency, an accusation of rape and at one point the threat of castration—but the genial spirit she has called into being manages to hold the dark clouds at bay.

So just what were the circumstances that brought this most uncharacteristic work—a kind of screwball comedy for the intelligentsia, the suburban and tenured—into being? Oates provides a multi-tiered explanation, beginning with proximity to the McCarter (she is currently the Roger S. Berlind Distinguished Professor in the Humanities at Princeton University) and her close friendship with Emily Mann, the theatre's artistic director.

"It was always understood that I would try to write something that might be suitable for the McCarter. Emily has always been very receptive to my work and I think because of her presence here I was encouraged to write a kind of play I would not have otherwise attempted. I also love to learn new things, and for me *The Perfectionist* is an experiment in genre."

Finally, Oates offers what may be the best reason of all for such a play: Life isn't all discord and anguish. "There really are romances in the world," she ventures. "People fall in love. Every day."

While her literary reputation rests securely on her prose fiction, Oates is becoming a conspicuous presence in American theatre. She is particularly active during the current season—which also finds her on terrain more familiar than the sunny realm of *The Perfectionist. Black*, a scalding drama of racial confrontation, will open March 7 in New York at Women's Project and Productions. Oates's 1972 play *Ontological Proof of My Existence*, about a kidnapper who struggles to possess a young girl while offering her for sale to the highest bidder, was revived by Chicago's Thunder Road Ensemble in November. *I Stand Before You Naked*, a "collage-play" first presented at New York's American Place Theatre in 1990, is entering its second year at the Theatre Marie Stuart in Paris.

Oates also recently completed a libretto for an opera based on her 1991 novella *Black Water*, a fictive retelling of the Chappaquiddick incident, which is to receive its world premiere in 1995 at the American Music Theater Festival of Philadelphia, as well as a screenplay for Martin Scorsese. She is currently at work on another full-length drama titled *Bad Girls*. The present season promises numerous performances of her one-act plays ("I love short plays because they get immediately to the drama," she remarks), which have proved extremely popular with college and small theatre groups because of their small casts and minimal production requirements.

But ironically, of all her recent projects, it is the one set closest to home that seems to have elicited the greatest creative stretch. Oates admits she would have really preferred to fashion *The Perfectionist* as "more of a brittle Restoration-type comedy. More sentimental and romantic comedy is not my own taste. I did graduate studies in English, so I read Restoration drama, and I admire Congreve and Wycherly immensely. But those comedies are so hard. *The Perfectionist* is set in a place like Princeton, it has people in it who I know, and I didn't have the hardness of heart to do that."

Part of the play's charm is that those on either side of the curtain are part of the same community, and the knowing laughter of Princeton audiences, who were quick to identify the comedy's familiar types and catch its thinly veiled references, fairly set the theatre spinning. It is not too much of an exaggeration to say that one walked out of the McCarter, which sits on the edge of the university's neatly clipped greensward, into the very world one had left behind.

Oates says she has been interested in drama as long as she can remember, though the circumstances of her formative years allowed her no direct contact with the stage. "I grew up in a rural community in upstate New York and we were so far from any kind of theatre. Drama wasn't taught but I remember reading Eugene O'Neill and Tennessee Williams when I was in high school. I began going to the theatre when I went to college in the late 1950s. I saw wonderful plays on Broadway—*Rashomon* and *Tea and Sympathy* and Archibald MacLeish's *J.B.*, which was quite an experience because it was a verse drama and a tragedy."

Oates's initiation into the theatre came in 1965 ("It all began so long ago—it's almost like another lifetime") when the director Frank Corsaro, sensing something dramatic in her published short stories, commissioned her first play, *The Sweet Enemy*, for the Actor's Studio Workshop. Other theatre pieces followed from time to time during the next two decades, most of them produced Off Broadway.

In 1990 she received a commission from Jon Jory and Actors Theatre of Louisville, and for the first time became an active participant in the theatrical process. "I never had much experience being in the theatre and working at rehearsals. Louisville got me started at that. Since then I've been writing plays virtually all the time." During the past three years her work has been seen at New York's American Place Theatre, Ensemble

Studio Theatre and the Contemporary American Play Festival, Massachusetts' Williamstown Theatre Festival, and Connecticut's Long Wharf Theatre.

Oates speaks of writing plays and writing novels as two entirely separate disciplines. "It's the difference between swimming and jogging. Both are exercises and can be very rewarding, but they use completely different muscles. The challenge of the theatre is to make the characters vivid enough to be alive on stage and carry the weight of action. The prose narrative voice doesn't require this; you're telling a story."

A play is also about forward momentum, and Oates likens its workings to that of an automobile. "It has to move. You can have a very beautiful Rolls Royce but if something is wrong with its engine and it just sits in the driveway, you'd be better off with another car that *moves*. Of course, content matters too, but I've learned that in the theatre pacing and velocity are very important. If people are falling asleep, you fail."

She typically begins a play by imagining an empty stage or room in which something will happen. "It takes a long while. I sit and fantasize. The characters are sort of there and they start moving around and talking. It's not like prose narrative. I can't tell the story—they have to tell their own stories. Usually I do the page over and over in my typewriter, reading it faster and faster to imagine visually how it will play on stage and so I hear the voices. I'm always listening."

In writing for the theatre, Oates must not only relinquish the controlling authorial voice of fiction—what she calls "the prose writer's sheltering cocoon of language"—but also her carefully shaped texts into the hands of others to alter and interpret. One might think that an author known to weigh each word and every piece of punctuation—and who acknowledges that she is in large part the perfectionist of her recent play's title—would yield up her creations with a certain reluctance, but this is not the case; she gives herself over to the collaborators freely and without hesitation. In fact, surrendering a play to "another's imagination" is part of what arouses her excitement about the theatre, for without "voices other than one's own," she believes, a playwright cannot truly experience his or her work. ("The joy of theatre," she recently told an interviewer, "is coming to a director or to actors with a work you thought was more or less finished, then having them read it and realizing how much more work you have to do.") When well-meaning people ask if it isn't troubling to have her characters taken over by other people her reply has always been, "But isn't that the point of writing for the theatre?"

Oates also prides herself on being a good collaborator. Emily Mann, who has come up against a few protective playwrights in her time, recalls that whenever she requested cuts or alterations—in one instance the elimination of an entire scene—Oates would invariably reply, "Just do it." ("I am the most agreeable of playwrights," Oates once declared. "To be any more agreeable, I would have to be posthumous.") Collaboration does, however, exact a toll. While Oates enjoys returning to the production to monitor the fluctuating response of the audience and the subtle changes from night to night as the company settles into the play, she admits to experiencing a sense of distance from the self-contained world she has set in motion. "I don't feel I'm the creator of those people up there. They're getting all the laughs and having the fun. I'm just a spectator. It's like I'm standing at a great distance and the little raft is drifting away."

Although she has been writing plays for nearly 30 years, Oates still speaks of herself as a beginning playwright and a novice in the theatre, and her regard for its practitioners seems positively wide-eyed. She got a big laugh at a post-performance discussion a few days after the opening of *The Perfectionist* when she told the audience that she's still "somewhat amazed that actors can memorize their lines" and they come out "sounding spontaneous." Her fascination with the live performer is clearly part of what keeps drawing her back to the theatre. "I'm really in awe of actors, in awe of their creativity, energy and courage. It's also a hard life for them. I'm a professor; I have a contract and a place, but an actor, even a good actor—where will he or she be in a year?" While Oates is interested in all the details of the theatre, especially the art of the director, she senses her limits. "I'm not like David Mamet or Sam Shepard, who have actually staged their own plays. I wouldn't be able to direct a play of mine and I wouldn't want to. To me that would be like trying to do my own brain surgery."

"The more one is around the theatre the more ideas one gets for the stage," Oates recently told an interviewer, and her activities bear this out. She continues to produce one or two novels a year (she has published 23 to date, in addition to countless volumes of short stories, poetry and essays—the late John Gardner once referred to her as "that alarming phenomenon"), but her newfound passion for playwriting has cut deeply into other activities: "I don't do a lot of short stories or book reviews anymore. I've already stopped writing poetry. Now I tend to do mainly plays." Oates also likes to keep abreast of what's going on in contemporary theatre; she maintains friendships with people in the profession, reads plays of all kinds and attends theatre regularly.

"Drama," Oates writes in her most recent collection of plays, "remains our highest communal celebration of the mystery of being, and of our being together, in relationships we struggle to define, and which define us. It makes the point, ceaselessly, that our lives are *now*, there is no history that is not *now*."

For the present, one of our preeminent novelists will continue to enter that "now," testing her protean talents and giving herself over to the reimaginings of others in that perilous if often exhilarating corner of the literary endeavor where "the sheerly imaginary" meets "the incontestably real."

Conversations with Joyce Carol Oates

Stig Björkman

The following excerpts are from a book-length interview published in Sweden in 2003. Reprinted by permission.

Stig Bjorkman: How do you contemplate your childhood and your parents? Which is your first and most vivid childhood memory?

Joyce Carol Oates: My most vivid childhood memories seem contradictory. A heavy snowfall, and my father (then very young, in his early thirties) bringing a Christmas tree into the house, and presents from my grandmother; and, a summertime memory, outside with my mother (then very young, in her late twenties, with wavy-curly honey-brown hair) playing in the grass with a mother cat and several kittens. (This memory has been bolstered by snapshots, so I know that the kittens are black.)

SB: What is your most important heritage from your parents?

JCO: My most important single heritage is perhaps an undaunted optimism, even when we have felt "pessimistic." That is, we have always been resilient, with a predilection for liking to work and to be active. My parents' retirement years, so-called, were particularly fruitful and enjoyable to them, though their earlier lives were somewhat arduous. My husband and I enjoyed visiting them and one of our most absorbing adventures together was visiting the U. K. some years ago. (My father died in May 2000.)

SB: Many of your early novels are set in a landscape reminiscent of the place where you grew up. I guess that memories and experiences from your childhood and adolescence are to be found in some of your work, explicit or implicit?

JCO: My writing is, at least in part, an attempt to memorialize my parents' vanished world, my parents' lives. Sometimes directly, sometimes in metaphor. *Marya: A Life* (1986), for instance, is an admixture of my mother's early life, some of my own adolescent and young adult experience, and fiction: reading *Marya*, as they read everything I wrote, they immediately recognized the setting— for of course it is the setting—that rural edge of Erie County just across the Tonawanda Creek from Niagara County, not far from the Erie Canal (and the Canal Road where Marya lives). The quintessential world of my fiction. *You Must Remember This* (1987) is set in a mythical western New York city that is an amalgam of Buffalo and Lockport, but primarily Lockport: the novel could not have been imaginatively launched without the Erie Canal, vertiginously steep-walled, cutting through its core. And though my father is not present in the fictional world of *You Must Remember This*, his shadow falls over it; it's a work in which I tried consciously to synthesize my father's and my own "visions" of an era now vanished. Felix Stevick is not my father except in his lifelong fascination with boxing and with what I consider the romance of violence, which excludes women; that conviction that there is a mysterious and terrible brotherhood of men by way of violence.

But it is in an early novel, *Wonderland* (1971), that my parents actually make an appearance. My beleaguered young hero Jesse stops his car in Millersport, wanders around my parents' property, happens to see, with a stab of envy, my young mother and me (a child of 3 or 4) swinging in our old wooden swing; and when my father notices Jesse watching he stares at him with a look of hostility. So I envisioned my father as a young man of 27— tall, husky, with black hair, intent in protecting his family against possible intrusion.

SB: When did you learn to read and write?

JCO: I began to "write" before I could read: I played at imitating adult handwriting, scribbling onto tablet paper in my enthusiasm and excitement at mimicking adult behavior. Writing seemed like something sacred to me, empowering and wonderful. Otherwise, I probably learned to read and write at about the age most children do. Four years old? Five? I was considered a "fast learner" in my first, one-room schoolhouse in Millersport, New York.

SB: What was the first important reading experience for you?

JCO: Lewis Carroll's *Alice in Wonderland* and *Alice Through the Looking Glass* had a lifelong influence upon me. Alice's no-nonsense yet playful personality and her sense that things can be brought under control were excellent models for a young impressionable child.

If you could transpose yourself into a girl of 8, in 1946, in a farming community in upstate New York north of Buffalo, imagining the excitement of opening so beautiful a book to read a story in which a girl of about your age is the heroine; imagine the excitement of being taken along with Alice, who talks to herself continually, just like you, whose signature phrase is "Curiouser and curiouser," on her fantastic yet somehow plausible adventure down the rabbit hole, and into the Wonderland world. I must have been the ideal reader: credulous, unjudging, eager, thrilled. I knew only that I believed in Alice, absolutely.

SB: When did you start to write yourself, and at what point in your life did you feel or decide that you would/could become a writer?

JCO: I don't believe that I ever consciously made any decision to be a "writer." That would have seemed rather arrogant to me. Rather, I enjoyed writing enormously. With the passage of time, I seem to "enjoy" it more, even as I spend more time revising and rewriting. The extraordinary richness of language is thrilling to me; the way sentences can be constructed, coiling and uncoiling, creating unexpected nests of meaning, is forever fascinating.

SB: Then, when you were studying at college, you sent a short story to the magazine *Mademoiselle*.

JCO: Well, it was a competition for college students, for people my age, so it seemed natural to do it. I think I just saw an announcement about it on the bulletin board. And then I won the prize. It was so exciting. God, it was so exciting! I think I won 500 dollars. To me, that was a fortune. I didn't have any money, and I was like intoxicated. I remember that vividly.

SB: When did you discover and start to make use of the "I" in your own writing?

JCO: As an adolescent, I was already using the device of the "I" narrator, though my characters were male. At the time, this didn't seem unusual to me. I would perhaps have thought that using the first-person from the point of view of a girl would suggest too autobiographical a perspective, which at the time had not much interest for me. I've always felt that literature should transcend the merely personal and local, and I've virtually never written "confessional" fiction. Even *I'll Take You There*, my 2002 novel in the memoirist-fiction mode (this may be a term I've invented, I don't know if others have employed it) is far more fiction than memoir.

SB: Female writers (like female artists or female filmmakers) and their works are sometimes being regarded and discussed solely in relation to gender, which, of course, only can be seen as discriminating. I'm not guessing, if I assume that your attitude concerning this is highly critical.

JCO: Yes, the classification "woman writer" is an anomalous thing, which is lacking a counterpart, a grammatical equivalent. For there are no "men writers." Persons of either sex who write define themselves as writers, but roughly half of us are defined (by others) as women writers. Problems of a metaphysical as well as practical nature arise.

SB: How does an ordinary day look for you?

JCO: An average day? I would start writing soon in the morning, and then I will write until about 1:30. I don't have breakfast, I have tea. So I try to get something established, like a vision I've had, try to get it in words. And I rewrite and rewrite. I rewrite all the time. Lots of revisions. Like most writers, or most artists.

My husband and I work every day, including weekends. I never take time off. I don't know why anybody would want to. Work is what gives us our identity. I use the word "work," but actually it isn't work. I don't know what to call it. It's a kind of exploration of language. I'm so caught up in the novels I'm writing that I don't want to take time off. It's like having an enraptured conversation with someone; you don't want to stop. I use my writing as a prismatic lens to look at America.

I am always working. I can be riding a bicycle or jogging, which I love to do, and I'm still working in my mind. I have a short-term photographic memory, so when I'm away from my writing I can see the pages I've written that morning, and I can edit them in my head—even punctuation.

SB: How do you write your manuscript? By hand, on a typewriter, on a computer?

JCO: I am more oriented towards writing with a pen and then going to the typewriter. I write my first drafts in longhand, usually on papers that have been used on the back, because I'm very frugal. I would have to be, having written so much. I have had many typewriters over the course of decades. I really love to write using a pen, because it's one's own handwriting. It's such an intimate act. To bring a mechanism between yourself and your writing, to me that seems too formal.

SB: *A Garden of Earthly Delights* is a novel divided into three parts, named after three of the main male characters, Carleton, Lowry and Swan. But the central character in the novel is Clara, and Carleton is her father, Lowry her lover and Swan her son. The novel is a kind of 'education sentimentale'—or, maybe, a very rough and down-to-earth education—of a young girl during the Depression years in the U. S. Could you see your novel as a kind of counterpart to Steinbeck's *The Grapes of Wrath* and Clara as a sister-figure to Tom Joad?

JCO: I wasn't thinking in particular of Steinbeck, but rather more of my childhood memories in composing the novel. Migrant farm workers were often seen in western New York when I was growing up, especially in Niagara County, which is mostly orchard- and farmland. Seeing these impassive-looking men, women, adolescents and children being driven along our country roads in battered buses, I wondered at their lives; I could imagine myself among them, a sister to the young girls. (The migrant workers I saw were predominantly Caucasian.) I grew up in a small family farm in Millersport, where the crops required picking by hand: pears, apples, cherries, tomatoes, strawberries. (Eggs, too, another sort of hand-picking.) Months of our lives were given up to "harvesting"—if we were lucky and had something to harvest—and I can attest that little romance accrues to such farm work, still less to sitting self-consciously by the side of the road at an improvised produce stand hoping that someone will stop and buy a pint, a quart, a peck, a bushel basket of your produce. (Early conditioning for the writer's solitary yet cruelly exposed position in a capitalist-consumer society!)

SB: What kind of research do you engage yourself in before writing these kinds of stories with a non-contemporary setting?

JCO: I do a fair amount of research while writing a novel, but use only a small fraction of what I've accumulated. For *Blonde* I had to severely edit and select this, the novel might have been ten times as long otherwise. Clara is a precursor of Norma Jeane Baker, I saw to my surprise. She too must "sell" herself in America—somehow! She is desperate, and out of that desperation springs cunning. She marries a man who will honor and support her and shield her against the world that destroyed her mother, Pearl. She marries a man to give her son a name and a place in life.

SB: You make of Clara a real heroine, a heroine who can be seen as an example.

JCO: Clara is certainly not a passive victim. Even Carleton, her father, is a driven, passionate individual. (In the new, revised version of the novel, Carleton comes to a somewhat different end; his death is self-determined, not through natural causes.) If anything, Clara is too manipulative, as she acquires more and more power as the wife of a well-to-do but unreflective farmer and investor.

SB: Toward the end of the novel, Swan purchases a gun. Why did you want to have Swan use his gun in the way he did at the end?

JCO: Swan's ending is pre-determined; he replicates the fate of his grandfather Carleton, whom he has never met. Self-destructive, because self-condemning. In reliving Swan Walpole's life, in my rewriting of much of *A Garden of Earthly Delights*, I see him as a kind of alter ego for whom the life of the imagination (he's a bookish child, in a world in which books are devalued) is finally repudiated, as it was not, of course for me, but rather more my salvation, if "salvation" isn't too melodramatic a term. Swan is burnt-out, self-loathing, and finally a suicide because his truest self has been denied, and that "true self" would have been a writer-self, an explorer of cultural and spiritual worlds. I would not have known in 1965-66 how this young man's experience would parallel the ways in which America would seem to have repudiated, in the 1970s, 1980s and 1990s, even into the morally debased and economically ravaged 21st century, a further loss of innocence of this nation at such odds with its own ideals and grandiloquent visions. *Swan, c'est moi!* (But only in fantasy.)

SB: At what stage during your writing do you decide the final fate of your characters? Do you always know it beforehand, when you start to write a novel? Or does the decision sometimes suggest itself after the novel is underway?

JCO: I usually know the "fate" beforehand of any character since this is part of the formal design of the work. I am a "formalist" to whom the forms of literature are as significant as their ostensible meanings. Form is very important to me; I have to divide the work into a structure that has coherence in its various parts. It's often divided in terms of years, certain spaces of time, and each space of time encompasses a development or movement in the narrative.

SB: You have said that *A Garden of Earthly Delights*, *Expensive People* and *them* form a trilogy. Why do you see these three novels in this way?

JCO: Yes, I see them as a trilogy. I think they have a lot in common, and what these three novels, which differ considerably in subject matter, language, and tone, have in common is the use of a youthful protagonist in his or her quintessentially American adventures. All three novels were conceived as critiques of America—American culture, American values, American dreams. And they are all about class consciousness.

Expensive People, with its climactic episode of self-destructive violence, was perceived as an expression of the radical discontent, the despair, the bewilderment and outrage of a generation of young and idealistic Americans confronted by an America of their elders so steeped in political hypocrisy and cynicism as to seem virtually irremediable except by the most extreme means.

What is assassination but a gesture of political impotence? What are most "crimes of passion" except gestures of self-destruction, self-annihilation? When the child murderer of *Expensive People* realizes that he has become, or in fact has been, all along, a mere "Minor Character" in his mother's life, he is made to realize absolute impotence and despair. He has slipped forever "out of focus." A desperate act of (premeditated) matricide will not restore his soul to him but will at least remove the living object of his love and grief.

A complex, multi-tiered novel can be an exercise in architectural design and it can be, in the writing, true labor. A novel like *Expensive People* with its relaxed first-person narration, its characteristically succinct and chatty chapters, and its direct guidance of the reader's reading experience, can ride upon the ease of its own melting, as Robert Frost said of the lyric poem. Of my numerous novels *Expensive People* glimmers in my memory as the most fluidly written in its first-draft version.

The most immediate model for the novel's peculiar tone was evidently Thomas Nashe's *The Unfortunate Traveler: or, the Life of Jack Wilton*, from 1594, often called "the first novel in English." My narrator alludes to "*that other unfortunate traveler* from whom I have stolen so much" in Part I, Chapter 23, but in rereading the ebullient sixteenth-century work I can see only occasional and glancing similarities.

SB: *Them* is prefaced by an Author's Note where you refer to the origin of your story. Why did you feel that the novel should be supplied with this preface?

JCO: I wanted to direct the reader's attention to the fact that the title refers to certain people and is not a shorthand "poetic" way of alluding to all Americans. Who are these people, Loretta and her children Jules and Maureen and their relatives? They are Americans of a certain class and era—infected, in part, by the glamour of America, the adventure of aggressive and futile dreams—but they are not Americans most of us know. Neither impoverished enough to be italicized against the prodigious wealth of their culture, nor affluent enough to be comfortably assimilated into it, the Wendalls exist—and they continue to exist—in a world for which, for the most part, despair itself is a luxury, incompletely understood, and failure unthinkable: because no American and no public models for failure are available with whom the disenfranchised might identify. If their lives are temporarily "unhappy," it never occurs to such people (not even the quick, intelligent, sweetly crafty Jules) that their dreams are at fault for having deluded them. They think instead, and indeed must continue to think, that success—that is, "happiness"—lies not far ahead in the future and can be grasped if only one knows how to play the game.

SB: To me, *Childwold* has strong cinematic qualities. Did you regard this novel as an experiment at the time you wrote it?

JCO: I did regard the novel as a kind of experiment in choral voices overlapping, occasionally contradicting one another. As, in childhood, we sometimes seem partly other people; our identities are more fluid, dreamlike in their transformations.

Childwold is a poet's novel. Yet how horrified my publishers were, when I told them! "We don't want to stress the 'poetic,'" they said. "It could certainly not sell books."

SB: Regarding the protagonist, Laney: does she remind you of girls in your neighborhood or girls you befriended when you were young?

JCO: Laney is partly myself in her yearning qualities, and her ability to see, hear, feel strongly. Yet she is also quite different, being somewhat self-destructive at times, and estranged from others. There were probably girls like this in the Millersport/ Lockport area.

SB: Kasch's infatuation with Laney, naturally, brings Nabokov's *Lolita* to mind.

JCO: I doubt that I was thinking very much of *Lolita* in writing this novel. Nabokov is not a favorite writer of mine, for his acute self-consciousness and superiority to his characters. The man's inflated sense of his own worth makes me shudder, it seems to suggest so vain, so shallow and ungenerous a soul. I've always felt that those individuals whom Nabokov would scorn and satirize have their own distinctive personalities; and know many truths that the mandarin author did not know.

SB: Kasch's acceptance of the love that Arlene offers makes him also more mature—and more vulnerable—than Nabokov's hero.

JCO: Kasch seeks a more authentic self, and can only find it by way of pursuing an unlikely, improbable, and yet irresistible "love" for one who seems to him genuine. In a way, he would like to be Laney/Evangeline and her family, trading places with them spiritually. (As he seems to have done by the end of the novel.)

SB: *Wonderland* is one of the most inventive and imaginative of your early novels. How was this novel conceived?

JCO: Of my early novels, *Wonderland* stands out in my memory as having been the most painful to write. The most painful in conception and in execution. The most painful even in retrospect. For it was evidently so mesmerizing, so haunting, so exhausting an effort, I must have willed it to be completed before, in that regulatory limbo of the unconscious to which we have no direct access, it was ready to be completed. As Graham Greene so eloquently says, "We remember the details of our story, we do not invent them."

SB: Some time after the first publication of *Wonderland* you reread and rewrote the ending of the novel. How come?

JCO: Yes, when I reread *Wonderland* after its hardcover publication, I knew that the ending I'd written was not the true ending; in the months between finishing the manuscript, and seeing it published, I had continued to be haunted by it, "dreaming" its truer trajectory. I knew then that I had to recast the ending, at least for the paperback edition and subsequent reprints. The original ending, and a brief hallucinatory prologue that framed the thirty years of the novel, were jettisoned, and the "true" ending supplied. *Wonderland* could not end with a small boat drifting helplessly to sea (specifically, Lake Ontario); it had to end with a gesture of demonic-paternal control. This was the tragedy of America in the 1960s, the story of a man who becomes the very figure he has been fleeing since boyhood: a son of the devouring Cronus who, unknowingly, becomes Cronus himself.

SB: In connection with the title, *Wonderland*, you have written "This book is for all of us who pursue the phantasmagoria of personality" as a kind of motto for the novel.

JCO: Yes, this dedication exposes the novel's secret heart.

The novel's deep verticality and inwardness is driven by convulsive narrative leaps; months and even years pass, but only those actions possessing psychic significance are dramatized. Opening with an act of despair that seems to us so tragically American—the slaughter of a family by its "head," who then kills himself—*Wonderland* moves from the Depression through World War II through the Korean War and the "Cold War" and the Vietnam War and the turbulent years of that decade (approximately 1963-73: from the assassination of President John F. Kennedy to the end of the Vietnam War) known as the Sixties. Background is foreground, in a sense, only in terms of the Depression, which has devastated Jesse Harte's father; the assassination of Kennedy, which is experienced by the Vogel family at a crucial time in their lives; and the grimly self-destructive yet intermittently radiant visions of the Sixties, to which both Jesse's mock-brother Trick Monk and his daughter Shelley fall victim.

Like virtually all my novels, *Wonderland* is political in genesis, however individualized its characters and settings. It could not have been conceived, still less written, at any other time than in post-1967 America, when divisive hatreds between the generations, over the war in Vietnam, and what was called, perhaps optimistically, the "counterculture," raged daily. (So too *them*, the novel immediately preceding *Wonderland*, could not have been written before the "long, hot summer" of urban race riots of 1967.) How specifically rooted in time and place *Wonderland* is, from the meticulously observed view of the Erie Canal, its cascading waterfalls and locks seen by Jesse from the perspective of a certain bridge in Lockport, to the demoralized street scene in Toronto, thirty years later, where the drug-addicted young, moribund, unsexed, affectless, begging from strangers, have "the appearance of victims of war." (Yes, that was Yonge Street, Toronto, in those days. A "street of the young" in any large North American city, in those days.)

For *Wonderland*, as a title, refers to both America, as a region of wonders, and the human brain, as a region of wonders. And "wonders" can be both dream and nightmare.

SB: *Bellefleur* is one of your most comprehensive and intricate novels. Constructing this imaginative story and determining the fates of the separate characters must have been both a time-consuming and adventurous challenge.

JCO: The "key" to most works of fiction is a voice, a rhythm, a unique music; a precise way of *seeing* and *hearing* that will give the writer access to the world he is trying to create. (Yet this world is sometimes so real in the imagination that its construction, in terms of formal art, seems rather like a re-creation, a re-construction.) Sometimes one must wait for a long time for this key to present itself—sometimes it comes rather quickly. In the case of *Bellefleur* I waited several years.

I would collect images along the way—a clavichord I saw, a snatch of conversation I heard—but I never could find the right voice. I would just throw the pages away; I was blocked.

For some reason I was not able to begin the novel until I moved to Princeton. But this move seemed to have unleashed or triggered a new interest in doing enormous amounts of research. I spent many hours doing research. It became a passion with me. I got very interested in 19th-century America, specifically as seen through the eyes of women. I read women's novels of the mid and late 1800's. Very popular literature, which seems to be marginal to the literary effort. I wanted to redeem, or reclaim, these genres which had been so much despised. And, of course, I used them in a postmodernist way. I loved the form. I do want to get back to it some time.

The entire novel grew out of a haunting image: there was a walled garden, luxurious but beginning to grow shabby; overgrown, "old," yet still possessing an extraordinary beauty. "Oh, I'd love to be there," I thought. It was a warm, penetrating, nostalgic image. In this mysterious garden the baby Germaine was to be rocked in her regal cradle; a less fortunate baby was to be carried off by an immense white bird of prey. My vision gave me the Bellefleur garden with an intimidating clarity, yet I could gain entry to it only by imagining all that surrounded it—the castle, the grounds, the waters of Lake Noir, the Chautauqua region, the state itself with its turbulent history, and the nation with its still more turbulent history.

In the foreground the Bellefleur family emerged as prismatic lenses by which the outer world is seen—an "outer" world abbreviated and in some cases mocked by the Bellefleurs' ambition for empire and wealth.

It took several years for me to acquire the voice, the rhythm, the tone of *Bellefleur*. Before I finally began writing it I had acquired more than 1000 pages of notes—some of them mere scraps of paper, some fairly complete dramatic scenes that would emerge, in the novel's narrative, without many changes. It became the most demanding and mesmerizing novel I have written.

SB: Are there novels of yours which are closer to your heart than others, and in that case which ones?

JCO: Well, writers are notoriously close to their most recent work, so sometimes one is blinded. Because your most recent work needs your heart and blood to keep it going. It's like your organs have been pumping life into this recent work. Then, after a period of time, I think we can gain perspective. But I would point to novels that are from my own background, like *A Garden of Earthly Delights*, *You Must Remember This*, and *I'll Take You There*. Some parts of *Because It Is Bitter and Because It Is My Heart*, because it is set in a city that I know. Then I have written many short stories that I feel very close to.

I think that D. H. Lawrence has said, that you shouldn't make choices like this. Or Picasso, or anyone who has been somewhat prolific. I think it was Picasso who said, that it wasn't up to him to make any aesthetic assessment of his work, that that belongs to other people. It's his role to create the work. I don't feel quite that detached from the critical function myself, because there are novels that do linger in my memory very powerfully. Who knows why!

SB: Is it harder for you to write with a male character as the central figure?

JCO: Not really. I think it is equally hard to write about anyone. In a way it might be harder to write about someone who's like yourself. You have to leave out most of your own life, you can't put in everything.

SB: Do you think that people connect novels like *Marya: A Life* or *Because It Is Bitter* or *I'll Take You There* with you and your own life and try to find autobiographical traits in them?

JCO: Yes, I think that they do. It's more composites of my life and my mother's life. Sometimes it's my parents' lives mixed in with myself. So it's an older generation, a generation beyond mine. *Marya* is very much my mother's world, and then I mix it again with my own world. But people tend to see things autobiographically, I think. No matter what you write, they seem to think: "That's you." It's a certain naivete.

SB: In a preface for the Franklin Library edition of *You Must Remember This* you say that the working title for the novel was *The Green Island*, which now is the title of the first section of the book.

JCO: Yes, during the approximately fifteen months of its composition I thought of this chronicle of the Stevick family suffused, in a sense, with greenness: green of romance, of nostalgia, of innocence; green of an epoch in our American history that, for all its hypocrisies, and its much-documented crimes against its own citizens, has come to represent an innocence of a peculiar American kind. And this greenness is an island: insular, self-contained, self-referential; doomed. Passion plays itself out on both the collective and the personal scale, and is best contemplated at a distance, by way of memory.

You Must Remember This was immediately conceived as a family chronicle of sorts, with its focus upon Enid and her uncle Felix. By way of passion Enid exorcizes an instinct for suicide; by way of passion, and its somber consequences, Felix exorcizes an instinct for self-destructive violence. The one I think quintessentially female, the other male: poles of masochism and sado-masochism. Which is not, of course, to suggest that we are defined by such poles, only that they exert a gravitational pull, weak in some, powerful in others.

The novel's primary excitement for me was its evocation of that now remote decade 1946-1956; its focusing upon certain selected areas of American life, notably politics (the antipodes of the Red Scare and the early, pioneering, anti-nuclear arms movement), popular culture (primarily music and Hollywood films) and professional prizefighting. The Stevicks live through an era and, to a degree, embody it; but should not be thought of as representative. They are too real, in my imagination at least, and surely too idiosyncratic, to bear the weight of allegory.

SB: *Because It Is Bitter and Because It Is My Heart* is a novel which can be seen a bit in the same light as *Marya* and *You Must Remember This.*

JCO: Yes, this novel is also very central to my body of work, as to my experience, and it was extremely difficult to write as well. So much of my heart seems to have gone into it. The first chapter alone must have been revised, sentence by sentence, as many as seventeen times. The voice was elusive—for many months, hovering just out of reach.

SB: Most fiction is written in past tense, but with *Because It Is Bitter* you have chosen to use present tense. How come?

JCO: Well, I wanted to write the novel in present tense, omniscient narrative, so that while we sometimes go into different people's heads, we're actually not in anybody's head;

we're experiencing everything from the outside. I wanted to write it this way because I'd never written in that form. Why I chose to do it the hard way I don't know.

SB: Can you see yourself in Iris, the main character?

JCO: Iris is very much based upon aspects of myself, but I did not have an alcoholic mother and father; that part is fiction. I did know someone, a very close friend, who died of alcoholism, and who is the model for Persia, Iris's mother. I think you can say that the characters in the novel are composite characters, sometimes taken from life, but more often invented.

I knew a young black boy who in some ways is reminiscent of two of the black boys in the novel, Jinx Fairchild and his brother. The novel is actually dedicated to him. I think he's no longer living—I've been out of contact with him for more than forty years—but the novel is fiction. This boy did not commit a murder, even in self-defense.

We were students at a junior high school in Lockport, New York. Being a white girl, I was in some cases very interested in the African-American students, who were at that time called Negro students. I was brought in by school bus to the city—I was from the outside—and I think I felt that they were outsiders too, and there was a kind of alliance. I don't want to make too much of this because I didn't know this boy very well. He just had a strong personality. He was the kind of boy who could have been a leader, if he hadn't been perhaps a little too rebellious.

One of the reasons I wrote the novel was to explain to myself, in some oblique way, how I came to Princeton. Why am I here? I'm so far from my own background; my whole world is left behind. Just the feeling that you look in the mirror and you say, "Well, here I am, and I am happy—but how did I get here?" I guess I wrote the novel also to show where I came from. Some people might think it's ugly, but to me it was my world; these kids swimming in the creek and jumping off the bridge, and the alleys and the railroad yards, and the river and the canal—it's also part of my background. They're all part of my background.

SB: In the early 1990s you wrote several very short novels, or novellas, all of them very intense, and very poetic in the execution of their themes.

JCO: *I Lock My Door Upon Myself*, *The Rise of Life on Earth*, and *Black Water* I can see as a trilogy of very short novels about young women, who are representative of their time or place or something beyond themselves. *The Rise of Life on Earth* is about a young nurse's aide in Detroit in the early and mid-1960s. My explicit desire was to write about somebody whom Dostoyevsky would have called "among the insulted and the injured." A woman of dull, normal sensibilities who becomes a nurse's aide, and sometimes murders her patients. She kills people in hospitals. Not that she is a murderer and that there's so much passion in what she does, but because she's acting out a kind of societal revenge on the world. I see our society as nourishing people so disenfranchised from our relative affluence as to be enemies to the society. And I see these people taking their revenge, and I can't judge them. I feel that what they're doing is perhaps wicked. At the same time, society must acknowledge its role in creating these people.

For the novelist, the act of writing even a short novel is an act of faith sustained through many months. It has been said by Aldous Huxley that all art is a quest for grace, and it has been said, by Flannery O'Connor among others, that merely to write fiction is an optimistic gesture: pessimists don't write novels. To write is to make a plea for some sort of human sympathy and communication. To write is to risk being rejected, ridiculed, misunderstood. To write is to attempt to make contact between the world *out there* and the world *in here*, both of them mysterious, perhaps ultimately unknowable.

SB: What made you interested in boxing?

JCO: My father took me to boxing matches when I was quite young. I entered that world of intense masculine drama when I was perhaps ten or eleven years old. At that age I didn't have any preconceived notions about morality or feminism. I was just looking at this world of men, which to me was like a window into a world very different from my own, and I found it fascinating. I became very interested in that whole world of appealing masculine endeavor. I guess that's one of the reasons I'm a novelist. I'm so interested in people who lead lives very different from my own.

Though one might claim any number of parallels, most of them theoretical, between the life of the fighter and that of the writer, it is probable that the writer conceives of himself, fundamentally, as a nurturer, a practical-minded dreamer, a creator who never creates out of nothing but out of a palpably living, immediate reality.

SB: You have been very much engaged in theatre work, and you have written some fifteen or twenty plays by now.

JCO: Yes, I wrote my first play in 1967, *The Sweet Enemy*, at the invitation of the director Frank Corsaro at the Actors Studio. Many years later, in the spring of 1990, I was commissioned by Jon Jory to write two linked one-act plays for the Humana Festival of New Plays in Louisville, and there I learned with much gratitude what can work—and what can't—on the stage. I wrote two short plays, "Tone Clusters" and "The Eclipse."

The first play began as a purely conceptual piece, devoid of story: an idea, a mood, a sequence of jarring and discordant sounds. "Tone clusters" refers to the eerie, haunting, dissonant music, primarily for piano, composed by Charles Ives and Henry Cowell in the early twentieth century. The music is unsettling and abrades the nerves, suggesting as it does a radical disjuncture of perception; a sense that the universe is not after all harmonious or logical. In conjunction with these tone clusters of sound I envisioned philosophical inquiries of the kind humankind has posed since the pre-Socratic philosophers, but rarely answered—"Is the universe predetermined in every particular, or is mankind 'free'?" "Where does identity reside?"—being put to an ordinary American couple of middle age, as in a hallucinatory television interview. The horror of the piece arises from its revelation that we reside in ignorance of, not only most of the information available to us, but our own lives, our own motives.

Only later, by degrees, in the writing of the play, did the nightmare interview become linked with a crime, thus with the specific, the timebound and finite. It is subsequently ironic to me that "Tone Clusters," which exists in my imagination as a purely experimental work about the fracturing of reality in an electronic era, is always, for others, "about" a crime.

When rehearsals were begun in Louisville, however, and I saw actors inhabiting the roles, I soon realized the impracticability of my original vision. Why, I thought, there the Gulicks are, and they are *real*. In my original idealism, or naivete, I had even wanted the play's dialogue to be random, with no lines assigned to either speaker; a kind of aleatory music. What madness!

SB: From what I understand, *What I Lived For* is one of your novels which you feel most satisfied with. One of your favorite novels, maybe?

JCO: Yes, I think so, though it was an immensely difficult novel to write. The writing of the novel took place over a period of maybe three years. I started the work in the form of notes to myself and drafts, and early chapters. Then I put that aside and worked on shorter novels. I wrote *Black Water* and *Foxfire*, and many short things in between. So much of the time when I was working on *What I Lived For* I was actually very, very unhappy with myself, very impatient, very angry with myself. And I passed many months in a state of perpetual anger with myself, for not being able to do what my vision instructed. I had a definite vision of the novel. I knew emotionally what it was, but I'd sit down to work and I just couldn't seem to get it. I work so much with dissatisfaction so much of the time, that to me it characterizes my writing life. Yes, *What I Lived For* was a difficult novel.

SB: Difficult in what way?

JCO: What was most difficult was to establish a narrative voice that reflected my protagonist's voice, and yet was not identical with his voice; and the meticulous interlocking of a plot that is both a "mystery" story and a highly tangled personal story. What I think about obsessively is the form that the work takes, the actual structure of the sentences, how long the chapters are, or how short, how long paragraphs and sentences are, and that kind of formal aspect of writing. Because I am a formalist. The characters come to me without much difficulty, rather smoothly. So, it's the form that I work on. Certainly, *What I Lived For* was massively difficult to arrange, to organize all the details.

When I conceived *Zombie*, which is the novel I wrote directly after *What I Lived For*, I knew immediately that the form of the novel would be in two parts, and that each of the chapters would be very short. And that there would be very few passages of what I would call "literary radiance." There are very few metaphors in the novel, because Zombie is not that kind of character. *What I Lived For* is rather like a prose poem in the account of a supposedly average American Caucasian male of the middle class. I wanted to make poetry out of his vulgarity.

SB: How did you conceive your character, Corky Corcoran?

JCO: My process as a writer is to build character simply by inhabiting him or her obsessively. During the course of writing a novel, I am immersed in my protagonists' souls virtually all my waking life. (And perhaps much of my dream life as well.) I see my own world, which I move through as myself, through "fictitious" eyes, and note what my characters would think or do in similar situations.

SB: *We Were the Mulvaneys* is told through the youngest member of the Mulvaney family, Judd. Why did you choose him as the narrator of the story?

JCO: Well, the youngest members of a family are always somewhat peripheral, they come along at the end, so they inherit many memories. It is said that the youngest members of families are told things, that become their memories. It's sort of sifted down to them, rather than being necessarily first-hand memories. Also, Judd is a writer. He's a reporter and an editor of a newspaper. So, he is someone who is a kind of witness. Judd says he is assembling a kind of family album, not writing a "confession."

SB: Judd is also left out from information about the drama and the tragedy that the family is being exposed to.

JCO: Yes, in the 1970s the whole consciousness of sexual crimes, sexual abuse, date rape, sexual harassment, all these words, and terms, with which we are very familiar today, had not existed.

SB: The theme of twins and twin relationships is recurrent in your novels. Why this fascination with twins and the relationship between twin souls?

JCO: I've always been very interested in the idea of twins. Part of it must be unconscious, a way that we can't understand, you know. The sense that there may be a soul mate in the world, someone we can relate to, who enhances us, who makes us complete. I think it's both a myth and possibly real. People meet someone in the world, and they have an instantaneous connection. I think it's quite genuine. It may not last. It may be morbid and not healthy, but it is real.

SB: You develop this theme of twins in some of the books you've written under the pseudonym of Rosamond Smith, like *Lives of the Twins* and *Double Delight* and *The Barrens*. Here the twin relationship becomes threatening.

JCO: Yes, I think that people who are artists have twin souls. There is a domestic self and then there is an imaginative self. Or it's symbolized by daytime and nighttime. The sleeping self, the dreamer, and then the good citizen of the world. These two are very often like twins who are at war with each other.

SB: Your novels differ so much in themes, and in form and in language. Do you sometimes feel that one type of a novel has to be followed by a novel of a very different kind? How do the ideas for your novels emerge?

JCO: I think I have to pursue them. For instance, after *Blonde* I wanted to write a comedy. Because *Blonde* is a tragedy. I wanted to write an American comedy. So I wrote *Middle Age: A Romance* and set it here in Princeton. A novel about seven middle-aged people. The tragedy of Marilyn Monroe is that she never became middle-aged. At the age of 36 she was still trying to be a girl. So I wanted to write a novel about Americans or anyone who becomes middle-aged and mature and understands that youth is over and that romance has to be a new kind of romance. So that was a kind of intellectual project.

Closer to the Bone

Rebecca Frankel

Originally appeared in *Moment* magazine, December 2004. Reprinted by permission.

The floor-to-ceiling windows that frame the Kennedy Center's balcony are dark, the night sky having flushed completely black. The hour is late but still she gives an intimate, unhurried attention to each admirer, long-time reader and would-be critic who approaches, eager to extend a hand to hers, exchange a word or two with literary great Joyce Carol Oates.

If her presence could be measured, it would be equal to her handshake—a combination of velvety warmth and surprising strength. It is a touch that suggests sincerity rather than pretense or formality.

The longtime Princeton professor has just seen the first reading of *The Tattooed Girl*, a Theater J production scheduled to debut in Washington, D.C. in January. Based on her 2003 novel of the same name, *The Tattooed Girl* revolves around disenchanted writer Joshua Seigl, author of a celebrated novel about the Holocaust who, at the onset of a debilitating nerve disease, hires an assistant, a troubled young woman marked with mysterious tattoos. He is unaware of her violent background and virulent anti-Semitism.

The audience members have been asked to critique the reading but are far more interested in questioning Oates on various unrelated topics. She indulges them, and from time to time a smile flickers on her face. Still there's a hint of melancholy in her large dark eyes.

From afar her downy voice paired with her slight shape and unassuming posture, makes her seem fragile. Yet her responses are firm and she does not raise her voice to be heard. She listens without interruption to each critique offered, at times unabashedly, by audience members, as though their insights are intrinsically valuable. It may be that Oates has grown accustomed to this kind of attention and is no longer overwhelmed by so many pairs of eyes. Her ego, if it exists at all, is not visible.

From the beginning, her path to becoming a writer was natural, intuitive. In her 1982 essay "Stories that Define Me," she describes her earliest narrative attempts as "stories I told to myself, and eventually to others in the family . . . tirelessly executed in pictures, in pencil or crayon . . . the unconscious pursuit of (as I couldn't have known then) the novel."

Instinctive as her path may have been, it was not painless. Oates attended a one-room schoolhouse near Lockport, New York, an out-of-the-way town not far from Niagara Falls. "In the company of other young children, I was repeatedly tormented by older children, pursued across a field funnily called a 'playground' until my heart knocked against my ribs and I came close to collapsing." Her childhood home and the cruel elements of human nature she suffered there have been fodder for many of her stories.

As a writer, Oates has never shied away from uncomfortable topics such as sexual abuse and violence. Her characters are known for their perverse appetites and sinister layers. An Oates novel does not often come tailored with a happy ending. "I'm a chronicler of the American experience," she once said. "We have historically been a nation prone to violence, and it would be unreal to ignore this fact." More recently, she has taken to dissecting the trials of American Jewish life, exploring an identity she discovered well into her adulthood.

After her grandmother passed away in 1987, she learned the true origins of her father's family. "My situation was so amazing because we didn't know my grandmother was Jewish," she says. "Her parents came over in 1890. They had left Germany, the pogroms and discrimination against Jews. They just wanted to forget. They changed their name and they weren't religious in any way, not at all, and so they just drifted into America."

Oates, who was raised a "nominal" Catholic and whose name is not usually associated with Judaism, wasn't able to retrieve as much of her Jewish past as she would have liked.

"My background is really very modest," she explains. "People were poor. They weren't educated people who would leave behind any letters or journals or diaries. They were a different kind of human being who lived much closer to the bone."

More than once called the most prolific writer of her time, Oates continues to produce titles at an outstanding rate. In a career that spans four decades she's published well over 50 pieces of work—novels, short story collections, chapbooks, novellas, plays, poetry and books for young adults and children—and been awarded some of the most prestigious honors the literary world has to offer.

The first of Oates' literary recognitions came while she was an undergraduate attending Syracuse University, when she won *Mademoiselle*'s writing contest. Not long after, during her master degree study at the University of Wisconsin, she met and married literary critic Raymond Smith. The couple moved to Princeton, New Jersey in the late 1970s, where they still live. In addition to teaching, Oates and Smith run a well-respected literary journal, *The Ontario Review*.

However, it is *The Tattooed Girl* that reviewers have called her most controversial work to date. Indeed, both the novel and the play are thick with an excruciating mix of disregard and brutality, revealing that there is much brewing beneath the placid exterior of the serene writer. Oates, who finds resurging anti-Semitism and Holocaust denial "disgusting," explores both themes in this particular work.

Oates hesitates to name a single inspiration, for as she says, "many inspirations go into writing a novel, like a river with many tributaries." When she wrote *The Tattooed Girl*, her family history played a significant part. Like Oates, Seigl has a Jewish father and a non-Jewish mother. Through Seigl she confronts complex issues of modern day Jewish identity. He grapples with feelings of shame over accusations that he's "expelled all that is Jewish in him." As a descendant of survivors, he's conflicted by the responsibility to preserve a grim heritage that is inextricably tied to Jewish living.

"It's such a complex issue," Oates says. "You could see why it would be important to emphasize the Jewish legacy. But then if it becomes a burden and a duty, the younger generation is not going to thrive or flourish. For me this is a very exciting area to write about and explore. But if I had been told I had to do it, that it was a responsibility, I would have a different feeling."

In a particularly affecting passage in the novel, Seigl remembers that his grandfather once told him "there would come a day when no one would believe what had been done to the Jews of Europe, in a calculated genocidal political action. Because 'no one living' would wish to believe such evil had been perpetrated."

Such a beautifully idealistic thought is also frightening. Would it be a day to curse or celebrate? Oates doesn't believe such a day will come to pass.

"Any erasure of something so significant in history is unacceptable. Anything of that magnitude has to be remembered. I personally don't think it will be forgotten. For all the people who are Holocaust deniers, there are hundreds of thousands of others who are not going to deny history."

Another of the novel's tributaries compelled her to social commentary. "It's a post-9-11 novel and I wanted to write about how hatred, ethnic and racial hatred, can translate into acts of terror and violence that derive from people's misconceptions."

Despite its tormented characters and darker themes, *The Tattooed Girl* becomes a hopeful model of how bigoted minds can shed their misperceptions of others. "Ethnic discriminations melt away when we're one on one," she says. "It's when we're isolated that we have feelings of detachment. If most anti-Semites just knew a little more, if they read more or if they met some Jews, they wouldn't be anti-Semites."

So how should society battle ideas like anti-Semitism and racism? How can the world rid itself of such poisonous notions?

"Oh, I have no idea." Oates laughs, though it is more of a sigh, suggesting only "education and the other things we've tried for decades to solve some of these problems."

While she chooses not to preach, Oates has long since realized that writers must never stop voicing what would otherwise be forgotten, inspiring readers to transcend their worldviews.

As she remarked more than 30 years ago, upon accepting the National Book Award, "The writer of prose is committed to re-creating the world through language. . . . The opposite of language is silence; silence for human beings is death."

Joyce Carol Oates on Marilyn Monroe

Lawrence Grobel

This interview originally appeared in *Ego* magazine, 2004. It is reprinted here with the permission of the author.

There are more books written about Marilyn Monroe than any other movie star. Now comes *Blonde*, a 738-page novel by one of America's premier writers, Joyce Carol Oates. Oates has always been fascinated with 'the other,' twins, with our dual nature, and the movie industry's creation of Marilyn Monroe contrasted with who she was before she became a movie star seems right up Oates's alley.

We know Monroe, of course, from the movies, from her two famous short-lived marriages with Joe DiMaggio and Arthur Miller, from her breathless singing of 'Happy Birthday' to President Kennedy and her mysterious death soon after, and from all those enticing photographs, beginning with that famous nude pinup which first appeared on a calendar and then in *Playboy*'s first issue, for which she was paid fifty dollars. Here's Oates on that shot that dreams are made of:

"'Miss Golden Dreams' had appeared in a 1950 glossy girlie calendar called *Beauties for All Seasons* . . . the kind of calendar to be found in gas stations, taverns, factories, police stations, and fire houses, men's clubs and barracks and dormitories. 'Miss Golden Dreams' with her eager, vulnerable smile and smooth bared armpit and beautiful breasts, belly, thighs, and legs, and her honey-blond hair tumbling down her back had inhabited how many thousands or tens of thousands of masculine dreams of no more harmful significance than any fleeting image that triggers orgasm and is forgotten upon waking."

There's a lot of introspection about the star's dual personality: as the girl she knew called Norma Jeane and the studio's creation, Marilyn Monroe. Norma Jeane could go out and not be bothered by people; Marilyn, though, was a different story. It took a lot of work to create Marilyn:

"The day of the [*Gentlemen Prefer*] *Blondes* premiere, a half-dozen expert hands laid into the Blond Actress as chicken pluckers might lay into poultry carcasses. Her hair was shampooed and given a permanent and its shadowy roots bleached with peroxide so powerful they had to turn a fan on the Blond Actress to save her from asphyxiation and her hair was then rinsed another time and set on enormous pink plastic rollers and a roaring dryer lowered onto her head like a machine devised to administer electric shock. Her face and throat were steamed, chilled, and creamed. Her body was bathed and oiled, its unsightly hairs removed; she was powdered, perfumed, painted, and set to dry. Her fingernails and toenails were painted a brilliant crimson to match her neon mouth. Whitey the makeup man had labored for more than an hour when he saw to his chagrin a subtle asymmetry in the Blond Actress's darkened eyebrows and removed them entirely and redid them. The beauty mark was relocated by a tenth of a fraction of an inch, then prudently restored to its original position. False eyelashes were glued into place." [417]

It's an epic of a novel, which might be boiled down to one sentence, neatly placed in italics towards the end of the book:

"Never forget this sleek blond pussy has claws."

LG: There are probably more books about Marilyn Monroe than any other film star, what inspired you to add to this particular canon?

JCO: My work is fiction and it's imaginative, so I was freed from any kind of biographical or historical constraints. I was particularly interested in writing about Norma Jeane Baker, beginning with her childhood and focusing on her girlhood and moving into the young woman who becomes a photographer's model, a starlet under contract, and then is given the name Marilyn Monroe. I was going to write a novella of about 175 pages and end it when Norma Jeane gets the name Marilyn Monroe. But then it became an epic. I was so involved with Norma Jeane as a person and felt I wanted to give her a little more depth and poetic significance than she has been granted. I wound up writing 1400 pages, which I will never do again. It was a once-in-a-lifetime.

LG: How long did it take to write?

JCO: It took a couple of years to take notes for it, because I write first in longhand and I have lots of notes. It was extremely exhausting, especially the last section which I call "The Afterlife," where she's entering a somewhat hallucinatory consciousness—taking drugs, things are disintegrating in her life. That section was difficult and painful to write.

LG: Why has our fascination with her lasted so long?

JCO: She may be the only female screen star of the 20th century that's going to endure. It must be because of her special qualities of extreme physical beauty and at the same time vulnerability and innocence mixed up with sexual glamour. She seems to have had all these traits. She also radiated an insecurity, oddly enough, so people can identify with her, they don't see her as somebody finished and perfect, but as somebody who is insecure as they are. In a role like Sugar Kane in *Some Like It Hot* she's very childlike. The world loves children.

LG: When you say the only screen star who might endure, you eliminate such actresses like Bette Davis and Meryl Streep.

JCO: I mean on an iconic level. I'm thinking of the poster level: Elvis Presley, James Dean, Mohammed Ali, Marilyn Monroe. I don't think young people today have a lot of feeling for Bette Davis. Or Joan Crawford, Lana Turner, Jean Harlow. But Marilyn Monroe is just universally recognizable.

LG: You describe her trying out for cheerleading, singing, drama—and failing at everything. Was she a normal girl growing up?

JCO: Yes and no. The difference between a normal girl and her was that she just kept trying. Instead of slinking away she'd say, 'Let me try again.' And they'd let her and she'd still fail, and they'd tell her to try next year. She told her mother she couldn't sing or play piano and her mother said, 'You will.' Most people give up. Marilyn Monroe didn't take dancing lessons until she was, in a sense, too old. And she didn't have singing lessons until she was even older. But somehow she managed to sing and dance in movies like *Gentlemen Prefer Blondes*. She had a desperate will, and that will is analogous to the terrible hunger that you find in some athletes, like the young Mike Tyson, who are so hungry and so yearning to succeed that they just wipe away all the competition.

LG: Is this one of the insights into her character you discovered as you were writing this book?

JCO: Yes, and the biographies suggest that. For instance, the scene when she's in Korea and she's being held outside the helicopter at her request. That's only about two sentences in the biographies, but I dramatized that because I felt that was such a demonstration of her desperation to be loved. That she would risk her life? I mean, most of us would never even go up in the helicopter. And she said repeatedly that that was the happiest time of her life. 30,000 strange men yelling and screaming at her. And that was her happiest day, more than getting married—that's a kind of desperation there that I thought was very piteous, and also sympathetic.

LG: How mentally unbalanced was her mother? How much of that passed over into her daughter?

JCO: The mother was paranoid-schizophrenic. Eventually she was released and went to live in Florida. She died many years after Marilyn died.

LG: Did Norma Jeane grow up believing that she was the reason her mother had no husband? That her father didn't want her?

JCO: She may have thought that. It may have been true. The mother talked about this absent father, but who could be sure who he was?

LG: At one point Marilyn believes her father might be Clark Gable.

JCO: Yeah. It's like saying your father is God.

LG: Why did she marry at 16? Was she forced into it by her foster parents?

JCO: She was shocked and not ready to get married, but typical of her, she's a survivor. A couple of days later she's fantasizing about him and babies. A few weeks later she's making casseroles for dinner. She was an individual so desirous of being loved and surviving that she could adapt to almost anything. That's why she was such a good actress, because she could take on the coloration of a new character.

LG: There is a lot of sex in the book—how important was sex to her? Was it her only way of feeling connected?

JCO: I guess it was, from what I gathered. Later on in her life when she became a sex goddess, like Mae West, it became ironic. But in the beginning it was her way of cuddling. She loved to cuddle and be held like a doll. The sex would be an outgrowth of that. When she saw how successful she was after *Niagara* and her pinups, she realized she had a sexual appeal which had nothing to do with her own need. The two are different.

LG: She had so many men, was she a nymphomaniac?

JCO: I don't think she had so many men compared to other actresses, not like Ava Gardner. No, I don't think she was a nymphomaniac.

LG: Was her greatest desire to be wanted?

JCO: Yes. To be loved. She didn't feel she deserved to live, or to be born. There are many people like that. These people are often very creative, very energetic, they're workaholics, they're trying to prove that they deserve to be alive. Then there's a whole large category of other people who don't feel that way, they just live ordinary lives, completely happy being unknown.

LG: You write that one could see the doom in her by the time she was 19. Was her life out of her control? Was she fated to be destroyed?

JCO: She came of a certain class, she's like the Okies in California. The photographer who takes her pinup shot thinks she's one of all these thousands of girls who come to Hollywood to be used and then tossed out.

LG: You write that she lost interest in the sexy, glamorous stars like Joan Crawford, Marlene Dietrich and Jean Harlow, "for what is glamour but phony. Hollywood phony." This is Norma Jeane before she's become Marilyn. Does she always equate glamour with being phony?

JCO: I think so. She realized it was a way of manipulating other people. Like shaking a red flag at a bull. She was somewhat calculating.

LG: Was she always in search of her father? And was this why she was attracted to older men?

JCO: Yes. It's very natural. Even those of us who know our parents, we do a lot in our lives that's in reference to them, to please them, to confirm their love for us, and in some unfortunate cases to win the love. I don't think you can win anybody's love, frankly. If the love isn't there to begin with, nothing's going to win it.

LG: How much of a victim of the casting couch was she? Did she have a choice?

JCO: She was absolutely a victim of the casting couch—that expression is valuable. She never had any choice about that. It went on for years and years. It's because she came from such a lower economic level. Obviously someone like Elizabeth Taylor could not have any experiences like that.

LG: Did she equate posing nude with a form of prostitution?

JCO: In the beginning, yes.

LG: Did Norma Jeane believe Marilyn Monroe was a fake? And thus she was too?

JCO: Norma Jeane knew that Marilyn Monroe was her creation, that she played roles in two or three movies, and one of them was Lorelei Lee of *Gentlemen Prefer Blondes*. But not the characters in *Niagara*, *Don't Bother to Knock*, *Bus Stop*, or *The Misfits*. It wasn't a fake, necessarily; it was more like something she could do. But obviously Marilyn was a fake in the sense that her hair was terribly bleached—near the end of her life her hair was quite damaged and getting thin. She did have some cosmetic surgery. She had to spend so many hours with makeup, this would be very discouraging.

LG: How much of a freak was she?

JCO: I wouldn't use that term. She was made to seem to be a freak by people who were trying to make money from her, sewing her into her clothes, putting her in spiked heels and black net stockings. She could barely walk. In *Bus Stop* she's hobbling around in this tight costume where all the other women in the movie are wearing slacks and flat-heeled shoes. She was made to be like a female impersonator.

LG: Had John Huston not admired her ass, which led to his casting her in *The Asphalt Jungle*, would her career have happened the way it did?

JCO: I guess not. I got that from your book [*The Hustons*]. That to me was really, really profound.

LG: Ultimately, was it her directors who best understood her?

JCO: Some of the directors who worked with her, like Arthur Penn, had a real insight into her acting ability and how quicksilver rapid she was, just her movements and her reflexes and what kind of magic she exerted on the screen.

LG: You describe her attempting to kill herself after discovering her lover Cass Chaplin in bed with Edward G. Robinson's son. In real life, apparently, it was Cass Chaplin who walked in on Marilyn with his brother Sydney.

JCO: Yeah, I got rid of some of these extra men.

LG: That's a pretty drastic change, though, going from a heterosexual to a homosexual scene. What made you change this?

JCO: I know the three of them were seen together, they were young, attractive people in Hollywood, a bit on the margins. One of them, it may have been Chaplin, introduced Marilyn to drugs. I'm just assuming this kind of drug, promiscuous sex life that I'm writing about.

LG: You describe her acting as "gut instinct." Assess her as an actor.

JCO: She had this instinctive desire to take on the character of somebody else in a script. It's like a novelist creating characters.

LG: You describe her agent telling Norma Jeane that "Marilyn doesn't have to understand or think . . . She only has to be. She's a knockout and she's got talent and nobody wants tortured metaphysical crap out of that luscious mouth." Was this what fed her sense of doom?

JCO: I think so, at that point. She had done her very best in *The Misfits*. It didn't make money and people didn't like it that much. She probably felt that was her last chance to be serious as an actress. She was cast in another sex comedy [*Something's Got to Give*], she's 36 years old, this can't go on much longer. She did feel it was kind of the end.

LG: How did she see her marriages to Joe DiMaggio and Arthur Miller?

JCO: She didn't really want to marry DiMaggio, he talked her into it and it only lasted a few months. He was very much attracted to her as a beautiful blonde girl. He had a taste for starlets and models. But the Arthur Miller marriage was much more stable, it lasted four years. He was much more thoughtful about the relationship. He obviously loved her as a person. He did feel that she was marrying him for reasons that were partly unconscious. He's a smart man, a substantive man. He must have understood that she was idolizing him and that ultimately it wasn't a realistic relationship, it was more like fantasy. But he's a very subtle thinker, much more subtle and sensitive than Joe DiMaggio.

LG: You write that Arthur Miller "would not bend truth even in the service of art." Is this a major failing in his work?

JCO: I do admire his work, though I don't think he's on the level of Chekhov, but who is? He's more of a moralist. If you compare him to Tennessee Williams, Williams is the greater artist because he could go into poetry and fantasy, whereas Arthur Miller is pretty dogmatic. But he's intelligent, he's a considerable playwright.

LG: You printed a list of lovers the FBI said Monroe had, among them Lassie. Was this your way of showing the absurdity?

JCO: Yeah, all this crazy stuff. There was a big file on her but I've never seen it. It may not even be available.

LG: What would you say were the three greatest disappointments of her life?

JCO: The first great disappointment would have been losing her mother, being put into an orphanage and then a foster home. Then the prevailing disappointment was never having a father who would acknowledge her. Then the third would be a combination of a failure to have a happy marriage and a failure to have a baby. They're all very personal and have nothing to do with the career.

LG: During *Some Like It Hot* you write that "Monroe was no more tempting to [Tony Curtis] than a puddle of fresh vomit." Why was she so offensive to him?

JCO: Because she was late, she didn't show up on the set, he was there ready to act. He felt as he kept waiting hour after hour his strength was ebbing and then she'd arrive and she'd be all fresh and he'd be tired. He just hated her for the reasons anybody would.

LG: One of the great influences on her life in the end was Paula Strasberg, but you chose not to write about her. Why not?

JCO: I didn't get into the Strasbergs. I didn't have time.

LG: How sordid was her relationship with JFK?

JCO: It was pretty bad. I didn't talk about her relationship with Frank Sinatra, Dean Martin . . . I guess all these men sort of passed her around to one another. It was kind of disgusting.

LG: What did you think of the Marilyn Monroe auction recently?

JCO: Sad. That other people were bidding so much money on things that when she had them were not worth that much, including her white piano. I saw the exhibit. People were stunned to see all the books she had. Until that moment they thought she was just "Marilyn Monroe."

LG: Your Marilyn is murdered by an injection to the heart from The Sharpshooter. Who does The Sharpshooter symbolize?

JCO: I was thinking of the extreme right wing which was very active in California and elsewhere in the 1950s, aligned with the FBI and J. Edgar Hoover. There was a terrible fear and paranoia about Communism and Communist sympathizers and homosexuals, Marxists, Jews, that would breed a figure like the Sharpshooter, who basically is just up for hire, he's a patriot. I was thinking of people like Timothy McVeigh or Lee Harvey Oswald. But also, he may well be her imagination. She has this somewhat hallucinatory imagination near the end of her life. She thinks somebody is spying on her. Historically, in fact, there was surveillance on Marilyn Monroe. Her phone was tapped and it may have been the FBI because of her involvement with John F. Kennedy.

LG: Do you think the real Marilyn was murdered?

JCO: There are three general theories: one that she committed suicide deliberately; one that she took an overdose of barbiturates in a befuddled state, didn't know what she was doing, and died accidentally; or that she was murdered by the FBI or the Secret Service, maybe the Kennedys, maybe J. Edgar Hoover.

LG: You combined all three in your novel.

JCO: I did, that's what I wanted to do, to make it like a poem or a dream sequence in a movie, where people if they thought about it could have different interpretations.

LG: What kind of life and career might she have had had she lived?

JCO: If she stayed in New York and worked in the theater she could still be acting, playing older roles in Chekhov, Ibsen. She didn't try hard enough with that side of her career.

LG: Do you feel you've given her back her humanity?

JCO: That's what I hope, her inner poetic self that has been lost. The spiritual self that we all have.

LG: What actress today might you compare with her?

JCO: People say Madonna or Julia Roberts, but they're nowhere near her. Madonna seems very shallow and two-dimensional.

LG: Do you think *Blonde* might be your most widely read book?

JCO: I don't know, but if so, it's because of Marilyn Monroe.

LG: Final question: Was Marilyn truly the creation of her makeup artist?

JCO: No, she had to have the face; otherwise we'd all look like Marilyn.

The New Monroe Doctrine

Aida Edemariam

Originally appeared in *The Guardian* (U.K.), 9 April 2004. Reprinted by permission.

When, five or six years ago, Joyce Carol Oates came to write *Blonde*, a 939-page re-imagining of the life of Marilyn Monroe, the trigger was not any particular interest in Monroe—"whom I scarcely knew, and didn't much admire because I didn't know"—but a photograph of Monroe taken when she was 17 and called Norma Jean Baker. "And she looks nothing like Marilyn Monroe. She looks like girls I went to high school with, or grade school. She reminded me in her wistful way of my own mother." Through Norma Jeane, as her name is spelled in *Blonde*, Oates could attempt to understand the world her much-loved parents came from ("so impoverished, and desperate")—but she had also found a story that contained, to a mythic degree, the preoccupations she has returned to throughout her career: the power and vulnerability of adolescent girls; the damned-if-you-do damned-if-you-don't trap of femininity, of beauty; the political theatre—the second world war, McCarthyism, JFK; the daydream/nightmare of 20th-century America, and above all "class struggle. I'm always writing in some way about class struggle. It's a subject that many American writers don't write about because they're so uncomfortable."

Oates is now herself one of the comfortable. She teaches at Princeton, and lives, with her husband Raymond Smith, in an affluent suburb of that New Jersey town, in a light-filled structure of wood and glass set among mature trees. The living-room walls are covered in art. On the occasional tables there is more art: three glass boxes filled with found objects—*Prizes I Won at Coney Island*, Oates's favorite; *Mirror, Mirror* (a confection spun from shards of glass); and *Marilyn and a Few Others*, inspired by *Blonde*—by Oates's friend, the New York socialite and heiress Gloria Vanderbilt. Like Monroe, Oates moves among household names.

She refuses to say which American writers she admires because, as she says in her nasal, unhurried voice, "these people are my friends, and I can't really name 12 friends."

And if Monroe (as opposed to Norma Jeane) was larger than life, so too is Oates the writer: however much she wishes it otherwise—she is distinctly sharp with those who broach the subject—it's difficult to avoid commenting on how much Oates there is. Nearly every review of an Oates book, it seems, begins with a list, which, from this autumn, is: 42 novels (nine under the pseudonym "Rosamond Smith," one by "Lauren Kelly"); five novellas; 19 short-story collections; eight books of poetry; seven volumes of plays; nine of essays; two books for young adults; and two books for children—94 in total, not counting the volumes she has edited; the book reviews and magazine pieces; the rumored stacks of unpublished manuscripts at her publishers' and in bottom drawers; or the dozen practice novels she wrote before she was 18.

She reads on a similar scale: her conversation ranges from Trollope to Dickinson, from "my friend Norman Mailer" to Hilary Mantel, from Poe to James (Henry and William) and back, again and again, to Lewis Carroll. Ask about how she writes, and she compares her method with D. H. Lawrence (forward-plunging, intuitive) and James Joyce (schematic, highly controlled, highly edited)—she believes she employs the latter, though others don't necessarily agree. "She writes an onrushing kind of prose crackling with emotional tumult," says the *New Yorker's* poetry editor Alice Quinn, who has published some of Oates's verse; she attempted to excerpt *Blonde* but it proved difficult to corral. "It has a mimetic quality, where the prose is mirroring the onrush of feeling."

Oates's critical reception has always lurched between the glowing and the virulent. For every critic or peer who argues that she ranks among the most important authors of 20th-century America, there's a Michiko Kakutani (who, as chief critic for the *New York Times* takes a position of serial disappointment); or a James Wolcott (she "slop[s] words across a page like a washerwoman flinging soiled water across the cobblestones"); or, occasionally, a Truman Capote: "To me, she's the most loathsome creature in America. She's a joke monster who ought to be beheaded in a public auditorium."

The latter two suffer, as reactions to Oates often do, from entangling the quality of her work with resentment of her productivity and a certain kind of misogyny. "I think it's less of an accusatory phenomenon if the writer is a man," says Oates, wearily. And she has had to pay no obvious price, adds her friend, critic Elaine Showalter. "She's not an alcoholic, not a drug addict, not crazy, she has no broken marriages—it's a visceral superstition, that to get away with this she must have a pact with the devil."

"We have a bond in that we've come out of similar backgrounds, and I too am accused of writing too much," says John Updike, who has corresponded with Oates for many years, "but if you approach the writing business seriously and try to set it up like an orderly activity, as opposed to devoting your energy to the pursuit of the good life and happiness and drugs and drink and celebrity, you write an alarming amount over the course of a lifetime. We're blue-collar writers." "I don't think I'm fanatic or obsessive about working," she answers, testily, when I ask if she's done any writing that morning. This depends on your definition of obsessive. "Wherever she is, she's writing," says Daniel Halpern, her editor at Ecco and a friend for 30 years. "In cars, in airports, on planes, if she's at a party and no one's talking to her she's writing. She's completely focused and makes use of every moment."

In a recent, and, according to Oates, perceptive *New York Review of Books* essay, Caroline Fraser argues that "Oates's primary subject is victimhood, and her work features a kind of Grand Guignol of every imaginable form of physical, psychological, and sexual violence: rape, incest, murder, molestation, cannibalism, torture, bestiality . . . no American writer has devoted herself with more disquieting intensity to the experience and consequences of being victimized, a devotion that seems, strangely, to have inspired a kind of reactionary violence all its own." (In turn, she has an unfortunate habit of replying robustly to negative reviews.)

"I think serious art is transgressive, and that if you upset people, they're likely to wish to punish you," says Oates, who appears to find such punishment nourishing: in an essay collected in *The Faith of a Writer: Life, Craft, Art* (2003) she writes, "I have to concede: the more we are hurt, the more we seek solace in the imagination. Ironically . . . the more imaginative work we create in this solitude, and publish, the more likely we are to be hurt by critical and public reaction to it; and so, again, we retreat into the imagination—assuring that more hurt will ensue. A bizarre cycle. Yet it makes a kind of sense." But beyond all the essentially extratextual responses is a legitimate unease about the nature of her vast achievement. "As she herself has said," says Updike, "she's a somewhat isolated figure, there's nobody really like her, not only in terms of the productivity and the versatility, but in terms of a certain Dreiserian earnestness." Furthermore, "the writers we tend to universally admire, like Beckett, or Kafka, or T. S. Eliot, are not very prolific. The small choice body of work is what we like and instead we get Joyce Carol Oates's Victorian productivity, without the Victorian audience. She is, in a way, out of her time."

And while he admires her project, her whole approach, "you don't very often, as you do in so many less productive writers, encounter a gem. There are very few stories or moments that couldn't be any better put. There's a slight hastiness to her prose, which prevents her perhaps from giving the kind of delight that some writers do."

Because of the violence and reach of her work, says novelist Russell Banks, who also taught at Princeton, "I expected to meet a formidable, large personality, so I was surprised, because she seemed so frail and vulnerable." Margaret Drabble, who became a friend when Oates and her husband went to London for a sabbatical year in 1971, remembers her being "extremely elegant in an extremely pale way, with very red lips—very Gothic, which was not at all the fashion. I was impressed that such a frail-looking person should have produced such iron work." Oates is tall, and strikingly pale. In her physical presence, as in her prose, "Joyce is not like other people," says former student Jonathan Safran Foer, who acknowledges that he would not have begun his Guardian First Book award-winning novel, *Everything Is Illuminated*, would not have aspired to write, without her encouragement; she read drafts every two weeks until it was finished. "She's ghostly, ethereal. It's almost like she doesn't touch surfaces." She can almost disappear in front of company, and yet, says Halpern, "put her in front of 2,000 people and she is hysterical. She's one of the best stand-up speakers among writers I've heard."

Oates believes, emphatically, "that our best selves, our most complex selves, are not our social selves. I consider myself a transparent personality." When we meet she's reading Colm Toibin's *The Master*, and "what I like about it is that the Henry James he is creating is like a ghost—he doesn't say much. It's a novel that's almost about nothing—but it's a novel that I can identify with. I feel that the writer is like an observer at the margin. So when I write about characters who seem to have my background, they're nothing like me in terms of personality."

Oates grew up in Millersport, New York, which "was hardly a community, it was a farm and another farm, and a creek." In "They All Just Went Away" (1995), collected in the *Best American Essays of the Century* (2000, edited by Oates and Robert Atwan), she writes that "ours was a happy, close-knit and unextraordinary family for our time, place, and economic status"—an experience unlike that of her parents. Her father, Frederic Oates, grew up fatherless, and left school for work as a sign painter very young, and then did various manufacturing jobs; after a lifetime of labor he went to university in the late 1980s. Joyce's mother Carolina was of Hungarian descent, one of nine children; when her father was beaten to death in a tavern brawl, her mother could not cope, and though Joyce did not discover this until middle age, "my mother was given away, she never knew her father. And Marilyn Monroe had a mother who didn't love her—couldn't love her, basically, because of her mental imbalance, and she never knew her father."

It's a typical Oates progression, and has its roots in a proper respect for the power of chance. She began her education in the same one-room schoolhouse as her mother, but changes in population meant she was bussed to a better city school; when the district changed again, she went to an even better school in a suburb of Buffalo, which was sending students to Harvard,

Princeton, Yale—she won a scholarship to Syracuse. These coincidences meant she was the first person in her family to finish high school, let alone university. "If I hadn't been able to go to high school, I basically wouldn't have anything—I wouldn't be here. It's a bittersweet thing, because you want to feel pride in what you've done, but when you come from that kind of background you remember when you were kids, and you don't feel that you're that different." She has a brother, Fred Jr., who is five years younger, and on Joyce's 18th birthday, a sister was born, Lynn Ann, who is severely autistic. "She's never uttered one word—she can't speak. It's very extreme, the brain is probably really damaged—so that could have been me, very easily. She and I look like each other. I think much of my life is a consequence of accident and luck."

It isn't far-fetched to say that a large amount of Oates's fiction can be seen as explorations into what might have been; generally, what could have gone wrong. (Though chance itself doesn't translate into fiction "because it doesn't make for a coherent narrative. It doesn't seem to mean anything.") So in Monroe's case, for example, genetic luck and hard work and talent played their part—only to be scuppered by neediness. When Oates was writing *Blonde*, "the most difficult novel for me to write," she told Greg Johnson, her biographer, that she pinned some invented words of Norma Jeane's by her desk: "I guess I never believed that I deserved to live. The way other people do. I needed to justify my life. How many of us, I wonder, feel exactly the same way!"

In "They All Just Went Away," she evokes the Hopperesque upstate New York landscape that formed her and is a constant in her work: "A gone-to-seed landscape had an authority that seemed to me incontestable: the powerful authority of silence in houses from which the human voice had vanished." She would explore these houses, staring in distaste at "filthy mattresses streaked with yellow and rust-colored stains . . . The most terrible punishment, I thought, would be to lie down on such a mattress." It is no surprise, then, that in the title story of *Haunted: Tales of the Grotesque* (1994), a girl is forced on to the mattress by a ghost who subjects her to unspoken things; the biographical nugget is revisited but shot through with darkness, supernatural dread.

Even before she could read she was making little books of pictures, and when her grandmother gave her a copy of *Alice's Adventures in Wonderland* she found in fiction both a salvation and, in the fierce young girl unfazed by monsters and the threatening mutability of dreams, a way of going forth into the world. For if she was lucky in some ways, in others she was not: the violence of her books is not so far from the reality she knew. The farm boys, trained to hunt animals, were accomplished bullies, and in her journal, Johnson writes, she recalls witnessing "so many brutal, meaningless acts . . . incredible cruelty, profanity, obscenity . . . even (it was bragged) incest between a boy of about 13 and his six-year-old sister."

Oates herself was semi-molested, an experience she revisits in her short story "The Molesters," for example, or in the elliptically autobiographical *Marya: A Life* (1986). Johnson makes the case for such writing as self-therapy, and she did finally come to see, as she puts it in a 1999 essay, "Running and Writing" (she is a keen runner), "that such abuse is generic, not personal . . . it allows us insight into the experiences of others, a sense of what a more enduring panic, entrapment, suffering, and despair must be truly like."

Oates is "unique in American literature in her compassion and understanding of adolescent girls," says Banks. "She has made them memorable—humanized and dignified them." She mines a rich vein of intense, fraught adolescence; its embattled, brief innocence and power, often combined with the particular difficulties of being clever in a rural area, or the self-protective watchfulness of a young woman who finds herself among those of a different class. "I connect so much to the young person," she says; and credits some of her characteristically mesmeric momentum—in *Wonderland*, for example, or *Because It Is Bitter*—to writing about "a young person evolving and having spiritual and intellectual and emotional discoveries."

She has often said that her first literary heroes were men—Faulkner, Carroll, Poe, Dostoyevsky, Lawrence; she writes well about men, and often from a male point of view; she seems especially fascinated by inarticulate male aggression and drive, shame and honor, not infrequently as they affect issues of race (some of her best writing, says Quinn, is about interracial love affairs); and she is a famously incongruous boxing fan. A common criticism is that women connected to these men are so often passive, suffering/accepting, but this is fairly consistent with the worldview of one who has asked: "Are there any adult women who have not been, in one way or another, sexually molested or threatened?" She has a tragic sense generally, says Showalter, but an especially tragic sense of femininity—"She thinks that women are often mistreated for being feminine, beautiful, or not beautiful enough"—and *Blonde*, of course, is "paradigmatic." In a story from 1970, "Unmailed, Unwritten Letters," Oates writes: "Women who are loved are in perpetual motion, dancing. We dance and men follow to the brink of madness and death, but what of us, the dancers?"

After Syracuse University, where she blossomed (though she also suffered a breakdown due to overwork, and discovered she had a heart condition), Oates studied for an M.A. at the University of Wisconsin, and there she met her husband, Ray. She did not enjoy the M.A., but Ray, a Ph.D. candidate who would become a professor of 18th-century literature, was her other great stroke of luck, "because my marriage is really a marriage of like minds—both my husband and I are so interested in literature and we read the same books; he'll be reading a book and then I'll read it—we trade and we talk about our reading at meal times." They run the Ontario Review Press, which publishes books, including some of Oates's, and a literary magazine. "We design covers for the books, we design the magazine—so it's a very collaborative and imaginative marriage, and that isn't typical of many marriages." And also, importantly, he is not in competition with her. Oates is like Simone de Beauvoir, says Showalter, "but there's no Jean-Paul Sartre, no egomaniacal little guy she's going to sacrifice herself for." They have never had children.

Smith's first teaching job was in Beaumont, Texas; they lasted a year, then, in 1962, moved to Detroit, where they both taught. Oates has done so ever since: her classes in creative writing and English literature keep her in touch with young people, and with the world in general; they also allow her to do "very close readings of Henry James or Faulkner or Hemingway, in a way that you never do with your friends." Prompted partly by the Vietnam war, partly by the 1967 Detroit race riots, but mainly by a joint job offer, they crossed Lake Ontario to the University of Windsor, in 1968; 10 years later they moved to Princeton.

Now that Oates has been publishing for 45 years, an arc is evident. The first phase, realist, traditional, Dreiserian, draws heavily on her rural youth, and on the grit and volatility of Detroit. The novel that made her famous, earning a National Book Award and putting her on the cover of *Newsweek*, was *them* (1969), a dystopian saga of a poor white Detroit family hurtling towards the conflagration of the race riots: it prompted Harold Bloom to say: "What I myself find most moving in Oates is her immense empathy with the insulted and injured, her deep identification with the American lower classes. She is not a political novelist, not a social revolutionary in any merely overt way, and yet she is our true proletarian novelist."

More successful, as a novel, is *Wonderland* (1971), a meditation on the "phantasmagoria of personality," which follows Jesse from rural New York State (his father, unmanned by the depression, kills the rest of the family in a murder-suicide), to a foster family, to success as a neurosurgeon: it was written, and reads, breathlessly, exhaustingly. "Like virtually all my novels," wrote Oates in an afterword added 20 years later, "*Wonderland* is political in genesis"; set against Vietnam and the assassination of JFK, "*Wonderland*, as a title, refers to both America, as a region of wonders, and the human brain, as a region of wonders. And 'wonders' can be both dream and nightmare."

One of the nightmares, recounted with vivid, stylized disgust, is Jesse's horrifically fat foster family; obesity is, for Oates, a "spiritual obscenity," and food, generally, a difficult area. In the essay "Food Mysteries" she describes the appeal of anorexia: "Without appetite, steadily losing weight and noting with grim pleasure how readily flesh melts from your bones, you experience the anorexic's fatally sweet revelation: *I* am not *this*, after all." Her literary voraciousness (you just mention a thing, says Showalter, and "Joyce will have the novel by next week") has got her into trouble: Johnson details how colleagues at the University of Windsor, for example, were unimpressed to find their private lives in stories. Gene McNamara, the possible model for a story about an adulterer whose lover's husband murders her, is tight-lipped about whether she wrote about him, but clear about how it made people feel: "Bitter." The collection, appropriately, was called *The Hungry Ghosts*. Anorexia is essentially about control; there is often the sense, in her fiction, that sanity is only just maintained, that superhuman effort is required to hold things together, or they will—in a recurring phrase—fly apart like "shattering glass." "I think I feel that less personally myself," Oates says now, "but I feel there's a certain madness in America, a frenzy, an intoxication, and we are, collectively, a very paranoid people who are forever projecting onto others our own ideas of who they are, like Bush—we're good people and they're evil people—it's so simple-minded."

In her second phase, most of the early 80s, she moved into other worlds, with five hugely complex, postmodernist gothic novels, her stated ambition to capture "America as viewed through the prismatic lens of its most popular genres." For the ever-present threat of the dissolution of self, says Oates, is also a "gothic theme, central in Poe, H. P. Lovecraft, the great gothic writers." In the introduction to her selection of major works of Lovecraft (Ecco, 1998), she calls the gothic tale "a form of psychic autobiography," and says now that "It seems to me that the gothic ties in with surrealism, and surrealism actually ties in with fairy tales, and my earliest love, *Alice*. It's not that much of a stretch to go from the Wonderland world, the looking-glass world, to Lovecraft—the monsters, and shifting shapes. I don't think of gothic as being that different from the writing of Kafka—it's psychologically surreal writing—I feel very much at home with that, because I think our minds are like that."

Bellefleur (1980) was her first bestseller, but the gothic novels are a very specific taste, and the rest did not do well. She returned to realism and as well as seizing upon and transmogrifying a moment in her own history, she has been writing more fiction based on stories in the public domain, such as *Black Water* (1992, based on Chappaquiddick); Zombie (1995, written from the point of view of a Jeffrey Dahmer-like serial killer), and, of course, *Blonde*. *Black Water* was nominated for a Pulitzer, as was *What I*

Lived For (1994); *We Were the Mulvaneys* (1996) was an Oprah choice. Short stories appear regularly, and although they receive less attention, many feel they are what will last. Increasingly, she is also writing plays: by 1995 there had been 60 productions in America, though they are not all enthusiastically received: the critic Vincent Canby has commented on her limited engagement with contemporary culture.

This year she publishes two novels, *The Tattooed Girl*, which tackles anti-semitism, and *The Falls*, a tragic love story set at Niagara Falls; another, *Blood at the Root*, about race relations in the aftermath of Watergate, is written. In a 1983 essay, "Notes on Failure," Oates offers an explanation, of sorts. "Success is distant and illusory, failure one's loyal companion, one's stimulus for imagining that the next book will be better, for otherwise, why write? The impulse can be made to sound theoretical, and even philosophical, but it is . . . as physical as our blood and marrow. 'This insatiable desire to write something before I die, this ravaging sense of the shortness and feverishness of life, make me cling . . . to my one anchor'—so Virginia Woolf, in her diary, speaks for us all."

Oates's Young Adult Novels

Various Online Interviewers

The following are excerpts from several online interviews. Reprinted by permission of Joyce Carol Oates.

Interviewer: What prompted you to start writing specifically for young adults?

Joyce Carol Oates: I was invited by Tara Weikum, who's an editor now at Harper Collins Children's Books, to assemble a collection of short stories about adolescents, because she had noticed I'd written quite a few. The collection is *Small Avalanches* (2003).

I've always written about adolescent girls. I think I just have a gravitational pull in that direction, and yet I've never written specifically for that audience. So, it was just a matter of rethinking how a story might be presented in a somewhat less complex way.

Then I wrote a young adult novel, which was just the next step. I always wanted to write about this Ugly Girl type who is a little bit like myself, I guess —she played basketball in high school and so forth. Basically it grew out of that and became *Big Mouth & Ugly Girl*. My writing generally begins with characters.

Now with *Freaky Green Eyes*, I remember very clearly that my husband and I were walking somewhere and we saw these pens in somebody's yard with animals inside. They didn't have any space really to turn around in. It just came over me: I would like to run in there and liberate all those animals. That was actually the thematic origin of Freaky as a character. Who would go in and let those animals out? Well, it wouldn't be me, Joyce Carol Oates, I'm a professor at Princeton. But who would? Well this girl Franky, who's 15, who is impulsive and has a sense of ethics.

Adults can live with compromises in a way that children and adolescents find grating. I'm just very drawn to the adolescent personality.

I: Is it coincidental that both *Big Mouth & Ugly Girl* [which revolves around a boy who jokes about a bomb threat and the girl who defends him] and *Freaky Green Eyes* are so topical?

JCO: Well, I'm not sure that ultimately they're that topical, *Big Mouth & Ugly Girl* sort of turns on somebody having a big mouth and saying things he doesn't mean in order to be funny to his friends. I wanted to focus on that phenomenon. The subject of a bomb threat or a situation like Columbine in a way is not necessary. He could have said something else that would get him in trouble at school.

Freaky Green Eyes obviously turns upon something like the O. J. Simpson case without the whole racial angle. Here I'm focusing on how a person who is a celebrity is so admired that he casts a kind of aura, that people stare at the aura, and they don't really want to see that the person himself is somewhat stunted, in fact, morally, that he's immature. To me, it's more like an archetype or an idea.

I: What are you hoping that readers will take away from Franky's story?

JCO: I would think that a girl reading the novel might feel that she could aspire to an ethical standard that was higher than just her own family's, that she doesn't have to protect a parent who may be a lawbreaker or a murderer just because this person is her father—that she can have a sense of the moral self within.

I: Are you working on another novel for young adults?

JCO: I just finished a book called *Sexy*. It's about a boy who's 16, and he is actually very shy; but he's very attractive. And unfortunately he's attractive to both girls and men. He is not himself gay, but he's attractive to older men, and so this is very upsetting to him and causes anxiety. It's a subject I've never really thought about until I was writing about it—the sexuality of a boy. There's so much crude humor about it that arises, I suppose, from anxiety.

I: Do you think you will continue writing for this age group?

JCO: I probably will, but I alternate different genres. If I do a young adult novel, the next thing would be a short story or an adult novel, or an essay or a play. It's probably like a cook, a chef who makes a certain meal and really puts all he has into it, then he won't make that meal again for a long time.

You put all that you have at one time into something and hope it's good enough, and then you have to release it. I definitely feel a little sad when I finish these young adult novels, because the kids are so much fun. I like the voice, and I feel a loss.

I: Not many young adults address school violence. Why?

JCO: I'm surprised. Maybe publishers are a little wary about getting into it. There isn't any school violence in *Big Mouth & Ugly Girl*—it's basically just the threat, the specter of it. The subject will be addressed; it just takes some time. It's like writing about September 11. Unless you're going to write about it in a really profound and significant way, you don't want to write something light. I know in my adult fiction, except for one very short piece I did for the London *Observer*, 9-11 is really non-incorporated in my writing. It's too important to just be in the background, and yet, unless you're going to write a whole piece about it, it can't be in the foreground either. You can't trivialize something like that.

I: A lot of young adult authors try to teach teens some kind of lesson. Did you feel compelled to do this in *Big Mouth & Ugly Girl*?

JCO: Not really. There's always a moral in my writing, although it's not necessarily explicit. In this little novel, these young people are made to realize certain flaws in their personalities and characters, which we all can learn. What's so wonderful about adolescents is that they change so rapidly. When you're forty or fifty or sixty years old, you just don't know how to change that well.

I: How is writing for young adults different from writing for adults?

JCO: It allows me to move swiftly without the layers of description and expository background that are more customary for adult fiction. Basically, it's just stripped-down adult fiction with more dialogue and less description. In adult fiction you do things with language—for example, you might repeat certain adjectives for atmospheric effect. In young adult fiction, that isn't done, and the chapters tend to be shorter. So I got the idea to write from one point of view and then another point of view, and that makes it move even faster.

I: What is it about adolescent characters that you find compelling?

JCO: I think many women still identify with adolescent selves, a feeling of uncertainty and a kind of awkwardness physically and not knowing your place in the world. I think adolescents are very sensitive about things that adults have learned to accept with more composure. I guess I just feel sympathetic with that age group. I feel at ease with them.

I: What kind of stories are teens looking for in their literature?

JCO: I think that they're looking for stories about their own lives—to get help with their own lives, ways to behave and analyze emotional situations. I think it's less character-driven, but they obviously would like to identify with some characters. It's more situational.

I: *Big Mouth & Ugly Girl* spans only about four months, but the characters grow up quite a bit.

JCO: Which is so typical. I've seen changes in my students, who are between the ages of eighteen and twenty-one, at Princeton. It's very interesting. They have such passionate friendships—it's so touching. And of course their hearts are broken so easily. I really identify with that. And then the young man, I should call him a boy—he's not a young man, he's a boy—he says things to be funny, he says the wrong thing, and he gets himself into trouble. And we've all had the temptation to say things, but when you're older, you bite your tongue, you learn to be more prudent.

I: He didn't even remember all that he said when he was joking about shooting people.

JCO: And you wouldn't, either. It's so sad, because this is going on in high schools. People are getting into trouble for what would possibly just be something in bad taste, making a joke about something that isn't funny.

I: You have written about many teenagers and tough girls over the years. Very few have survived their coming of age and outsider status with such success and optimism as Ursula Riggs and Matt Donaghy in *Big Mouth & Ugly Girl*. Did you resist a more catastrophic or twisted end for any of the characters because this was a book for young adults?

JCO: Since I have worked with "young adults" for many years as a professor, and have often visited prep schools and high schools,

I'm vividly aware of how individuals can change, sometimes virtually overnight, and certainly within a semester. It isn't a characteristic of older people, but it is definitely a characteristic of adolescents. Therefore, to me, "young adult" fiction is written in a spirit of more optimism about the ability to change, to behave in ways strategic for survival and success. I saw such behavior in a number of my contemporaries and, I suppose, to some degree in myself. Fiction for adults is likely to be more charged with irony, skepticism, and a tragic sense of life and history.

I: Do you sense a loss of sanguinity and enthusiasm among the current adolescents?

JCO: No, I don't really. I don't believe that adolescence is susceptible to the sort of long-range enervation one might experience among adults. My Princeton students are very intelligent, very hard working, and often very ambitious, and their doubts about life simply don't lodge as deeply as the doubts of their older contemporaries.

Why? I think the answer is simply nature; our species is bred to be optimistic, to live in the future, to plan ahead, to yearn for ideals. Even at a time when public ideals have conspicuously corroded, you will find highly idealistic young people. Irony, the predominant mode of postmodernist fiction, doesn't come naturally to young adults.

I: Do they need more happy endings?

JCO: I don't think adolescents need "happy endings" as such. I think that popular culture provides for them possible ways of living. Some works of art are cautionary tales: warnings that, if you behave in this way, if you make certain choices, you may invite disaster. Shakespeare's great tragedies are cautionary tales: behave like Macbeth, you will invite Macbeth's fate. On another level, young adult fiction provides its readers with models for behavior, both exemplary and unwise. My adolescent characters —who number quite a few—are always meant to be both individuals and representative. In my adult writing, I have numerous portraits of adolescents, an age group with which I feel enormous sympathy and identity.

I: You have captured the rhythm and content of teenage con-versations completely. Were there special considerations when creating teen characters? Was it a challenge to create and maintain tension and emotion without many of the usual teen staples?

JCO: I wasn't aware of the teen staples/stereotypes, though now that you mention them, I suppose I am. My experience with young adults has been more or less direct, and my sense of their ways of speaking and behaving is taken more from life than from popular culture. (One thing that is very difficult to communicate in prose is the predilection for humor among young people. This is an enormously funny age group. Whimsical, goofy, imaginative, insightful—a daunting task for a writer, though it's ideal material for video.)

I think of adults as fairly well meaning when confronted by the complexity of their adolescent children's dramas. I do think that, in the sometimes claustrophobic world of adolescents, there are those who bully and prey upon others, and that their power over their peers is remarkable, a phenomenon of immaturity and the confined society of high school. When we're more adult, we can escape such people relatively easily. (Unless they are family members.) Therefore, I believe that there are legitimate "villainous" individuals in the lives of some adolescents, who probably don't seem nearly so difficult or dangerous, or possessed of such outsized power by adults, who tend often to myopia, seeing only what they want to see and underestimating their children's vulnerability vis-à-vis other children.

I: Ursula Riggs is a complicated and admirable character with a strict, albeit idiosyncratic, code of ethics. Was her threat of blackmail by "speaking to Dad" (the employer of Trevor's dad) about Trevor's malevolence, a violation of her principles? Did the end justify the means?

JCO: Ursula meant to help her friends in ways available to her, and her loyalty to Matt would override her sense of fair play with Trevor. But I did mean to indicate a certain playfulness in their behavior. Trevor objects, "That's like something little kids would do," and Ursula responds, "We are little kids" (meaning that they are not fully mature adults, after all). Ursula would not in any case have said anything other than the truth in speaking to her father about Trevor's behavior.

I: Did introducing e-mailed text (including deleted passages) allow for greater options to examine Matt's inner life? Are young people, reared on e-mail, showing more fluency as writers?

JCO: E-mail is an extraordinary invention of our time. Yes, I think it makes for greater fluency and ease of expression. I'm not sure that it will make much difference in terms of literary writing, though it may. Writing per se isn't the issue, for young people are generally quite fluent, but selecting the stronger aspects of writing, and self-editing. Talking is very different from writing since it has no form.

I: Are there any books for young adults that you have particularly enjoyed?

JCO: When I was of junior high school age, I read avidly, continuously. I read everything I could get my hands on in the library, that was accessible to me. So answering this question is virtually impossible. The single book that shaped my childhood imaginings and perhaps my subsequent life as a writer was Lewis Carroll's *Alice in Wonderland* and *Alice Through the Looking Glass*, which is presumably for children, not young adults.

Fictions of the New Millennium:
An Interview with Joyce Carol Oates

Greg Johnson

Excerpts of this interview originally appeared in *Prairie Schooner* (Fall 2001) and in *Michigan Quarterly Review* (Spring 2006). Reprinted by permission.

Since the year 2000, the fiction of Joyce Carol Oates has been as varied, as ambitious, and as abundant as ever. In the six-year period between January of 2000 and December of 2005, Oates published an astonishing nineteen books, and four more are scheduled for 2006 publication. Her novels of this period are *Blonde* (2000), *Middle Age: A Romance* (2001), *I'll Take You There* (2002), *The Tattooed Girl* (2003), *The Falls* (2004), and *Missing Mom* (2005). During these same years she published two novellas, *Beasts* (2002) and *Rape: A Love Story* (2003); two story collections, *Faithless: Tales of Transgression* (2001) and *I Am No One You Know* (2004); one novel under the pseudonym Rosamond Smith, *The Barrens* (2001); two novels under the pseudonym Lauren Kelly, *Take Me, Take Me With You* (2004) and *The Stolen Heart* (2005); four books for young adults, the novels *Big Mouth & Ugly Girl* (2002), *Freaky Green Eyes* (2003), and *Sexy* (2005), and the story collection *Small Avalanches* (2003); a children's book, *Where Is Little Reynard?* (2003); and a collection of essays, *Uncensored: Views and (Re)views* (2005). She also produced revised versions, for Modern Library editions, of her early novels *A Garden of Earthly Delights* (1967) and *them* (1969). And this list does not take into account the dozens of plays, short stories, poems, essays, and book reviews published during this period; her work as an editor for the small press she and her husband, Raymond J. Smith, founded in 1974, Ontario Review Press, and their literary magazine *Ontario Review*; her full-time teaching at Princeton University, where she is the Roger S. Berlind Distinguished Professor of Humanities; and the dozens of talks, lectures and readings she gives each year around the country and internationally.

At 67, Oates clearly remains a major force in American writing. Nonetheless she recently found time for an interview, conducted at various times between 2001 and 2006 from her home in Princeton, New Jersey.

Greg Johnson: What was the genesis of *Blonde*? What prompted you to choose Marilyn Monroe as the focus of a novel?

Joyce Carol Oates: Some years ago I happened to see a photograph of the 17-year-old Norma Jeane Baker. With her longish dark curly hair, artificial flowers on her head, locket around her neck, she looked nothing like the iconic "Marilyn Monroe." I felt an immediate sense of something like recognition; this young, hopefully smiling girl, so very American, reminded me powerfully of girls of my childhood, some of them from broken homes. For days I felt an almost rapturous sense of excitement, that I might give life to this lost, lone girl, whom the iconic consumer-product "Marilyn Monroe" would soon overwhelm and obliterate. I saw her story as mythical, archetypal; it would end when she loses her baptismal name Norma Jeane, and takes on the studio name "Marilyn Monroe." She would also have to bleach her brown hair to platinum blonde, endure some facial surgery, and dress provocatively. I'd planned a 175-page novella, and the last line would have been "Marilyn Monroe." The mode of storytelling would have been fairy tale-like, as poetic as I could make appropriate.

GJ: Obviously, you've produced a long novel, not a novella. What happened?

JCO: In the writing, characteristically, the "novella" acquired a deeper, more urgent and epic life, and grew into a full-length novel. "What happened" is what usually happens in these cases. *Blonde* has several styles, but the predominant is that of psychological realism rather than the fairy tale/surreal mode. The novel is a posthumous narration by the subject.

After I abandoned the novella form, I created an "epic" form to accommodate the complexities of the life. It was my intention to create a female portrait as emblematic of her time and place as Emma Bovary was of hers. (Of course, Norma Jeane is actually more complex, and certainly more admirable, than Emma Bovary.)

GJ: What led you to choose this unusual point of view, a "posthumous narration" by Norma Jeane herself?

JCO: This is a difficult question to answer. The voice, point of view, ironic perspective, mythic distance: this curious distancing effect is my approximation of how an individual might feel dreaming back over his or her own life at the very conclusion of that life, on the brink of extinction even as, as in a fairy tale, the individual life enters an abstract, communal "posterity." Norma Jeane dies, and "Marilyn Monroe" the role, the concoction, the artifice, would seem to endure.

GJ: At over 700 printed pages, this is your longest novel but your original manuscript was even longer—1,400 typed pages. Why did you cut the novel so substantially?

JCO: At 1,400 pages, the novel had to be cut, and some sections, surgically removed from the manuscript, will be published independently. They are all part of Norma Jeane's living, organic life. To me, the language of Norma Jeane is somehow "real."

Still, a novel of such length is a problem. Rights have been sold, according to my agent, to "nearly all languages" except Japanese where, if the novel were to be translated it would grow again by between one-third and one-half in length. In German, for instance, it will be massive enough!

GJ: You wrote and extensively revised this huge novel in less than a year. It must have been an intense writing experience.

JCO: I think, looking back on the experience, that it is one I would not wish to relive. In psychoanalytic terms—though we can't of course "analyze" ourselves—I believe I was trying to give life to Norma Jeane Baker, and to keep her living, in a very obsessive way, because she came to represent certain "life-elements" in my own experience and, I hope, in the life of America. A young girl, born into poverty, cast off by her father and eventually by her mother, who, as in a fairy tale, becomes an iconic "Fair Princess" and is posthumously celebrated as "The Sex Symbol of the 20th Century," making millions of dollars for other people—it's just too sad, too ironic.

GJ: Could you describe your writing process as this novel evolved?

JCO: With a novel of such length, it was necessary to keep the narrative voice consistent and fluid. I was continually going back and rewriting, and when I entered the last phase of about 200 pages, I began simultaneously to rewrite the novel from the first page to about page 300, to assure this consistency of voice. (Though the voice changes, too, as Norma Jeane ages.) Actually, I recommend this technique for all novelists, even with shorter work. It's akin to aerating soil, if you're a gardener.

GJ: Since the 1960s, a number of well-known writers—Capote, Vidal, Mailer, DeLillo and others—have focused ambitious novels on famous, and sometimes infamous, historical figures. Do you consider *Blonde* as falling into this tradition of the "nonfiction novel"?

JCO: The line of descent, so to speak, may derive from John Dos Passos's *U.S.A.* with its lively, inventive portraits of "real people" mixed with fictional characters. Dos Passos's Henry Ford, for instance, is an obvious ancestor of E. L. Doctorow's emboldened portraits in *Ragtime*. Some of these are rather more playful/caricatured than serious portrayals of "real people."

So much of *Blonde* is obviously fiction, to call it "non-fiction" would be misleading. (I explain in my preface: if you want historical veracity, you must go to the biographies. Even while perhaps not 100% accurate, they are at least predicated upon literal truth, while the novel aspires to a spiritual/poetic truth.)

GJ: Were you concerned that the glare of Marilyn Monroe's celebrity and myth might divert attention from your artistic goals? What was the advantage to you, as a writer, of using the skeletal reality of her life, instead of creating a wholly fictional actress-character to dramatize the "spiritual/poetic truth" you sought?

JCO: I'd hoped to evoke a poetic, spiritual, "inner" truth by selecting incidents, images, representative figures from the life, and had absolutely no interest in a purely biographical or historic book. Pre-publication responses and interviews so far have indicated quite sympathetic and intelligent readings of the novel. Of course, there will be others, but angry or dismissive reviews can happen to us regardless of what we write, whether purely fiction or fiction based upon history. The writer may as well pursue his or her vision, and not be distracted by how others will respond in their myriad and unpredictable ways.

GJ: You did considerable research into Monroe's life and into the art of acting. Did you come to see parallels between acting and writing? Did you develop a sense of kinship with Monroe as you wrote the novel?

JCO: Not "considerable research" compared to my biographer/scholar friends. Rather, I created an outline or skeleton of the "life," collated with the "life of the time." (*Blonde* is also a political novel, in part. The rise of Red Scare paranoia, the betrayals and back-stabbings in Hollywood; the assumptions of what we might call Cold War theology: we are God's nation, the Soviet Union belongs to Satan.) All of my longer novels are political, but not obtrusively so, I hope.

Theater/acting fascinate, as a phenomenon of human experience. Why do we wish to "believe" the actor in performance, why are we moved to true emotions in a context which we know is artificial? Since 1990 I've been involved quite actively in theater, and have come to greatly admire both directors and actors. Norma Jeane seems to have been a naturally gifted actress because, perhaps, she so lacked an inner core of identity. "I guess I never believed that I deserved to live. The way other people do. I needed to justify my life." These were words of Norma Jeane's I affixed to the wall beside my desk. How many of us, I wonder, feel exactly the same way!

GJ: What concerns did you have in dealing with living people—for example, Monroe's third husband, the playwright Arthur Miller—in a fictional context? Did you contact or interview Miller, or anyone else who knew Monroe?

JCO: No, I didn't interview anyone about "Marilyn Monroe." It was not "Marilyn Monroe" about whom I wrote. Norma Jeane marries mythic individuals, not "historic" figures. Her husbands include the Ex-Athlete and the Playwright. (If I wanted to write about Joe DiMaggio and Arthur Miller, I would need to write about these complex men in a different mode. Though, in fact, the Playwright is presented from the inside, often. It's clear that I identify with the Playwright, and that he becomes, eventually, the voice of conscience in the latter part of the novel. But I certainly didn't read Arthur Miller's memoir or any interviews with him about "Monroe.")

GJ: Monroe's reputation as an actress remains controversial. What is your assessment of her achievement as an artist?

JCO: She was a naturally gifted, often uncanny actress. Her fellow actors began by condescending to her, but ended by feeling awe for her on-film presence; she "out-acted" most of them. In movies, as in art, it isn't what goes in, but what comes out, that matters. Your process of, for instance, acting, or writing, is not important; only what it leads you to matters. And the process, mysteriously, would seem to have little to do with that final product.

GJ: Did the writing of *Blonde* change your own view of Norma Jeane Baker?

JCO: Ultimately, I didn't think of Norma Jeane as an isolated, idiosyncratic individual signifying nothing but herself, a specimen without a species; I came to think of her as a universal figure. I certainly hope that my portrait of her transcends sex and gender, and that male readers can identify as readily with her as female readers. But I don't recommend, for anyone, writing a psychologically realistic novel about any "historic" individual who is said to have committed suicide. It's just too . . . painful.

GJ: You've published over 700 short stories in your career, yet I'm impressed by how each collection is organized carefully around a central theme. Your most recent volume, *I Am No One You Know*, explores (as its title suggests) the theme of self-identity and the identity of a mysterious "other"—as in, for example, the college teacher's dramatic confrontation with a student who is a former death row inmate in "The Instructor"; a young girl's memories of a sexually threatening uncle in "Upholstery"; two college students' discovery that they are in a bookstore at the same time as Marilyn Monroe in "Three Girls." Do you consciously write a batch of stories focused on a theme in this way, to collect them together, or do you write each story independently and then go back and discover the unifying theme? And please say anything else about the process of selecting and ordering a story collection.

JCO: My story collections are always organized around themes, and usually presented in three sections. Generally, the stories move from what might be called realism to "surrealism"; there's a bending of perceived reality toward the "meaningful distortion" of the unconscious. This isn't so much the case in *I Am No One You Know* which is more or less realism throughout, though ending with "The Mutants" which seems to peer into the future, but it's always the case with its predecessors *Faithless* and *Will You Always Love Me?* and especially *The Collector of Hearts* (in which the fifth, final section is a single story that adumbrates the "journey" of the writer who is, or has been, writing *The Collector of Hearts* and other, preceding books). *Heat,* which has four sections, begins in realism and bends into the surreal in the final section, and even into the dystopian future in "Family" (which is one of my favorite stories of my own, though seemingly unknown to anyone else!). The sections within each collection tend to be tonally and geographically and "class"-related (i.e., social class), and with the "rural" stories in the second position. The only reviewer/critic who ever seems to have noticed these divisions was Anatole Broyard (speaking of *Last Days* in which the divisions are meant to be dramatic). Within the sections, the stories are arranged in what I think of as "rhythmic modes"— longer stories bracketed by shorter. There are some "miniature narratives" among the stories, though not often. (I love the miniature narrative mode—I think the term is my invention— which is something like a prose poem overlaid with embryonic plots, or hints of plots, or fossil-like remains or glimmers of plots, as in, for instance, "Area Man Found Crucified" and "The Wig" in *Where Is Here?* and "Two Doors" in *The Assignation.* . . .)

I don't consciously write stories in relationship to one another unless I am writing a novel-in-stories (like *Marya: A Life*), but naturally there are predominant themes, recurring images, and the like. Writers, like most artists, are very likely in the grip of powerful unconscious processes, that are recurring, obsessive, thrilling and filled with dread simultaneously, so that simply to write (to paint, like Van Gogh in his final fevered days) will be to express linked material, with no deliberate effort. Of a number of stories written in a calendar year, some will be meritorious enough to warrant being brought together into hardcover, and some will not. I've never been able to collect several stories of mine that appeared years ago in the *O. Henry Awards* and the *Best American Short Stories* for one or another of these reasons, unfortunately.

GJ: Also in the newest collection, "The Mutants" deals with the events of 9/11. Lately a number of novels and stories have taken up this subject, with perhaps mixed results. Do you anticipate writing more specifically 9/11 fiction or, in some sense, is your post-9/11 work influenced by its events in any kind of ongoing way?

JCO: I don't anticipate writing anything specifically related to 9/11, but of course I can't predict what I might do. (I realize that, over the years, I've told you that I have decided not to do something, like never again to review, but then, a few months later, I've changed my mind. I suppose that's what a mind is for, perhaps a woman's mind: to be changed.)

GJ: You've often been drawn to the novella form, most recently in *Rape: A Love Story*. Other than the obvious one of length, are there particular qualities of the novella that make this form attractive to you?

JCO: In the afterword for *I Lock My Door Upon Myself*, I've said a few things about the "blessed novella" (James's famous definition). Of the literary prose forms, the novella is the most difficult, at least for me. I seem to have an imagination bent upon enhancing, "developing," investigating alternate points of view, not ideal for novellas which should move through choppy water like sailboats, not ships or barges. The novella requires a sleight-of-hand technique, to suggest more than one is going to spell out clearly, while the novel is such a large, loose form, it can accommodate any number of approaches. I am trying to work out a novella now, and have enough notes already for a novel, which is discouraging. But if I try to start with a short story, and expand it, somehow this doesn't work, either. What challenges me most is trying to work out the proportion of dramatized scenes and narrated/summarized/skipped-over scenes. And of course I need the final scene, the final line of the novella, or I can't begin. And I need the narrative voice. (I was very happy with the hovering/impersonal voice of *The Rise of Life on Earth*, a virtually unknown novella of mine, which seemed to me experimental, like nothing I'd quite done before.)

GJ: You recently wrote a play version of your novel *The Tattooed Girl*. What made you choose that particular novel for dramatic treatment?

JCO: I wrote the play-version of *The Tattooed Girl* more or less simultaneously with the novel, as I'd done with most of *Blonde*. Working out dramatic scenes, then re-imagining them in prose. The novel is comprised of chapters that can be reduced to scenes. So this seemed logical, in the way that another novel, like for instance *Middle Age: A Romance* or *What I Lived For*, would not have been so. Some of the chapters involving Seigel and Alma, on the nature of the Holocaust and on the nature of "art," are virtually debates. . . . I've come to realize that while I love to write plays, I am not by temperament a playwright, who's typically someone who loves to hang out at theaters, absolutely thrives on rehearsals, etc. To me, rehearsals are maddeningly repetitive and exhausting. I don't actually mind revising—if I can stay home and fax the revisions to the director. So probably, with such an attitude, I should not be writing plays at all.

GJ: Lately you've been writing young adult novels. What drew you to this form, relatively late in your career? Compared to your adult fiction, are these books less or more challenging to write? Have you gotten much response from adolescents to the books?

JCO: A young editor named Tara Weikum, who has been reading my work since high school, invited me to assemble a collection of short stories, which became *Small Avalanches*. Tara encouraged me to write a young adult novel, which, for me, became an experiment in genre: how to present a narrative in the most succinct and dramatic way, relying mostly upon dialogue, a minimum of interior narration, virtually no description, exposition, or background. In adult fiction, the act of describing, for instance, a high school cafeteria could be a tour de force of sharp, sensory writing, but a young adult editor will simply cross out such a description with the gentle admonition: "Teenagers know what a high school cafeteria is, you don't have to tell them." Much of adult writing is nostalgic, but virtually no young adult or children's fiction is, for obvious reasons. It's a considerable challenge for one accustomed to composing complex atmospheric passages like mosaics, to pare back language to such an extreme. Much of what I love about reading is, in fact, these "atmospheric" passages, so the experiment in abandoning them was part of the interest in writing young adult novels: *Big Mouth & Ugly Girl* (incorporating material I'd originally written for the story "Ugly"), *Freaky Green Eyes* (set in Seattle, where we'd visited when my play *Miss Golden Dreams* was being performed at the A.C.T. Theatre there: this is a "geographically specific" story with some of the ethical issues of the O.J. Simpson case), *Sexy* (imagined originally as an "adult" story with a tragic ending), and the upcoming *After the Wreck I Picked Myself Up Spread My Wings and Flew Away* (a first-person narrative by a fifteen-year-old girl who believes that she caused an automobile accident that killed her mother, set in more or less the locale of *Sexy*). The young adult genre is for me an arena in which to dramatize ethical issues in a manner that would be too obvious or obtrusive for "adult fiction"; also, it's a genre that allows for quite plausible happy endings/positive resolutions. Young adults do change rapidly; they are enormously impressionable, and subject to influences both good and bad. In this genre, I would never involve adolescent characters in the sort of extreme, often tragic situations that seem quite plausible, if not inevitable, in adult fiction. (Yes, I've gotten quite a lot of response to the young adult novels. Readers of such fiction react almost solely in personal terms, like readers associated with the Oprah Book Club. The "how" of literature means very little set beside the "what"—what identification the reader makes with the material.)

GJ: Lately you've also undertaken a new pseudonymous identity, Lauren Kelly. Does that name have any particular significance, as the previous pseudonym Rosamond Smith did? Do the Kelly novels *Take Me, Take Me With You* and *The Stolen Heart* differ formally from the types of novels you wrote as Rosamond Smith?

Why the change? Is Rosamond Smith "finished," or will you continue to write novels under both pseudonyms?

JCO: Rosamond Smith seems to have metamorphosed into Lauren Kelly, a somewhat younger variant; more svelte, seemingly, since the novels are shorter, more succinct and narrative-driven, though turning still upon the phenomenon of linked doubles, twins, "soul mates." Originally, *The Tattooed Girl* was to be a suspense/psychological pseudonym novel, but it grew more ambitious and obviously longer.

GJ: In your post-2000 fiction, as in earlier work, you often deal with race issues, often involving a white woman's involvement with a black boy or man (this is the focus of *I'll Take You There* in particular), and I understand that you have a forthcoming novel, *Black Girl, White Girl*, which focuses on a relationship between two college girls, one black and one white. What kinds of challenges does it pose for you, as a Caucasian author, to deal with black characters? Do you "research" such fictions in much detail? Has your consideration of race evolved in any significant ways since such earlier books as *I Lock My Door Upon Myself* and *Because It Is Bitter, and Because It Is My Heart*?

JCO: It's a highly complex and obviously sensitive issue. For me, with my interest in individual/class-nuanced voices, the issue is probably more with choosing the appropriate "voice" for a character regardless of his or her race. People of color don't in fact have anything like a uniformity of voice, though obviously "black dialect" is a subspecies of American English and some people speak it naturally. I've tended to focus on a Caucasian girl or woman's vision of a black boy or man, for obvious reasons. My few black (at that time Negro) classmates at North Park Junior High in Lockport made a strong impression on me since there were no Negroes in the rural area where I lived. Caucasians do tend to feel an emotional attraction to blacks, both male and female. It may be similar to the rapport many (most?) women feel for gay men.

I haven't researched the novels that deal with race. *Black Girl, White Girl* is vaguely scheduled for Fall 2006. It will be a controversial novel, I'm afraid, since the young black girl with whom the narrator rooms at college is, shall we say, not trying to win any popularity contests.

GJ: Your recent work continues to explore the theme of sexually or physically abused young girls and women: Norma Jeane Baker in *Blonde*, the eponymous character in *The Tattooed Girl*, the young woman in your most recent Lauren Kelly novel, *The Stolen Heart*, and characters in stories like "The Girl with the Blackened Eye." What accounts for your abiding obsession with this theme? Does it result in part from your childhood experiences with male bullies at the one-room schoolhouse you attended, or are you taking more of a sociological perspective, simply reporting what happens? Or perhaps a mixture of both?

JCO: I suppose it is, as you say, an "abiding obsession." I think that we are all drawn to imagining and dramatizing stories in which there are victims whose experiences might otherwise remain unacknowledged, lacking language. The occasional complicity between victim and aggressor—overt, unconscious— is significant, too. Most of my stories about "victims" evolve into stories of adjustments and growth, strategies of survival. I was struck by the Jean-Paul Sartre quote I've used as an epigraph for *Blonde*: "Genius is not a gift, but the way in which a person invents in desperate circumstances." (I don't actually know the original French quotation.)

Very likely, the emotional identification is, as you suggest, my childhood memories. Yet, it should be stressed, the occasionally cruel/crude things that happened to me and in my presence weren't at all unusual or uncommon in that time and place, and surely are not now, in many social settings.

GJ: You've said that your most recently published novel, *Missing Mom*, was written deliberately leaving out any "trace of irony." You've been a master ironist in your past and other recent work, so how difficult was this experiment? What led you to attempt it?

JCO: As you know, I'd originally hoped to publish *Missing Mom*, if at all, under a new pseudonym, with a woman editor at another publisher. It seemed to me at the time exclusively a woman's novel, with clear, direct, mostly simple sentences, a limited vocabulary, little or no irony (except the profound, tragic irony that good-hearted individuals can't comprehend how their very good-heartedness may be an invitation to their destruction), little or no dramatic conflict, resolutely "nice" characters (like our own relatives and friends, who rarely populate literary fiction), a "normal" romance/love relationship (virtually unheard-of in literary fiction). I had wanted to write a novel that my mother might have found congenial in its tone and setting, many of its details taken from her world, or a near analogue to it.

I did imagine the writing of the novel as a kind of literary experiment, and *Missing Mom* (the title was there from the start) as a genre novel of the very kind I'm not drawn to read. In the U.K., the title is *Mother, Missing*. (The Brits don't use "Mom" and their "Mum" is much too colloquial.) Essentially, beyond literary experimentation, the novel is an attempt to preserve the elusive memory of one now vanished from the world, though leaving behind a trail of entangled memories, emotions. When Nikki discovers her mother dead is a very painful scene for me even now to read, for it's meant to be an analogue to the telephone call I received from my brother telling me that my mother had died of a stroke, evidently in her sleep. She had had no prior strokes, had not seemed unwell, and was, so abruptly, gone. My father's death, too, seemed sudden, though he'd been seriously ill for a long time. In his case, he simply "fell asleep" as the hospice nurses said, and "never woke up." Both deaths occurred in May, often the most lovely month, though occasionally, capriciously, cold and rainy. The smell of lilac is a strong association with my Millersport childhood, preserved in *Missing Mom*, I hope not too overtly.

GJ: Your recent novels, like *Middle Age: A Romance* and *The Falls*, as well as *Missing Mom*, feature animals prominently as characters in their own right. I found the cat Smokey in *Missing Mom* to be especially vivid. I don't remember many animal characters from your early novels. What accounts for this recent development? I know that you've always owned cats and that nowadays you like to watch "Animal Planet" on television.

JCO: Animal characters! I'm glad that you see them as possessing "characters," which makes them very like us, though perhaps not quite as complex and brooding as we are. There was a powerful/magical cat Mahalaleel in *Bellefleur* and probably there have been animals scattered throughout my writing, but in recent years there have been more, who knows why? Acquaintance with animals can redeem your faith in nature! I'd love to write an entire novel, perhaps a comedy of manners, from the point of view of an animal resident of a household, cat or dog. (If your dachshunds could speak . . . !) I'm glad that you liked Smokey [in *Missing Mom*], a very definite "animal character." Smokey has been traumatized but anyway is not a "nice cat." All of Nikki's observations about this cat are taken from life, of course.

GJ: Since 2000, all your novels and novellas have focused on female characters (though *The Falls* and *The Tattooed Girl* had prominent male characters as well). I understand that your forthcoming novels *Black Girl, White Girl* and *The Gravedigger's Daughter* focus on women as well, and you have a story collection forthcoming entitled *The Female of the Species*. Is this concentration more or less accidental, or have you consciously focused on female experience in recent years? Can you see yourself doing another long novel like *Wonderland* or *What I Lived For* that is focused almost wholly on a male character?

JCO: I had not particularly realized that so many of my protagonists are female characters. I suppose I feel as most writers do that there is more of a sense of legitimacy to the voice of one's own gender, so to speak. In fact it isn't "easier"—or "harder"—as you probably know from your own writing experience. To discover and cultivate a voice that is engaging (to the writer) is the challenge no matter the gender. The differentiation tends to be along strata of education, intelligence, insight, sensitivity, perhaps race.

GJ: You dedicated *Middle Age: A Romance* to "my Princeton friends, nowhere in these pages." You used the same dedication for your 1989 novel *American Appetites*, which is also in an academic setting. Is it a ticklish situation to set a novel in a place very much like Princeton, where you reside? Do people tend to see, or think they see, themselves in such works? Is using your own habitat harder than using your rural background, say, as a setting?

JCO: Princeton has been the setting for relatively little of my fiction because it's less engaging to me emotionally, I suppose.

Here, nearly everyone is from somewhere else and we are all, in many ways, very like one another: verbal, bookish, "educated," reflective, and 100% liberal. (There are plenty of conservatives in the older, wealthier Princeton, but we rarely encounter them. Our own wealthy friends, like Seward and Joyce Johnson, are bracingly liberal.) Since I don't actually write about real people, but am inclined to use real settings, it hasn't happened, so far, that people have "seen themselves" in the novels. Henry Bienen [former Princeton professor, now president of Northwestern University] liked to tell people that he was the model for the protagonist of *American Appetites* but there was so little resemblance between them, it was meant as a kind of joke. The only Princeton-set novel that embeds an obviously "real" event, one which received a good deal of publicity at the time, is *Nemesis*, a Rosamond Smith novel; but here again, the characters are all distinctly different from their real-life counterparts. (The villain was much, much more attractive, in fact.) In *Middle Age: A Romance*, I wanted to evoke the vulnerability of individuals who, seen from a distance, rarely engender much sympathy in fiction: very well-to-do, seemingly successful, seemingly complacent middle-aged and older men and women. Why the true travails of the rich seem the stuff of comedy and not tragedy, to one with a proletarian heart like my own, I don't know. I am so much more emotionally engaged with Maureen Wendall [a character in the 1969 novel *them*] yearning to live in one of the large beautiful houses in a certain Detroit neighborhood than I am with individuals who live in these houses, though, at one time, I myself lived in one of these houses, in fact.

GJ: I find your novel *I'll Take You There* to be one of your most impressive, and you've said it's written more or less in your own voice, as opposed to a crafted fictional voice, and of course it's one of your most autobiographical novels, with its Syracuse/sorority house setting. What was that writing experience like for you? Did you identify more strongly with the heroine than with characters in your other recent novels?

JCO: The unnamed narrator of *I'll Take You There* obviously speaks with my voice, virtually unmediated. Always, or usually, I work with mediated fictional voices, not my own, in some cases antithetical to my own like Quentin in *Zombie* or Kathleen of *The Rise of Life on Earth*, which are two favorites of my own. Annelia, as she came to be called, is a just slightly fictionalized version of myself, even more blundering and naively trusting/vulnerable than I was, as her sorority "sisters" are outsized/demonic versions of my own "sisters" in Phi Mu. (Whom I continue to meet, over the years! It is really quite amazing, how little some of them have changed physically. If they've read the novel, they can see that the sorority isn't ours, so there are not disgruntled feelings so far as I know. I've been invited to participate in Phi Mu national activities. The obvious antipathy of the girl narrator to "sisterhood" seems not to be picked up by these readers who take fiction somewhat literally, and perhaps this is a good thing.) *I'll Take You There* meant, to me, exploring the "philosophy" side of my undergraduate experience, not the "literary." When the novel appeared, Bob Phillips [a friend from Oates's Syracuse University days] naturally expected it to deal at least obliquely with the Syracuse U. he also remembers very clearly, our excellent professors, talented and interesting writer-friends, perhaps with Bob himself, and may have been surprised when it does not. So *Broke Heart Blues* would seem to enshrine some of my colorful high school classmates and events of our high school years, but in fact it's totally fiction, except for the power of "nostalgia" in our imaginative lives. I think it's the case with many writers that actual people can't be nearly so interesting as those we imagine; certainly, their dialogue can't compare. What I most respond to about real places is the physical setting, the inexplicable and atmospheric *thereness* of a place. People who've gone to S.U. and/or have lived in upstate New York understand the preponderance of weather and skies in the novel in that strange moody region susceptible to what's called the "lake effect." (If you've wondered why so many odd characters have come from that part of the world, the founder of the Mormon church John Smith, for instance, the first "spiritualists" and "séance" operators, John Ashbery [Sodus, right on Lake Ontario] and some others, the "lake effect" may be why.)

GJ: In addition to all the books you've written since 2000, you also took the time to do revisions of your early novels *A Garden of Earthly Delights* (1967) and *them* (1969), revisions that were particularly extensive for *Garden*. What led you to revise these early novels, which had already garnered so much acclaim in their original versions? Do you anticipate doing revisions to other novels, perhaps in the manner of the later Henry James doing his New York Edition?

JCO: Revising *them* and *A Garden of Earthly Delights* was a mesmerizing experience for me. *them* didn't really require much revising, but *Garden* had been only my second published novel, and required trimming in places and tightening /dramatizing/ bringing into sharper focus in others. I felt that I was looking through a slightly fogged lens, and could polish that lens without altering any of the chapters essentially. It was in some way an intensely spiritual experience as if I were revisiting a past, seemingly lost time in my life, in a way I could never have anticipated. I kept thanking David Ebershoff, editor of Modern Library, for giving me such a rare opportunity. I don't think that other novels of mine would require such attentive revising and re-imagining. Such an experience is uncanny: it's as if you were living again a sustained, intensely emotional period of your life except, this time, you know the outcome, and even the outcome beyond the novel itself: the fact that the novel will be published, and will find some readers. Initially, we haven't a clue what awaits our exhausting efforts.

GJ: In the past, you would take a "respite" from writing a novel by spending six weeks or so writing poetry. I haven't seen very much poetry from you these past few years, so I wondered if you still follow this practice, or has the writing of fiction lately tended to trump your work in poetry?

JCO: The interim between emotionally draining novels seems to be taken up now, in my writing life, by young adult fiction, Lauren Kelly pseudonym novels, and lengthy review-essays for *New York Review of Books*. A few years ago, I tended to write poetry at such times, and plays; for some reason, I seem to have shifted interests, at least temporarily. The response is so much more evident, the entire writing experience so much more engaging, I'm afraid, than the writing of poetry is.

GJ: Even as we are conducting this interview, a new eighty-page novella, "The Corn Maiden," has appeared in the anthology *Transgressions*, edited by the late Ed McBain (pseudonym for Evan Hunter). In the author's note, you say that the novella—which deals with several young girls who kidnap, torment, and plan to "sacrifice" another, more vulnerable young girl—is based on stories of Native American sacrifice rituals. I've learned to take your author's notes with a grain of salt, so I wonder if these were rituals you actually read about, or did you make up the story out of whole cloth?

JCO: The idea for the novella probably did come to me from my reading of some Native American sacrificial rituals. Some of these, like the Sundance ritual, are more gruesome than others. "The Corn Maiden" is a composite of several, very similar ceremonies. I'm intrigued by the undercurrent of "sacrifice" in our so-called civilized lives that is so overt and codified in so-called primitive societies. I'd read of Indians in the Niagara Falls area, and their sacrifices to the god of the Falls.

The difference in contemporary civilized society seems to be mainly statistical. Thousands of young people are "sacrificed" in rapacious and quixotic adventures of acquisition like the Iraqi War while the Native Americans sacrificed carefully selected individuals, usually a very few.

GJ: Also during the brief period of this interview, you have begun and completed yet another Lauren Kelly novel entitled *Blood Mask*, which will appear in summer 2006. What I want to address is the issue of your productivity, and the way you manage your time: how do you manage to produce so much?

JCO: I'm not sure how to reply to your question. Now that I've returned to playing piano, or trying to play piano, the analogue seems clear: we are drawn to certain activities that may or may not "express" us but which demand thinking/calculating/care/precision/ problem-solving of one kind or another. Some people believe that time is "infinite" and some that time is "finite"; some that time is, as it certainly seems to be, "flowing," and some that it is static, a sort of fourth dimension which is perceived by us as "flowing." When we are intensely involved in problem-solving of one kind or another, or "creating," we seem to slip into another dimension, and what seems a short time to others can seem very long to us. In the world of *Blonde*, for instance, I was lost for what seemed like years. Also in *What I Lived For*. Even *Blood Mask* seemed to take a very long time. . . . They say that three-minute rounds for boxers are extremely long, which I wouldn't doubt.